Sustainability in Higher Education

Urban and Industrial Environments

Series editor: Robert Gottlieb, Henry R. Luce Professor of Urban and Environmental Policy, Occidental College

For a complete list of books published in this series, please see the back of the book.

Sustainability in Higher Education

Stories and Strategies for Transformation

Edited by Peggy F. Barlett and Geoffrey W. Chase

The MIT Press
Cambridge, Massachusetts
London, England

© 2013 Massachusetts Institute of Technology
All rights reserved. No part of this book may be reproduced in any form by any electronic or mechanical means (including photocopying, recording, or information storage and retrieval) without permission in writing from the publisher.

MIT Press books may be purchased at special quantity discounts for business or sales promotional use. For information, please email special_sales@mitpress.mit.edu or write to Special Sales Department, The MIT Press, 55 Hayward Street, Cambridge, MA 02142.

This book was set in Sabon by the MIT Press. Printed and bound in the United States of America.

Library of Congress Cataloging-in-Publication Data

Sustainability in higher education : stories and strategies for transformation / edited by Peggy F. Barlett and Geoffrey W. Chase.
    pages cm
Includes bibliographical references and index.
ISBN 978-0-262-01949-1 (hardcover : alk. paper) — ISBN 978-0-262-51965-6 (pbk. : alk. paper) 1. Campus planning—Environmental aspects—United States. 2. Universities and colleges—Environmental aspects—United States. 3. Environmental management—United States. I. Barlett, Peggy F., 1947- II. Chase, Geoffrey W.
LB3223.3.S88 2013
378.1'070973—dc23
2013000046

10 9 8 7 6 5 4 3 2 1

To all our students, past and future

Contents

Preface and Acknowledgments

Ten years ago, when we first began to convene groups of campus leaders from around the country to consider how they could support changes for sustainability on their campuses, they spoke of their isolation and their sense that the transformation of higher education toward sustainability was an overwhelming challenge. But, they avidly absorbed and shared strategies and returned home with renewed energy for the work. They also renewed our energy and opened a window for us on a societal transformation—one unfolding in higher education in its own unique way, but echoed by changes in businesses, communities, and homes across the country.

As the sustainability movement has unfolded, campus champions are now supported by collegial networks, organizations, publications—and even, at times, by their peers. Whether they are drawn from students, staff, faculty, or administrators, campus leaders for sustainability still often feel daunted by the challenges, but no longer are so isolated. In some institutions, boards of trustees and sustainability councils mandate change. Student groups and alumni demand new academic programs, engaged learning, new skills, and revitalized educational structures. Employers, governments, and granting agencies alike share a sense of urgency and turn to colleges and universities to provide solutions and trained minds. As we have watched the innovations emerge—the pilot projects evolving into pioneering policies—we have a sense of urgency as well to share these powerful stories.

This volume emerged from our appreciation of the transformational efforts of individuals and coalitions in all kinds of colleges and universities around the United States—and indeed, around the world. From our travels, from workshops, and from the generous time in reflective conversation offered by colleagues, we have come to learn how institutions find a revised sense of mission, new goals, new curricula, and new habits of mind. Not only do we understand more clearly the emerging practices of sustainability, but we see that the paradigm itself is emerging in multiple forms. As we have recruited the authors in this volume, we have seen how they are working with—and sometimes moving beyond—the conventional structures of the academy. Their voices document the struggles, disappointments, and breakthroughs that have helped their schools move beyond business as usual and in the process offer us all a glimpse into the workings of a society in motion.

The pressures on higher education today are intense and are likely to intensify. We hear calls from legislators, taxpayers, and others for a fundamental transformation of higher education that ensures that more students graduate with the skills and abilities to meet the challenges of the twenty-first century. We also hear that higher education may be on the cusp of transformations in technology, access, and funding. Over and over again, we hear calls for higher education to do more to meet the needs of society.

Because of our work in higher education over the last thirty years—and our work specifically related to sustainability in higher education over the last twenty years—we believe that it is time to connect the dots, to draw lines that link accountability, achievement, and access, while documenting how higher education has responded to the larger sustainability challenges we face. Whether from our big cities, sprawling suburbs, small towns, open farmland, or rural communities, we seek pathways to address climate change, water scarcity, food insecurity, new sources of energy, adequate healthcare, and a host of other issues. We know that higher education can play a critical role in supporting a vibrant quality of life, renewed communities, and restored ecosystems. As we explore new social and political strategies to act decisively for the common good, we hope the stories we share here will inspire further transformative changes in colleges and universities—and in a broad range of institutions and communities—as we seek a more sustainable future.

We are delighted to work once again with the MIT Press. Special thanks go to Clay Morgan, our editor, and Bob Gottlieb, series editor, who have shepherded this work with great professionalism. Mary Bagg did a lovely job of the copyediting, and we would like to thank Yasuyo Iguchi for the beautiful cover. This volume has benefited from the advice of anonymous reviewers, and although we cannot thank them by name, we are grateful for their thoughtful engagement with our work.

We are deeply grateful to all the authors of this volume who have taken the time to record and share their stories here. We appreciate these contributions—and their hard work. We also want to thank families and friends—theirs as well as our own—for the encouragement and support we have all received. In addition, we are acutely aware that there is a larger community of support without which this volume would not be possible. A special thanks in that regard go to Anna Avendano, Tony Cortese, Ciannat Howett, Mariah Hudson, Nancy Marlin, Deborah Rowe, Paul Rowland, Leith Sharp, and the many hundreds of faculty and sustainability leaders with whom we have worked over the years. This volume has been a collaborative effort from the beginning, and we have always been mindful that such efforts emerge from and are, indeed, community efforts.

Introduction

Geoffrey W. Chase and Peggy F. Barlett

Almost ten years ago, we published *Sustainability on Campus: Stories and Strategies for Change* (Barlett and Chase 2004) to capture what we saw as some of the significant first steps and pilot projects around sustainability on college and university campuses. These efforts had begun to emerge as faculty, staff, administrators, and students began to embrace the idea that higher education has a key role to play in the move toward a more sustainable world. Through the research conducted on campuses, stewardship of operations, engagement with local communities, and especially through curriculum change efforts, these authors shared stories of how colleges and universities could serve as significant leverage points to support environmental integrity, economic vitality, and social justice for present and future generations. These individuals reflected the commitment articulated by David Orr in 1994: "It is not education, but education of a certain kind, that will save us" (Orr 1994, 8).

Today, we find ourselves in a higher education landscape more changed than we imagined in 2004. More and more faculty are outgrowing the narrow confines of their disciplinary training to join multidisciplinary efforts to address urgent societal problems, not only with other scholars, but through new forms of pedagogy and practice with students, administrative staff, international organizations, and local groups. We see administrators embracing ambitious agendas of institutional change around sustainability that bring into dialog historically separate realms of operations and academics, students and staff, town and gown. As Leith Sharp and Cindy Pollock Shea have stated, "Sustainability is no longer an elective. It is a prerequisite" (Sharp and Shea 2012, 79).

Remarkable shifts in institutional rhetoric and personal commitment to addressing sustainability challenges are also visible. In some cases we see major reorganization of university divisions, new multiyear general education curricula, new degree programs, new faculty development efforts, and new governance structures such as sustainability councils. As the authors in this volume share what they have done in the classroom, in the boardroom, in faculty and student meetings, in reflection practices, and in community development efforts, they also share ways that working for sustainability have been transformational for themselves, not just for their institutions.

This volume offers stories of how diverse colleges and universities from across the United States have begun to rethink and restructure programs, processes, and pedagogies in ways that illustrate shifting tectonic plates of higher education and speak to personal transformation. In their narratives, authors share some of the difficult questions about what it means to move toward sustainability, how critical reflection can be part of our efforts, and how we can overcome setbacks and embrace the doubts that inevitably accompany such work. As with *Sustainability on Campus: Stories and Strategies for Change*, we emphasize accounts of what happened, recognizing that these are inevitably partial. Nevertheless, we hope these snapshots of institutional strategies and cultural change will provide practical advice and inspiration.

A Vibrant Context

The narratives collected here emerge from an energetic context of national sustainability efforts aimed at capitalizing on higher education as an important engine for societal change. Today, there is more support from disciplinary and professional organizations for sustainability, green building is a commonly understood commitment (though not yet a common practice), sustainability positions (directors and coordinators) are more prevalent, and even popular culture supports sustainability-related change in ways that were not true in the year 2000. In *Sustainability on Campus: Stories and Strategies for Change*, we referred to the roles of organizations and programs such as Second Nature, University Leaders for a Sustainable Future, the National Wildlife Federation and its Campus Ecology Program, and cited important sustainability-related documents such as the Talloires Declaration and the Brundtland Report. But there has been in the last eight years an amazing evolution of organizations and projects.

Perhaps most significant of these is the Association for the Advancement of Sustainability in Higher Education (AASHE), with 1,100 institutional members and an annual meeting that draws more than 2,000 attendees. An advocacy and educational organization, AASHE brings together sustainability directors, administrative officers, students, faculty, business leaders, product and service providers, and nonprofits to share best practices, disseminate knowledge, support professional development, foster policy efforts, and encourage national networking that has buttressed efforts on many campuses. Beyond AASHE, many campuses have benefitted from the dynamic intervention of the Disciplinary Associations Network for Sustainability (DANS), which supports change led from within each discipline, and the Higher Education Associations Sustainability Consortium (HEASC) that brings together many associations connected to higher education. In addition, Focus the Nation, the U.S. Green Building Council, and especially the American College and University Presidents' Climate Commitment (ACUPCC), which has now been signed by more than 670 presidents, offer a support structure for campuses that seek to find leverage toward sustainability. In some fields, support for change around sustainability has even been incorporated into formal accreditation processes and textbook updates.

An additional change in the national context for higher education and sustainability is STARS (Sustainability Tracking, Assessment, & Rating System, developed by AASHE), a strategy for continuing to track momentum in a coherent and consistent ways through clearly described metrics. STARS is built on years of work by the National Wildlife Federation in the Campus Ecology network, the U.S. Green Building Council's rating system, and various other report cards and ratings. While it remains to be seen whether STARS and other award and rating systems will flourish, they offer some incentive to institutions to take a comprehensive approach and to attend to the persistence over time of the multiple dimensions of the sustainability efforts.

We also find it significant that many new published accounts—books, articles, and journals—have emerged to describe sustainability efforts on campuses in the United States and across the globe. Evolving from a focus on environmental education, the broader sustainability paradigm is evident in *Sustainability: A Journal of Record* and *The International Journal of Sustainability in Higher Education*, and in more disciplinary journals such as *Environment, College Teaching, The International Journal of Sustainable Engineering*, and *Journal of the Academy of Marketing Science*. Insight into current curriculum innovation and visions for a more robust academic engagement in the future can be seen in many excellent recent edited volumes (Blewitt and Cullingford 2004; Jones, Selby, and Sterling 2010; Leal Filho 2011; Timpson et al. 2006).

Accounts of broad sustainability engagement across the university, such as at the University of New Hampshire (Aber, Kelly, and Mallory 2009) and the University of Victoria (M'Gonigle and Starke 2006), include not only curriculum but also research, operations, community engagement, and the importance of coordination among them. Leal Filho (2009), in *Sustainability at Universities: Opportunities, Challenges, and Trends*, highlights international examples as well as metrics for assessment. James Farrell (2010), in *The Nature of College*, explores place-based pedagogical strategies with humor and wisdom, and Andres Edwards (2010), in *Thriving Beyond Sustainability: Pathways to a Resilient Society*, offers an overview of both issues and case studies.

Focused approaches have also received recent attention in documenting and guiding the sustainability movement in higher education, such as climate change efforts at Tufts (Rappaport and Creighton 2007) and internationally (Leal Filho 2010), environmental literacy at Indiana University (Reynolds, Brondizio, and Robinson 2010) and internationally (Stibbe 2010), economic development and interdisciplinary civic engagement (Forrant and Silka 2006), and guidance for academic administrators and institutional researchers (Bardaglio and Putman 2009, Litten and Geronimo Terkla 2007, and Martin and Samels 2012).

In addition to these publications, we find sustainability work supported by an expanding acceptance of interdisciplinary research and teaching, including greater attention to the reward structures that may inhibit such work. Engaged learning for both students and faculty also appears as a valuable addition to the curriculum in a number of the accounts we share here. Many institutions now offer practical experiences outside the classroom that support skills in teamwork, respect for multiple ways of knowing, and the habits of civility, all of which allow us to address complex societal problems that have no simple answers.

The Stories in This Volume

Within the context of this academic landscape, faculty, staff, and students express deep interest in the stories of how individuals and institutions have found their way to support sustainability. Responding to these interests (and recognizing that higher education is notoriously slow to change and that much remains to be accomplished), we wanted, first, to provide evidence of the changes taking place, to collect a panorama of ways in which institutions have begun to organize (or re-organize themselves fundamentally) to support sustainability. Second, we sought to present stories about *how* such change occurs, stories that would serve as pathways and directions from which we can borrow to guide our own campuses. We have left to other writers the task of untangling the philosophical roots of the sustainability movement and the visionary articulation of what we *ought* to be doing.

We recruited the authors in this volume through our personal networks, drawing heavily from the past participants in our curriculum development workshops for faculty leaders, which we have offered through AASHE. Our intent was to focus less on operations and campus greening, and more on the institutional structures (especially on efforts around the fundamental academic mission of the university). This leaves out important kinds of efforts and institutions; many of these accounts, fortunately, appear in the excellent new volumes noted already. We have also focused once again on the United States, leaving out significant breakthroughs in Canada, the United Kingdom, Europe, Australia, Korea, and elsewhere around the world. While we know that colleges and universities in the United States have much to learn from international colleagues, we realized that this book could not comprehensively explore all that is being done.

As a result, each of the chapters in this volume tells a story that is just the tip of an iceberg. Authors were constrained by space limitations and also by the complexity of the histories they recount. Unlike accounts of first steps, many schools by this time have seen multiple initiatives, involving many leaders. Each chapter, then, of necessity, tells only a partial story, omitting many actors, side-efforts, and bumps in the road. We know, too, that many institutions not represented in this volume have experienced significant change and have embraced sustainability in ways from which we can all benefit. Thus, we see the stories here as representative of work that is being undertaken at hundreds of institutions, and while these chapters provide directions, they do not capture every path on the map.

Major Threads

The endpoint of the multiple paths to sustainability is elusive because of the dynamic, evolving, and transient nature of our understandings of both the challenges and the solutions, both locally and around the world today. Thus, while the stories in this volume provide inspiration partly because they reflect so much dedicated work on the part of faculty, staff, students, and administrators at remarkably different kinds of institutions, they do not provide a single set of guidelines about how to move forward on all campuses. What is transformational change on one campus may not be on another, and appropriate starting points may differ. Sometimes these starting points are the result of intentional actions and decisions, and at other times they seem almost accidental or arising from opportunities presented by chance. Nevertheless, several key themes emerged from nearly all of these chapters, providing an arc of how sustainability continues to emerge and develop in higher education.

Sources of momentum in this unfolding have come from both within and from without. Many campus champions refer to their own internal disquiet with business as usual, as their scholarly and ethical awareness of the need for change has grown. Sometimes the intellectual demands of a compelling problem—such as refining economic development theory and practice to include environmental and social justice issues—lead to new cross-disciplinary or international partnerships, such as those at Arizona State University and the University of South Florida. These partnerships sometimes lead to new centers of collaboration, new forms of scholarly dissemination, and demands to rethink reward structures.

Momentum has also come from within disciplines and from peer institutions, accreditation processes, and forms of evaluation and ranking, including sustainability scorecards and prizes that highlight transformational steps at path-breaking colleges and universities. Funding sources— federal, state, and especially local philanthropy—have been critical in certain cases (Cortese 2012, 30). Finally, the existence of international accords, agreements, and organizations, whether focused around sustainability or around climate change or a post-petroleum world, has spurred many schools to new efforts.

In a very real sense, all of these pieces deal primarily with *leadership and commitment* in one form or another. Sometimes the leadership being described is formal, housed in the office of a senior administrator, as is the case with David Shi at Furman University or Mitchell Thomashow at Unity College. Just as often leadership related to sustainability emerges from students like Grant Mack at San Diego State University, who describes himself as knowing or caring little about the environment until he was inspired by the business ecology club and came to hold positions in student government, which led to new initiatives that transformed business as usual in the university, or from faculty members like Wendy Anderson at Drury University, who with hesitation accepted the role of sustainability champion, which led to broad collaborations, a regional hub for innovation (the Ozarks Center for Sustainable Solutions), and a proposed School of the Environment. Sometimes the leadership stems from an office of sustainability, like Julie Newman's at Yale or Angela Halfacre's at Furman, or from the boardroom debate among trustees, or from the interactions of diverse leaders at Florida A&M University, each championing a different component of the work. Reading these chapters with leadership in mind reinforces the idea that effective leadership for sustainability can occur almost anywhere on a campus.

Second, all these chapters in some way or another also speak to change—change extending beyond the modest internal shifts within institutions—and examine ways in which *institutions themselves are changing and reformulating their mission*. The diversity of institutions—community colleges, liberal arts colleges, state-supported universities, historically black colleges and universities (HBCUs), and tribal colleges—represented in this volume illustrates how sustainability can serve as a broad, overarching paradigm that can focus and enhance the mission and purpose at institutions as diverse as Santa Clara University (Jesuit), Florida Agricultural and Mechanical University (Florida A&M University, a state-supported HBCU), Spelman College (a private HBCU), the College of Menominee Nation (Tribal College), and the University of Michigan (state supported). These stories underscore such efforts not as part of a narrow, political, or limited agenda but rather as they reflect a broader paradigm that constantly asks us to re-situate ourselves in the world.

As powerful and transformational as the changes recounted here may be, they remind us that the journey to a sustainable world is a work in progress. As John Tallmadge (2009, 4) notes, sustainability always manifests "itself in some place with some people; it always has a local, personal flavor. And because conditions and people change, sustainability always appears dynamic and evolving." The stories from Arizona State University, the University of Wisconsin Oshkosh, Kapiʻolani Community College, and the University of South Carolina illustrate that *sustainability is dynamic and evolving*, and that local conditions contribute significantly to that evolution. These stories then provide an opportunity not only to see what has been achieved, but to begin to see what sustainability may become. As we work our way through the realities of this paradigm, we begin to understand the complexity of sustainability, its deeper levels and constructions—and the questions it presents.

Sustainability thus becomes more complex, subtle, and ultimately richer as we read Jean MacGregor's account of regional approaches to curriculum change on many campuses, Bill Throop's discussion of curriculum change at Green Mountain College, and Margo Flood's description of long-term change and administrative commitment at Warren Wilson

College. Our understanding of what constitutes a move to sustainability is enhanced and broadened by the institutions themselves, by how commitments to sustainability are manifested on diverse campuses. Often, somewhat ephemeral early steps toward curriculum change and larger system-wide, institutionalized commitments extend our understanding of sustainability itself and what it means for learning communities.

Dimensions of Transformation

In addition to these several overarching themes running throughout this book, readers will find narratives that offer insights and strategies for sustainability efforts in many arenas. The way we have chosen to organize these chapters foregrounds some of these approaches, but each of the chapters interacts in multiple ways with others in the volume.

In Part I, "Leadership and Commitment," Wendy Anderson describes how the intersection of both her personal and professional commitments led her to take on a leadership role at Drury University in Missouri. David Whiteman describes how he used democratic processes and inclusive approaches to governance to support the development of a "critical mass of student activists" at the University of South Carolina. Richard Schulterbrandt Gragg III, LaRae Donnellan, Ryan Mitchell, Clayton Clark II, and Viniece Jennings at Florida A&M University, the university with the largest number of African American students with science, technology, engineering, and mathematics (STEM) degrees, tell the story of how they combined efforts to ensure that underrepresented students make critical connections between climate change, environmental literacy, research, and public service. In their account, as in many others in the volume, leadership on the part of a few individuals inspires broader leadership around sustainability at other levels of the institution. Finally, Julie Snow, at Slippery Rock State University in Pennsylvania, explores the importance of resilience for anyone undertaking the challenging task of change on a campus, and recounts how bonds of loyalty in a group of committed individuals can make a significant difference in the face of limited resources.

In Part II, "Curricular Transformation," authors underscore the creative energy that emerges from teaching and engagement with the curriculum. Jean MacGregor provides a description of how the Curriculum for the Bioregion project in the Pacific Northwest helps faculty from fifty institutions consider how they might integrate sustainability into a wide range of courses on many different types of campuses. Place-based perspectives are critical in this effort, and many other chapters as well signal that closer attention to local issues and conditions is central to their sustainability work. MacGregor and her colleagues find sustainability is not an add-on, not a branch on each disciplinary tree, nor yet an ornament to be hung on the branch. It is part of the trunk and roots of each discipline. By linking to the "big ideas" in each field, the Curriculum for the Bioregion initiative works within the silos and departmental structures of higher education.

Bill Throop, at Green Mountain College in Vermont, describes how a commitment to sustainability can lead faculty to rededication of institutional vision, in their case to becoming an "environmental liberal arts college." Through the development of a dynamic general education program, faculty have worked across disciplinary boundaries to create place-based education for students that addresses financial aspects of college life and an entrepreneurial disposition to sustainability challenges

Jim Zaffiro's chapter tells the story of how the Prairie Project, a curriculum development initiative at Central College in Iowa, provided the opportunity for faculty to create a global sustainability minor linked to community-based service learning. Through these efforts, half the departments and almost a third of the faculty are now involved in new general education offerings grounded in sustainability issues. John Cusick at the University of Hawai'i Manoa describes how the ecological challenges Hawaii faces inspired an institute through which student leaders from many countries are brought together around global environmental and sustainability issues—and how students are transformed by those experiences.

In the last chapter in this section, William Van Lopik talks about the development of a general education course on sustainability at the College of Menominee Nation in Wisconsin and outlines how this course helped both him and his students rethink the relationship between sustainability and the traditional knowledge of the Menominee tribe. Drawing on his analysis of five hundred end-of-term essays, he provides insights into how students discover powerful connections with their own interests.

One of the emerging hallmarks of sustainability pedagogy as shown in these and other chapters is the expanded educational mission within local communities. Hands-on experiences for students—whether local or international—blur the boundaries of the campus and extend learning. Christian Wells in Part III, Chuck Redman in Part IV, and others throughout the book note that research, teaching, and practice go hand in hand, build stronger skills, and lead to more profound learning for students, but they also create new community service opportunities and establish important partnerships for higher education.

In Part III, "Defining the Paradigm for Change," the authors reflect on how the commitment to sustainability leads us to define, question, and develop deeper understandings of how institutions of higher education can embrace sustainability. In the first chapter in this section, Mike Shriberg and co-authors John Callewaert, Andrew Horning, Katherine Lund, and Donald Scavia from the University of Michigan illustrate how structures of careful guidance and support of student leaders at a large, research-focused university foster new forms of decision making and coordinated action. In this and other chapters, we see students gaining confidence and developing effective leadership skills. Christian Wells, from the University of South Florida, expands the notion of sustainability through the metaphor of urban metabolism and describes how embracing such a metaphor can help create a resiliency framework to engage stakeholders both on and off campus. The Campus Metabolism Mapping Project at USF offers students and faculty both research opportunities and new perspectives on campus functioning. Both chapters illustrate how the establishment of cross-boundary relationships leads to organizational change.

In the final chapter in this section, Krista Hiser at Kapi'olani Community College in Honolulu, shows how the diminishment of resources—the drying up of travel funds for faculty—caused her and others to rethink how faculty might sustain themselves. Creativity emerges from a "leaderless," decentralized model of faculty support that builds on transformative networks for academic renewal.

Part IV, "Institutional Mission and the Culture of Sustainability," provides accounts of institutional transformation that occur through inspirational leadership and through the way institutions become learning organizations that engage a set of core values. Beverly Daniel Tatum, the president of Spelman College, describes movingly how linking Spelman's mission—the education of black women—with its history, global issues, and the fundamental question about how Spelman women are taking care of their health, can energize and focus a college while helping us understand more deeply the fundamental interconnectedness from which sustainability can develop. Sherry Booth, Lindsey Cromwell Kalkbrenner, Leslie Gray, and Amy Shachter at Santa Clara University, a Jesuit campus in Silicon Valley, show how a culture of sustainability can emerge as an ongoing commitment when it is linked to the historic social justice mission of the institution and supported by aligned initiatives from the top and from the faculty and students at large. At Santa Clara, sectors of curriculum, residence life, student research, and campus operations have all embraced sustainability commitments, illustrating the importance of partnerships across campus to support new competencies and collaborative momentum (Kezar and Lester 2009).

In her chapter, Margo Flood describes how Warren Wilson, a college in North Carolina with a long tradition of combining academic learning, work on campus, and service, embraced sustainability at the administrative level in ways that advanced its mission while also honoring its history. She highlights "Warren Wilson's cultural approach to change: principled debate, careful examination of semantics, congruence with legacy, grounding in moral imperatives, and ultimately, formal community commitments."

Mitchell Thomashow, who served as president of Unity College in Maine from 2006 to 2011, describes how sustainability became a compelling narrative for helping a college define its sense of purpose while also contributing to the national dialog on higher education. He illustrates how presidents can use their positions to deepen engagement and how senior administrators can inspire innovation while understanding the need for patience, compassion, and tradition. Finally in this section, Angela Halfacre describes the significant impact David Shi, president of Furman University in South Carolina, had on a conservative campus culture that did not initially embrace the premises and principles of sustainability. Her story explores how Shi over many years helped convince a campus community that sustainability constituted an essential strategic priority. He extended his leadership into the fabric of the institution so that Furman will continue to serve as a model of sustainability in higher education long into the future.

"Accountability," part V of this volume, includes chapters that address how the maturation of sustainability efforts inevitably confronts issues of responsibility, compliance, and measurement. Grassroots efforts begin with enthusiasm and pilot projects, but as serious commitments to change are made, benchmarks of progress are adopted, even though those benchmarks may difficult to describe or may be contested. In the first chapter in this section, Julie Newman at Yale University in Connecticut articulates from her vantage point as the director of the Office of Sustainability the critical importance of setting goals, making commitments to accountability, and being transparent about achievements in order to maintain momentum over time when results depend on an entire community. Translating sustainability pledges into institutional policy allows them to be protected from competing priorities, financial setbacks, emergencies, and the inevitable personnel changes. Development of clear, incremental steps and systematic, reliable data is essential for long-term momentum. In the second chapter in this section, Chuck Redman describes how the School of Sustainability at Arizona State University was established and how the pioneering clarification of learning outcomes that have been adopted there address issues of accountability with regard to student learning.

Jim Feldman and David Barnhill then describe how the University of Wisconsin Oshkosh became the first Fair Trade University in the United States in an attempt to develop commitments that spanned the whole university, and thus to adopt a campus-wide approach to ethical sourcing. Student experience with Fair Trade practices on the ground in Latin America led to fruitful campus debate and deeper sophistication around the issues.

Grant Mack, in the final chapter of this section, tells the story of how over a number of years student leaders at San Diego State University came together to develop support for sustainability efforts across campus, including a new LEED platinum-certified student center. Through their efforts to develop principles and financial support, the student body as a whole took responsibility for sustainability advancements and in doing so developed accountability measures for themselves.

All of the chapters in this volume speak on one level to the personal satisfaction—and at times, elation—that takes place when we are fully engaged in a transformative task or project. But transformation on a more profound personal level is also evident, and it echoes the assumption that if we expect to change our institutions, we must begin with ourselves. In Part VI, the final section, "Professional and Personal Transformation," three chapters describe the deep changes that emerge from connection, commitment, and reflective practice. In "Living the Questions: Contemplative and Reflective Practices in Sustainability Education," Marie Eaton, Kate Davies, Michael Gillespie, Karen Harding, and Sharon Daloz Parks, all from diverse communities in the Pacific Northwest, describe how their collaborative practice over time has helped them consider the deeper levels of change for sustainability and apply what they have learned to their teaching. Through this deep engagement, these colleagues attend to quiet and reflection in a world of electronic over-stimulation, which helps them to reassess behavior patterns that privilege consumption and busy-ness. Hope and gratitude offer a balance also to the despair that can accompany the search for sustainable ways of living.

Bobbi Patterson at Emory University in Atlanta describes altered assumptions and a renewed sense of resilience that she and her students have experienced over the past decade as the result of pedagogies of transformation, reflection, and structured inquiry. Finally, in "Awakening to the Hero's Journey in Teaching and Learning," Christopher Uhl and Greg Lankenau describe how even a large lecture class can lead us to reconsider on a profound level our relationship to students, to our subject matter, to the earth, and to each other. Echoing the other writers in Part VI, Uhl describes a transformation toward a pedagogy that includes "awe, delight, compassion, wonder, and possibility." Sustainability challenges call us to new understandings and relationships to the earth and the peoples around us, and together the chapters in this section offer pioneering insights into the ways our classroom practices can respond.

Challenges and Opportunities

Among the challenges we face, which many of these chapters address either implicitly or explicitly, is defining next steps, maintaining momentum, and continuing to foster deep engagement. Amid the celebration for giant steps—and small steps—we also see that our work can be episodic. Efforts begin, but they can also fade. Funding, in particular, can follow fads, and finding a way to support long-term efforts is a critical challenge. As Jean MacGregor points out from her vantage point in the Curriculum for the Bioregion, it takes persistent energies and support to build new communities of trust to foster the breakthroughs we need to meet sustainability challenges. That is especially true for multi-institutional networks of institutions, but also for disciplinary re-visioning.

In the introduction to *Sustainability on Campus: Stories and Strategies for Change*, we noted that there are many barriers to sustainability-related change in higher education—disciplinary boundaries, silos and scale, multiple stakeholders, and financial pressures—and all of these still exist. But some of these, most notably financial pressures, are more pronounced today than they were in 2004. In terms of budgets alone, the challenges are increasingly daunting. Student loan debt now exceeds one trillion dollars, and state support for higher education (institutions that, collectively, enroll 75 percent of the students in higher education) has dropped significantly (Knapp, Kelly-Reid, and Ginder 2010; State Higher Education Executive Officers 2012). At the same time, concerns are being raised about the value of higher education and the success rates of students in their programs of study. Today, fewer than 60 percent of students who begin in colleges and universities graduate within six years, and the achievement gap among majority students and underrepresented minorities persists (Arum and Roska 2011; Knapp, Kelly-Reid, and

Ginder 2010). According to national surveys, employers do not believe that the students who do graduate are well prepared to enter the work force (Kuh 2008, 5).

Although not always included in discussions of sustainability in higher education, these issues—cost, achievement, equity, and student learning—speak directly to what it means to live in a sustainable world. We also recognize that there are forces and trends—digital information, online colleges and universities, federal research and student loan programs, and accreditation requirements, for example—acting upon higher education that will also shape the future. It is unclear whether these forces will support the transformation of institutions toward sustainability or inhibit our ability to do so.

As we read these accounts, we applaud what we see as an amazing rate of change at some institutions. There are new sustainability positions, broadened mission statements, transformed curricula, new habits of building and purchasing, new attention to endowments. But we also wonder, at schools of 20,000 students—or 30,000 or 40,000—how many students and faculty are really affected? Since the early strong signals from the United Nations Intergovernmental Panel on Climate Change called for curbs to greenhouse gas emissions, how many institutions have really responded? We are reminded that sustainability in higher education is, as we have already noted, multilayered, complex, and diffuse. Taken together, the stories here provide a window onto the culture of sustainability that is still emerging in higher education, but how it will evolve in the future is unclear. In some ways, the not-inconsiderable extent to which business as usual prevails on campus can be counted as a failure of our response.

In this regard, one opportunity signaled by this work is for thoughtful research to assess the breadth, depth, and durability of sustainability-related change in higher education. Cultural change in the form of institutional rhetoric, staffing, course offerings, and operational practices is unquestionable, yet fuller understandings of personal meanings, daily habits, and institutional aspirations would be useful to document fully the unfolding of this historical moment. As part of this research, attention to the ways reward structures and evaluation procedures are adapting will be particularly insightful.

For many of us, understandably, these broader trends in higher education can seem at times overwhelming and beyond our control. These forces can inspire creative responses, but they are certainly challenging. What is gratifying and reassuring is that the stories in this volume, while not addressing these national challenges directly, nevertheless point to thoughtful, structural engagement with sustainability issues at very diverse institutions. Though we sometimes experience discouragement at the pace of change, we also at times experience satisfaction. It is not clear whether we will be able to act in time to avoid great human suffering from the degradation of our natural systems, rising populations, and social inequalities. What is clear is that many individuals and some truly path-breaking educational institutions have moved ahead in the last ten years in extraordinary ways. These narratives generate important questions as well and, ultimately, if we can embrace these questions, they will serve our sustainability efforts in profound ways.

Sustainability in higher education calls us to new sets of relationships—with our students, with each other, with what we learn, and with ourselves. Throughout these stories, we see efforts accompanied by joy in new relationships, in teamwork across institutional boundaries, and also across wider communities as well. These relationships of trust nurture extended understandings of sustainability principles and also generate creativity and new collaborations. As projects face boulders in the road (or even crevasses), the deep satisfactions from teamwork—shared engagement with purposeful and meaningful action—can help overcome discouragement and maintain momentum.

Higher education is about the future, about preparing people for better lives, and about increasing their ability to strengthen their communities through art, research, technology, innovation, and entrepreneurial activity. Colleges and universities exist to contribute to a better world where there is less hunger, less disease, more prosperity, more joy, more freedom, and more love. Being aware that we will not ever see the end of disease or witness universal freedom or live in a world where there is no hunger, does not free us from seeking to achieve these goals; it makes it all the more important that we commit ourselves to these ends. In her chapter, Krista Hiser draws on how a starfish moves to describe the process of change at Kapiʻolani University: "in a process that no one fully understands, one part of the organism starts to move and persuades the others to cooperate and move." What all the chapters in this book—and all the stories we have heard that we were not able to include—illustrate and reinforce is that the "somehows" happen differently at every institution. These steps cannot be easily codified, summed up, or presented as concrete steps for action; there is no one blueprint. Taken together, these chapters provide hope, inspiration, and the opportunity to reflect on the paths and commitments we seek to follow.

References

Aber, John, Tom Kelly, and Bruce Mallory. 2009. *The Sustainable Learning Community: One University's Journey to The Future.* Durham, NH: University of New Hampshire Press.

Arum, Richard, and Josipa Roska. 2011. *Academically Adrift: Limited Learning on College Campuses.* Chicago, IL: University of Chicago Press.

Bardaglio, Peter, and Andrea Putman. 2009. *Boldly Sustainable: Hope and Opportunity for Higher Education in the Age of Climate Change.* Washington, DC: National Association of College and University Business Officers.

Barlett, Peggy F., and Geoffrey W. Chase. 2004. *Sustainability on Campus: Stories and Strategies for Change.* Cambridge, MA: The MIT Press.

Blewitt, John, and Cedric Cullingford. 2004. *The Sustainability Curriculum: The Challenge for Higher Education.* London: Routledge.

Cortese, Anthony D. 2012. Promises Made and Promises Lost: A Candid Assessment of Higher Education Leadership and the Sustainability Agenda. In *The Sustainable University: Green Goals and New Challenges for Higher Education Leaders,* ed. James Martin and James E. Samels, 17–31. Baltimore, MD: The Johns Hopkins University Press.

Edwards, Andres R. 2010. *Thriving Beyond Sustainability: Pathways to a Resilient Society.* Gabriola Island, BC: New Society Publishers.

Farrell, James. 2010. *The Nature of College.* Minneapolis, Minnesota: Milkweed Editions.

Forrant, Robert, and Linda Silka, eds. 2006. *Inside and Out: Universities and Education for Sustainable Development.* Amityville, NY: Baywood.

Jones, Paula, David Selby, and Stephen Sterling. 2010. *Sustainability Education: Perspectives and Practice across Higher Education.* London: Earthscan.

Kezar, Adrianna J., and Jaime Lester. 2009. *Organizing Higher Education for Collaboration: A Guide for Campus Leaders.* San Francisco: Jossey-Bass.

Knapp, Laura G., Janice E. Kelly-Reid, and Scott A. Ginder. 2010. *Enrollment in Postsecondary Institutions, Fall 2008; Graduation Rates, 2002 & 2005 Cohorts; and Financial Statistics, Fiscal Year 2008* (NCES 2010–152). U.S. Department of Education. Washington, DC: National Center for Education Statistics. http://nces. ed.gov/pubsearch.

Kuh, George D. 2008. *High-Impact Educational Practices: What They Are, Who Has Access to Them, and Why They Matter.* Washington, DC: Association of American Colleges and Universities.

Leal Filho, Walter. 2009. *Sustainability at Universities—Opportunities, Challenges, and Trends.* Frankfurt: Peter Lang Scientific Publishers.

Leal Filho, Walter. 2010. *Universities and Climate Change—Introducing Climate Change at University Programmes.* Berlin: Springer.

Leal Filho, Walter. 2011. *World Trends in Education for Sustainable Development.* Frankfurt: Peter Lang Scientific Publishers.

Litten, Larry H, and Dawn Geronimo Terkla. 2007. *Sustainability in Higher Education: New Directions for Institutional Research*. Hoboken, NJ: Jossey-Bass.

Martin, James, and James E. Samels, eds. 2012. *The Sustainable University: Green Goals and New Challenges for Higher Education Leaders*. Baltimore, MD: The Johns Hopkins University Press.

M'Gonigle, Michael, and Justine Starke. 2006. *Planet U: Sustaining the World, Reinventing the University*. Gabriola Island, BC: New Society Publishers.

Orr, David W. 1994. *Earth in Mind: On Education, Environment, and the Human Prospect*. Washington, DC: Island Press.

Rappaport, Ann, and Sarah Hammond Creighton. 2007. *Degrees That Matter: Climate Change and the University*. Cambridge, MA: The MIT Press.

Reynolds, Heather L., Eduardo S. Brondizio, and Jennifer M. Robinson. 2010. *Teaching Environmental Literacy: Across Campus and Across the Curriculum*. Bloomington, IN: Indiana University Press.

Sharp, Leith, and Cindy Pollock Shea. 2012. Institutionalizing Sustainability: Achieving Transformation from the Inside. In *The Sustainable University: Green Goals and New Challenges for Higher Education Leaders*, ed. James Martin and James E. Samels, 63–82. Baltimore, MD: The Johns Hopkins University Press.

State Higher Education Executive Officers (SHEEO). 2012. *State Higher Education Finance 2011*. Boulder, CO: http://www.sheeo.org.

Stibbe, Arran. 2010. The Handbook of Sustainable Literacy: Skills for a Changing World. Darlinton, Devon, UK: Green Books.

Tallmadge, John. 2009. What is Creative Sustainability? *Hawk and Handsaw: The Journal of Creative Sustainability* [Unity College: Unity, ME] 2:4–5.

Timpson, Walter M., Brian Dunbar, Gailmarie Kimmel, Brett Bruyere, Peter Newman, and Hillary Mizia. 2006. *147 Practical Tips for Teaching Sustainability: Connecting the Environment, the Economy, and Society*. Madison, WI: Atwood Press.

I

Leadership and Commitment

1

Drury University: A Story of Personal and Institutional Transformation

Wendy B. Anderson

Drury University, a small university grounded in the liberal arts tradition with several professional schools, serves 1,650 traditional students in the residential "Drury College" and 2,500 students through continuing studies and graduate programs. Embedded in the Ozark Mountain region of southern Missouri, Drury's main campus includes 80 shady acres that are poised between the two historic centers of Springfield on the ridge overlooking Jordan Creek, which flows through a revitalized downtown.

Within each institution that is on the journey toward sustainability are individuals whose stories are intricately woven into the institution's story of transformation. What follows is a story of my personal transformation, as one of the sustainability champions at Drury University. My story pivots around powerful events and key individuals that touched, motivated, inspired, and bolstered me as Drury's first "Director of Campus Sustainability." Through the countless obstacles that Drury and I have encountered, I had to redefine my roles to support Drury's, the Ozark region's, and the world's shift toward a more sustainable way of being.

A Reluctant Awakening

I came to Drury University in 1998 straight out of my PhD years at Vanderbilt. I was hired to be a plant ecologist—or, more specifically, to teach botany and ecology courses in the Biology Department. I studied the patterns and processes of cross-ecosystem flux as it influences food web structure and dynamics on pristine islands in remote locales, recognizing that all ecosystems are intricately connected to each other. In layman's terms, I was a plant expert who loitered on islands in the Gulf of California, Mexico, and the San Juan Islands of Washington State. At Drury, though, I found that many people—even my departmental colleagues—assumed that an ecologist was inevitably an "environmentalist."

I bristled every time someone referred to me as the biology department's new "environmentalist." I found myself fielding phone calls about why we had no recycling bins on campus and why the groundskeepers were always watering the sidewalks. Not only did I not see that as my job, I could have cared less about that stuff! They had nothing to do with the theoretical, ecological principles on which I was so intentionally maintaining my focus. I wanted to write NSF grants, *Ecology* papers, and academic books, not traipse around campus digging aluminum cans out of trash bins.

And then it happened in 2004. I had a baby. Beautiful, bright, clear, clarifying, Clara. Darn those pregnancy and postnatal hormones. Darn the mushy mommy brain. Darn her piercing blue eyes that peered into my soul—eyes that seemed to beg, "Will you protect me and make sure that the world is a safe place for me?" Mid-career motherhood did not set me back, but it did set me on an entirely different course.

During one of my six-minute contractions, while I was frantically photocopying data sheets for my class's field trip that my colleague would lead for me the following week while I enjoyed a ten-day maternity leave, the Vice President for Academic Affairs tracked me down to inform me that I had earned tenure. Going into labor and delivery with the assurance of job security was a relief. What I did not realize was the burden of tenure—the responsibility to leverage that job security and academic freedom for even greater feats of labor and delivery. A few weeks later, I was roped into serving in my first significant administrative role as the Theme Year Director. Each year, Drury organizes its weekly convocation series around a unifying theme, which also informs the general education curriculum and the campus-wide conversation. The faculty had chosen "sustainability" to be the 2005–06 theme, and the Biology Department's "environmentalist" was pegged to organize and host twenty-plus speakers and events for the year. I didn't even know what "sustainability" meant, but I went home and looked into those clear, blue eyes gazing up at me while I fed my daughter, and I began to understand something about "the future."

In 2004–05, I wandered through the haze of new motherhood, managed countless phone calls with faculty colleagues sharing a gazillion suggestions for convocation events, negotiated with agents demanding $25K for Dr. Famous Speaker, and tried to pick some "nature music" with the Springfield Symphony conductor for a special event. I longed to be in our Mexican field station trying to remember which blender was for the margaritas and which was for grinding guano!

Later in September, a group of six Drury faculty, staff, and students attended our first Greening of the Campus Conference in Muncie, Indiana. Our group included the web editor, the grounds director, a physics professor (a champion who had pushed hard for environmental initiatives since the early 1970s), an environmental economics professor, and an undergraduate senior. We moved through each day, mouths agape at the other schools that were launching laudable sustainability initiatives. We also realized that Drury had more going on than we had realized, and that nobody was telling our story. Upon returning to Drury, we six convened regularly throughout the year as a self-appointed ad hoc sustainability council, and developed a document: "Drury University Road Map to Sustainability."

The year unfolded with several compelling speakers and events. I fielded more phone calls about recycling—still with no answers. I talked to the press every week about what sustainability was and why Drury was hosting a year-long series about it. Each week, I got a little better at answering their questions and telling our story.

Terry Tempest Williams was our final speaker of the year in April 2006. She spent two days on our campus listening to students, staff, and faculty as they told our story and sought her wisdom. Our student leader on the sustainability council, Amy Strickland, and I dined with Terry the first night and pondered with her our futures as sustainability leaders. On her second evening, as she addressed a packed house in our sacred campus chapel, Terry surprised me. I thought she would tell us her own stories as she so eloquently writes in *Refuge, Red: Passion and Patience in the Desert,* or *The Open Space of Democracy.* But she mostly told our own story right back to us, weaving seamlessly the pieces she had picked up in her thirty-six hours with us. She shined light on our potential and issued challenges by name to our emerging sustainability champions, including the Drury president. She empowered us to claim our momentum and carry it forward. A wiggly but quiet two-year-old Clara looked up into my face and whispered, "Mommy, why are you crying?"

Later that summer of 2006, to celebrate the end of my Theme Year Director duties, my fellow-biologist husband and I went on a rare date. After a high carbon footprint meal at a fancy steakhouse, we went to see *An Inconvenient Truth* at the local, independent theater. We both came out of that silent, stunned, overwhelmed, awakened. We sat in the front seat of the car for a long time, quiet, thinking. I said to him, "I think this is what we have to do. In this conservative region the evolution-creation battles we've both engaged in are inconsequential compared to this. Our research on food webs on islands doesn't matter right now. We *must* use our credentials to lead the conversation about climate change in our community, on our campuses, and across the nation. This is all that really matters right now, if we want to ensure that Clara and her children will have a place to live on a healthy planet." So, we did. We shifted. We made a commitment to stay engaged in campus sustainability issues and to lead these charges on our respective campuses.

Evolving into Operations and Administration

Luckily, the Sustainability Theme Year awakened Drury to a reality: our mission mandated that we embrace sustainability both operationally and in our academic frameworks. With a rich campus conversation already underway, launching some new initiatives was easy. We landed a couple of small grants to fund some energetic and innovative students to launch a campus-wide, comprehensive recycling program. We began addressing our obvious energy hemorrhages across campus, and we started being much more thoughtful about water conservation. Like so many institutions, operational sustainability initiatives popped up all over campus: tray-less dining, a bike-loan program, solar panels, geothermal systems, a new LEED-certified arena, dormitory, and standards for construction, a transition to electric vehicles in the campus fleet, and so on. Over the next six years, this slowly became our way of thinking about ourselves, particularly after we hired in 2011 a new visionary Facilities Director and a new Grounds Director passionate about sustainability.

In 2006, our president, John Sellars, saw the potential for our six-person ad hoc sustainability council to lead an important charge, so he renamed it, expanded it, and empowered it as the "President's Council on Sustainability." One of the first things the council recommended was the creation of a Sustainability Director position. We crafted the job description with blatant plagiarism of Middlebury's position description. We hoped that the position could be a full-time staff position, and that Amy, our student representative on the council who was about to graduate, would be our first Sustainability Director. But, knowing that the university had little money to allocate, we offered the president two models: a full-time staff position with salary and benefits, or a half-time position for a faculty member with compensation to their home department for a half-time teaching release. Perhaps not surprisingly, the president chose the less-expensive model and appointed me as Drury's first Director of Campus Sustainability. That backfired. I didn't really want it, and Amy really did! But, I accepted it, assuming it would be temporary. The position came with no administrative stipend, no budget, no empowerment beyond my own tenured status, and no office space beyond my disorganized, overfull, teensy faculty office.

Also in spring 2007, President Sellars became one of the early signatories on the American College and University President's Climate Commitment (ACUPCC). Indeed, he would need a go-to person to ensure that greenhouse gas emissions inventories were conducted each year, and that a Climate Action Plan would be developed and implemented. This became the raison d'être for the Sustainability Director position, although the position itself also interfaced with campus facilities planning and management, fund raising and alumni relations, curriculum development, community outreach, student life initiatives, and public relations.

President Sellars signed the ACUPCC, and then a few weeks later resigned! An interim president was appointed, Todd Parnell, a retired local banker, community leader, and environmental philanthropist. Todd and his family were passionate about water quality issues in the Ozarks. During his first week as the interim Drury president, Todd attended the first ACUPCC Leadership Summit in Washington, DC, to participate in the public signing of The Commitment. A reporter from the *New York Times* took his picture signing it and used that picture in the article. Todd emailed me from the summit late one evening after hearing Jim Hansen speak about climate change. He wrote, "I had no idea about the severity and urgency of climate change. I am so glad Drury is taking a lead on this." I knew then that the Sellars-to-Parnell transition was going to turn out OK. Todd also recognized shortly thereafter that we could achieve our goals so much more effectively if I had a budget and some dedicated office space.

Over the next four to five years, I supervised a growing number of student employees who ran the ever-expanding recycling program, helped with special event planning, conducted detailed energy audits, ran the bike maintenance shop, and served as internal liaisons to other campus units. I realized that my role as an educator was shifting to this more applied context of coaching my student employees, working with students from across campus who were doing class projects related to campus sustainability, and providing guest lectures to classes in numerous departments. I still taught half-time, but no longer biology classes to majors. I chose to shift my teaching to general education arenas to offer a Science of Sustainability course to non-science students, which I co-taught with colleagues from a variety of other disciplines including architecture, geography, environmental policy, and environmental management. While temporarily setting aside my field research, I continued to publish articles and an academic book from field data I had collected in 2005 and earlier. Somewhere in all that, I tried to make quality time for Clara. Yes, Clara . . . the true raison d'être . . . lest I forget that all of those long hours away from my child are the trade-off for feeling like I am doing my part to ensure her healthy future.

Each initiative was birthed—not always by me—with the usual writhing effort and pain that accompanies any birth. In my role, I had the joy of being the nexus of communication among all these initiatives popping up across campus—endorsing, funding, facilitating, nurturing, encouraging and informing projects, and sometimes bringing new ideas to the table. I also had the privilege to communicate our successes to our campus community, board of trustees, Springfield community, and national audiences, always being careful to acknowledge the hard work of so many leaders across our campus. But, those joys of the job were continually balanced by the daily uphill battle of trying to effect change within an organizational structure that was simply not very malleable. Regular run-ins with the former VP for Administration or the former director of Facilities Services would raise my blood pressure and send me retreating to my office to scream silently. The VPA only wanted to talk about costs and not about the potential for savings, not to mention intangible value for recruitment and retention. The Facilities Director just wanted me to keep my female and faculty nose out of his shop's business. The tendency to be a bold, mouthy, tenured faculty member really got me into trouble sometimes . . . trouble I could afford professionally, but not always emotionally.

Nonetheless, as per our ACUPCC obligations, we began in 2007 to establish our baseline greenhouse gas inventory. It was not so different from most other similar schools. We began working on our Climate Action Plan, but, even with the help of the President's Council on Sustainability, I felt like I was operating in a vacuum because the members of the executive leadership team were not involved in it, as they were in a state of constant transition with retirements, resignations, and reappointments. It was impossible to see how implementation would actually happen.

In January 2008, as Todd Parnell was settling into his presidency, he took me out to lunch at the posh, private Tower Club to discuss some of his thoughts on reorganizing the administration. My intuition told me that he was going to establish a VP for Sustainability position, and that he would appoint me to it. He told me his plans for a larger reorganization and got to the point where, as I had imagined, he said he wanted to establish a new position, "Vice President of Operations and Sustain-ability." I smiled cautiously and took a deep breath while Todd contin-ued, ". . . and I have offered this new position to Pete Radecki. What do you think about that? Can you work with Pete? I want you two to be a team." My fork dropped to the table, my jaw dropped to the floor, and I tried desperately for tears not to drop out of my eyes. Pete? Pete! Our VP for Institutional Advancement? Are you kidding me?!? Why not *me*? Had I not proven my leadership abilities thus far? Was it because I was a woman? A mom to a young child? Had he even *thought* of me? No, he hadn't. Of course I choked back my surprise and weakly answered, "Sure, yeah, I can work with Pete." Really, what Todd was thinking was that he needed a VP for Operations who would ensure that operations were done *sustainably*, not a VP of Sustainability.

I struggled through that spring of 2008 to establish the partnership with Pete. I moved my sustainability resources from my faculty office in the science building up to the Pete's office suite in the central administra-tion building—to put a stake in the ground for the centrality of sustain-ability in our institution, to work closely with Pete, and to take advantage of proximity to the president. It quickly became clear to me that Pete's primary motivations to implement any sustainability initiatives were the potential for cost savings and hedging against inevitable increases in ener-gy prices rather than some deep-rooted concern about climate change. We would spar, sometimes find consensus, usually not, and I would retreat to my office, close my door, and figuratively pound my head on the wall.

And then the economy imploded. Like many universities, our endow-ment tanked, and banks started breathing down our necks about our sud-den change in debt-to-endowment ratio. Sustainability initiatives were off the table, as were diversity initiatives, gender issues, and employee raises. Any motivation to work on the Climate Action Plan was lost. In spite of the fact that many of the initiatives in a Climate Action Plan would actu-ally *save* us money, the upfront capital to do them would simply not be forthcoming. But, we had a retired, independent banker at the helm with the knowledge, the leadership ability, and the guts to stand up to Bank of America and renegotiate our covenants with them. We pulled through it, as most other institutions did, and were stronger, leaner, and more certain of our new strategic directions than ever before.

As we rolled into fall 2010, with the BP oil gusher still fresh on our minds, Todd said, "Wendy, I'm getting hounded by the ACUPCC and some other signatory presidents about getting our overdue Climate Ac-tion Plan submitted. It's time now to get this done." Todd, Pete, the new, more progressive VPA, and I met to discuss what our goal should be. After much discussion about the relative value of energy efficiency, renewable energy credits, and onsite renewable energy production, we finally agreed on a plan that would prioritize implementation of energy efficiency measures, as well as other initiatives on transportation, water conservation, solid waste, and forest preservation and regeneration. We arbitrarily chose 2030 as our target date. Of course, this would ultimately need to be approved by the board of trustees.

Somehow, over the last four years, Pete and I learned to work together. Our early days of butting heads were slowly replaced with learning how we complemented each other in our biologist-versus-engineer skill sets, our worldviews, our gender, and our personalities. We learned how to set common goals and how to trade off on playing good cop versus bad cop in tactically moving certain initiatives through different channels. I threw my tenured, full-professor weight around, and he threw his vice presidential weight around. We started to get stuff done. Every chance we had to address the board of trustees, I would give a cheerleading, feel-good report on our latest sustainability successes, and Pete would pound on the topic of the growing deferred maintenance needs and beg for some sort of allocation in the annual operating budget to build such a fund.

When the time came in May 2011 for Pete and me to present to the board of trustees the Climate Action Plan (now renamed "Sustainability Action Plan" to appease the climate skeptics on the board), we were well prepared for a fight. Pete was determined to focus on the funding mechanism of a green revolving fund, using a complicated but realistic model of escalating energy prices and associated utility liability for the university, rather than let the board members get too lost in the weeds of the details of the implementation of the whole plan. (While green revolving funds can be complicated to set up and manage, the simple premise behind them involves a loan mechanism to pay upfront costs for energy renewal or efficiency programs onsite and to use the reduction in energy costs to generate the source of capital that repays the loan.)

Knowing that this was the culmination of four years' effort and the hurdle that must be jumped to move forward, Todd and I sat listening to Pete's detailed analysis and compelling argument to the operations committee of the board on a Thursday afternoon. Board members started challenging his model assumptions—6 percent energy cost escalators, campus growth predictions, and so forth. They picked his arguments apart, and things started to spiral downward quickly. I could sense the tension in Todd next to me. I, too, was incredibly frustrated. My iPhone vibrated on my lap, and I looked down to see a text from my dear friend and supporter, a campus groundskeeper. He said, "Don't forget to breathe." I took a deep breath, and then another. Todd, subconsciously, started to breathe with me. A brief pause ensued in the conversation, and I jumped in with a genuine, pleading smile. "Look, everyone, we could quibble over the details of the energy cost model all day, but we're really asking for something very simple here. We want to *monitor* our energy savings, *capture* our energy savings, and *reinvest* our energy savings. This makes sense. Dozens of other universities are doing it, and Drury only stands to gain."

Much collaborative discussion followed that eventually led to a consensus among the committee for how they would present it to the full board for final approval the next morning. As the meeting broke up and Pete was wiping the sweat from his brow, Todd turned to me and, forgetting decorum, hugged me, saying, "We *did* it! We get to *do* this!" I smiled, and said cautiously, "We still have to get through tomorrow morning."

The next morning, we presented to the full board. I gave an introduction for how the Sustainability Action Plan fit into the mission of the university and the purpose of higher education, and challenged the board to accept that, beyond just being the "right thing to do," it was a strategic business decision for the institution to move in this direction. Then Pete repeated a simplified version of his energy-cost-hedging argument. More board members picked it apart. One member criticized the whole Sustainability Action Plan as entirely unnecessary; he considered climate change no real threat. Another member, one whom I had been expecting to be an ally, said, "This *is* 'the right thing to do.' It is so much 'the right thing to do' that I don't even know why we are having a conversation about this. But, since we are, I'd like to say that *everything* we do at Drury ought to be 'the right thing to do,' and given that this green revolving fund *is* going to generate some substantial savings and cash flow, I would like to suggest that 50 percent of that be returned to either the operating budget or to other initiatives that we also believe are important, such as diversity, disability accessibility, or gender equity issues. Pete began to argue that we needed to reinvest 100 percent to build the fund, but I interrupted and said, "I'll take 50, 50 percent's good."

Another board member chimed in, pulling out a hard copy of *Greening the Bottom Line* that I had sent to the board a week earlier (Weisbord, Dautremont-Smith, and Orlowski 2011). She said, "Did any of you even read this document on green revolving funds? If you had, we wouldn't be arguing right now. This makes sense. This explains *how* it works and how other universities have benefited greatly from this. We would be foolish to not get immediately on board with establishing such a fund and, for that matter, implementing as soon as possible the initiatives in the Sustainability Action Plan."

And with that, the chairman of the board called the question. With just a voice vote, the nays were about as loud as the ayes. Pete had sweat rolling down his cheeks. My heart was racing. Todd, who was sitting in front of where I was standing, kept turning around to look at me. The chairman said, "Well, I suppose we'll need to vote with a show of hands then. All in favor say aye: 22. All opposed say nay: 9." Success! Drury's Sustainability Action Plan, with a green revolving fund as the primary funding mechanism, had finally been approved, only eighteen months past the ACUPCC due date! And, as is usually the case at Drury after a heated debate, we closed the ranks and moved forward.

Since May 2011, changes in banking industry economics have opened up the opportunity for us to spend $5 million in much-needed deferred maintenance projects, including several energy-related projects, spending that supports the growth of the green revolving fund. Many of the goals in the Sustainability Action Plan (e.g., improvements in building envelopes, HVAC systems, and lighting) will be realized much sooner than we had planned. Carbon neutrality looks closer than I ever thought it could be.

Returning to My Academic Roots

In the meantime, sustainability was starting to bubble over on the academic side, as well. Given that the Sustainability Action Plan included not just operational initiatives but academic, research, and outreach goals, too, the plan's approval was timely for infusing momentum into several growing initiatives in those realms.

Sustainability in general education and within disciplines other than Environmental Studies blossomed between 2005 and 2012. Several faculty across campus voluntarily developed new units on sustainability in their courses, such as a public relations course that tackled ways to promote campus sustainability initiatives more effectively. They developed entirely new courses with sustainability-related themes, such as a Psychology of Sustainability course, and my Science of Sustainability course, which fulfilled a general education science requirement. The School of Architecture even developed an entire focus area on sustainable design and technology, and infused sustainable design and planning into community-based projects through their Center for Community Studies, their design-build studios, including a LEED Platinum-rated Habitat for Humanity home, and other outreach activities.

On the formal environmental education front, starting in 1978, Drury was the first school in Missouri to offer any sort of environmental program. Our Environmental Studies major has produced some incredible national and international business and government leaders. We launched an Environmental Science major in 1999, and then an Environmental Health Science major in 2001. This collection of major offerings, which we loosely called the Environmental Programs, was not really a department, with not really a budget, and its director worked without a stipend or administrative release time, but it nurtured a course infrastructure, a growing number of alumni, and a strong contribution to general education offerings that began to attract a growing number of students. With Dr. Teresa Carroll taking the reins of the Environmental Programs in 2009 from the retired founding director, she infused new life and energy into those majors.

Teresa worked with the affiliated faculty of the Environmental Programs to revamp the curricula of the three majors, to ramp up recruitment of students, to develop opportunities to partner with community organizations, and to nurture student interest in adding one of the programs as a second major or minor. Her tireless efforts translated into over 600 percent growth in student enrollment in these majors from 2009 to 2011.

On a parallel track, in summer 2008, we launched the Ozarks Center for Sustainable Solutions (OCSS), a new pollution prevention center at Drury that would provide non-regulatory, technical assistance to area businesses and organizations to help them reduce waste, conserve energy, and cut costs. Led by two talented staff, including Amy Strickland, Drury's OCSS has channeled more than $4 million in state and federal funds into the Ozarks region to stimulate sustainability initiatives.[1] Dozens of student interns majoring in business, economics, architecture, sociology, biology, public relations, and our various environmental programs have worked with local manufacturers, hospitals, municipalities, retailers, and hotel groups to identify and implement projects. More importantly, the OCSS became Drury's public face and outreach arm for helping lead the region's transformation toward sustainability. However, the university seemed oblivious to the value the OCSS was providing to our students, the institution, or our region and seemed unwilling to provide any sort of long-term support to ensure the center's sustainability, as upcoming grant cycles were promising to be leaner.

It began to dawn on us in fall 2009 that we were going to have to create a new model for our environmental education and outreach efforts. Our environmental courses were bursting at the seams, and we were relying too heavily on adjuncts to teach them. Our campus sustainability initiatives, the OCSS, and our Environmental Programs were duplicating efforts and not working as synergistically as they should have been. Drury was missing an opportunity to brand itself as the Missouri and regional leader in environmental education and sustainable operations. We decided that a School of the Environment would integrate our academic experiences within the context of the living laboratory of a sustainably operating campus and train students to be able to go out into the community to lead sustainability efforts.

Teresa and I met with the president in 2009 to float this idea, and he challenged us to develop this as a "new and unique niche" that Drury could fill. We set to work creating the vision, collecting feedback from dozens of community leaders and potential employers of our students, researching other schools, centers, and institutes at other universities, assessing our existing resources, and writing proposals for different audiences. We chugged along, making slow but steady progress, although not at the pace that I might have liked.

We ran into various obstacles. As the faculty revised the general education curriculum, the university as a whole prepared for a re-accreditation visit and then launched a comprehensive strategic planning effort, and one of the strategic imperatives was to restructure the academic organization. The VP for Academic Affairs preferred to postpone the development of a School of the Environment until those bigger issues could be resolved. But, we plugged ahead with the president's blessings and commitment to bring in a couple of external consultants in fall 2011 to help us craft the concept further and position it in the national context. First, we had Dr. Norm Christensen, founding dean of Duke University's School of the Environment, visit for a day with board members, administrators, faculty, and students. His wisdom and insights from decades of experience on the academic side of higher education were invaluable. Most importantly, though, was his quiet confidence and optimism that Drury could, should, and would pull this off. His advice for strategic processes and structures—such as insisting on a certain degree of university investment in the launching of the school, ensuring endowment separation and budgetary autonomy from other units, and building a dedicated advisory board of alumni and community stakeholders—is proving essential.

We also hosted Leith Sharp, founding director of Harvard's Office of Sustainability, who brought more operational perspectives and an understanding of how best to train students for jobs in a growing green economy. Leith happened to land in Springfield during a week in fall 2011 when everything was blowing up again. The final version of the institutional revision of our general education curriculum was coming to the faculty for a vote. Many of us were frustrated because the core courses that we had imagined would create the platform for sustainability themes had mysteriously disappeared from the curriculum in the latest iterations. As part of the goals of the Sustainability Action Plan, we needed to have sustainability strongly positioned at the center of our general education curriculum, as well as infused across all disciplines. We were in the final days of battling to replace and define the core sustainability-oriented courses in the general education sequence. Leith offered not just great wisdom and insight, but also her calm assurances to Teresa and me that it would all work out OK—and that if, somehow, things fell through, which they wouldn't, but if they did, that we both had great research careers to return to with passion and satisfaction.

The following week, the faculty finally approved an amendment to the general education curriculum, now called, "The Drury Core: Engaging Our World." This additional Global Connections course will provide a much-needed overview, conceptual framework, and tool kit for making connections across disciplines on issues relating to environmental, social, and economic sustainability, and will serve as a foundation for four more globally- or sustainability-oriented courses within the disciplines.

After Norm's and Leith's visits, the chairman of the board of trustees instructed the VP for Academic Affairs to include Teresa and me on the agenda for the meeting of the academic committee of the board of trustees. Teresa and I planned long and hard for that, crafting a powerful but concise two-page document for them to read ahead of time and honing our pitch to three minutes or less. Despite being placed next to last on an overfull agenda, with ten minutes left in the meeting, they got to us. Teresa said her piece. A couple of questions followed. I answered with more detail. Then one board member slowly responded, "This is a big mistake. . . ." Gulp! He didn't want us to link this effort with the larger process of restructuring of the university because *that* process would (or should) take too long. He thought this was important, urgent, and absolutely the highest priority and must be done immediately. "Now *this* is skating to where the hockey puck is going to *be*!" another member said. The rest of the committee members agreed unanimously and enthusiastically. They made it clear that they wanted a full proposal to the full board by May 2012 and would like to be ready to launch by fall.

As of this writing, funding issues have placed the School of the Environment on hold, but nonetheless, potential donors are emerging from the most unexpected places. Individuals, families, corporations, and foundations are starting to hear about our plans and asking how they can get involved. In early November 2011, I was walking back from a meeting across campus with Todd. Todd, who had recently announced his plan to retire from the presidency in May 2013, leaned in and whispered, "I have something to tell you. The School of the Environment has been designated as the recipient of an estate gift. Of course, somebody has to die first, and we hope that won't happen anytime soon, but the designation is a powerful symbol and beacon to others to consider the importance of this role for Drury in our community." I looked at him, thrilled, and asked, "Can I ask who designated the gift?" He paused, smiled, and answered, "Betty and me." I stopped and looked at him, shocked. "I can't hug you on the sidewalk, can I?" "No," he answered, and we both laughed. He acknowledged their conviction that establishing a School of the Environment should be one of the highest priorities for the university and for the university's relationship to the Ozarks region, and the gift was their way of expressing it.

The convergence of Drury's operational commitments to sustainability—sustainability across the curriculum, an emerging School of the Environment, and numerous outreach efforts to the region—leads me to believe that Drury may be finally transforming into the sustainability leader for our region, joining many other institutions that are also transforming themselves and their regions in powerful ways to ensure that, as a society, we are poised to adapt to this rapidly changing planet.

I took a sabbatical in the spring 2012 semester—a much-needed time for rest, reflection, writing, and field research. I continued my work on islands in the San Juan archipelago of Washington because I am, after all, an ecologist, not an "environmentalist." Most importantly, I spent some long overdue quality time with Clara as she celebrated her eighth birthday, learned to ride a bicycle, and lost her fifth tooth. As I reflect on the journey we have all made—my personal journey and Drury's—I am in awe at how powerful the outcome has been thus far, despite the overwhelming messiness, the battle scars, the investments lost and gained. I am amazed at how we got here. I look toward the next ten years at Drury under a new president, ten years during which Clara will finish grade school and high school and move on into higher education. Most likely she will find herself at a school that has similarly matured into its commitment to sustainability. And through her experiences with me on this journey and her experiences in college, she will most certainly emerge as a visionary, entrepreneurial, risk-taking leader for change in a much different world.

Notes

1. Amy Strickland is now the executive director of Partnership for Sustainability, the successor of OCSS, which includes universities, hospital systems, city and county government, the utility company, and public school systems. The consortium collectively controls 65 percent of the landmass and buildings in Springfield, employs 75 percent of Springfield's workforce, and consumes more than 60 percent of the energy produced by the utility company.

References

Weisbord, Dano, Julian Dautremont-Smith, and Mark Orlowski. 2011. *Greening the Bottom Line*. Cambridge, MA: Sustainable Endowments Institute. http://greenbillion.org/wp-content/uploads/2011/10/GreeningTheBottomLine.pdf.

2

Building a Decentralized, Grassroots, Campus Sustainability Organization and Community: The Transformational Impact of Green Values

David Whiteman

The University of South Carolina, chartered in 1801, is a comprehensive, urban research university with over 29,500 students in 324 degree programs. Located two blocks from the State House in downtown Columbia, the 570-acre campus provides the perfect laboratory for experimenting with social, economic, and environmental sustainability.

As I left the campus early one evening, I peered through the glass walls separating the rooms in the LEED-certified Learning Center in which I work: in one room a yoga class, in another a meeting of our campus student environmental group, in a third a presentation on solar energy, and in our conference room a meeting of the executive committee of the local Sierra Club chapter. Five years ago, when I was first appointed to a leadership position for campus sustainability, the Learning Center stood empty at night. What has happened since then has been a wild ride, and the most fulfilling period of my thirty-year career as a professor of political science.

The creation over the past five years of what has come to be called Sustainable Carolina has provided great professional and personal satisfaction for me. Intellectually, I have been pleased to be part of an experiment that demonstrates how "green values" can be successfully implemented in the real world. Organizationally, I have been intrigued by the ways in which a grassroots, decentralized, non-hierarchical organization can survive and even flourish within a classic hierarchical university structure. And personally, for the first time, I have been part of a real community on a university campus, a community that continues to grow and attract others (beginning with three staff in 2006, doubling each year to forty-seven by the fall of 2011 and then nearly doubling again to eighty-seven in the spring of 2012).

My preparation for this transformational process began in the mid-1990s, when I began experimenting with a much smaller-scale version of this project. At the time, no one in my political science department was teaching a course on the environment, and that seemed to be an inexcusable omission in our curriculum. Despite having no direct academic background in the area, having been trained as a specialist in congressional behavior, I proposed to teach a course on Green Politics (though the title was deemed to be too radical at that time, so for the first decade the course was entitled Ecology and Politics). My idea was for students not just to learn *about* green political thought but also to *experience* green values in the way the course was actually taught—which according to my reading meant turning over as much of the course as possible to the students themselves, creating a cooperative learning community governed by non-hierarchical, consensus-based decision making. In 2006, when I was appointed as the Faculty Principal of the Green Quad and the Director of the Learning Center for Sustainable Futures, and by default one of the key players in campus sustainability efforts, I wanted to see if this model would work on a campus-wide scale. And, to an amazing degree, it has.

Fast-forward five years, and Sustainable Carolina is an "umbrella organization" that integrates three major sustainability-related organizations on campus: the Office of Sustainability, the Learning Center for Sustainable Futures, and the Green Quad Living-Learning Community. As detailed in table 2.1, the eighty-seven staff members of Sustainable Carolina are organized into a decentralized set of seventeen project teams, focused on topics such as campus food systems, transportation and energy, sustainable design, campus planning, experiential learning, global sustainability, green leadership, assessment, marketing, and curriculum. For most teams, the project coordinator is a graduate or undergraduate student (paid or receiving course credit). All teams are a mix of students, faculty, staff, and community members—during the spring 2012 semester there were sixty-three undergraduate students, ten graduate students, two faculty members, ten university staff members, and two community members. All staff members participate in a series of leadership development workshops, created by the Green Leadership Team, which provide training in a broad set of organizational and communication skills. And the Assessment Team monitors both the process of each project team and the performance of individual team members.

But it wasn't always so. In spite of the fact there had been an innovative Sustainable Universities Initiative, which had spurred attention to a wide scope of campus sustainability issues (Schmidt et al. 2004) in the 1990s, when I was first appointed as the Faculty Principal of the Green Quad in 2006, campus sustainability efforts were at a low point. Within a span of six months, the three primary faculty and administrative leaders for campus sustainability (and for the Sustainable Universities Initiative) had all left the university (the dean of the School of Environment, the director of the Sustainable Universities Initiative, and the Sustainability Coordinator). Thus, at the time of my appointment as Faculty Principal, there was a relative vacuum in leadership of campus sustainability efforts.

What followed was a gradual but continual growth of our grass-roots campus "movement," developing the support and enthusiasm and resources that have led to the establishment of Sustainable Carolina. Our success was due in part to some amazing individuals who have been involved over the years as undergraduate and graduate students, full-time staff members, faculty members, and community volunteers. It was also due to significant changes in the cultural landscape over the period from 2006 to 2011, as "green" went from a word slightly outside the mainstream (at least in South Carolina) to the ubiquitous adjective for every product that it is today. And also crucial was the overall support of the larger university, which initially took the form of tolerance of our experiments and gradually shifted (due partly to the appointment of a new president and partly to the strong advocacy of Gene Luna, my official supervisor in Student Affairs) to more positive appreciation of our accomplishments, particularly because they so often enhanced the standing of the university. Looking back, the growth of Sustainable Carolina followed three general principles: create energy, make connections, and grow green.

Creating Energy

As I began my first year as Faculty Principal of the Green Quad, my staff consisted of an administrative assistant and a graduate assistant. Our first moves were designed to bring energy to the Green Quad and the Learning Center by cultivating a critical mass of students who were motivated to take action on sustainability issues. We pursued this objective in three ways: convincing the primary activist student group on campus to adopt the Learning Center as its base of operations, creating a Green Learning Community within the Green Quad to become the core of activity, and creating a new course for first-year students interested in sustainability to attract them to the Learning Center. The first was the easiest. As the advisor to the campus environmental group, Students Advocating a Greener Environment (SAGE), I encouraged them to begin meeting here by offering to provide them with office space and programming resources. We

Table 2.1
Sustainable Carolina Structure

GREEN COUNCIL (meets once a month, consensus decision making)
• All staff members
COORDINATING COUNCIL (meets weekly, consensus decision making)
• Full-time staff members (Faculty Principal of Green Quad, Residence Life Coordinator of the Green Quad, Assistant Director of Learning Center, Director of Office of Sustainability, Program Assistant for the Office of Sustainability, Housing Sustainability Coordinator, Facilities Sustainability Coordinator, Recycling Coordinator)
• Graduate assistants
PROJECT TEAMS (meet weekly, teams divided by category: education, transformation, and resource)

Education Teams
• Curriculum Team: Strengthen and expand campus-wide curricular opportunities.
• Campus-Wide Programming Team: Build campus-wide green education, awareness, and sustainability programming and events.
• Greening the Mind Team: Promote green pedagogy, green philosophy, and green lifestyles.
• Experiential Learning Team: Promote experiential and service learning, undergraduate research, and opportunities in the natural world.
• Global Sustainability Team: Promote education, research, and action on sustainability (including social justice issues) across the globe.
• Green Quad Community Education Team: Promote integrative learning and green exploration for residents of the Green Quad Living-Learning Community.
• Eco-Reps Team: Promote and expand sustainable living practices in on-campus and off-campus student housing.

Transformation Teams
• Campus Planning Team: Coordinate campus sustainability policy and planning and support campus "Green Teams."
• Green Leadership Team: Train and support campus sustainability leaders and Sustainable Carolina staff.
• Assessment Team: Assess campus sustainability, Sustainable Carolina project teams, and individual staff members.
• Marketing Team: Coordinate marketing, public relations, and campus and community outreach.
• Local Environmental Action Team: Promote education, research, and action on local environmental and social justice issues.
• Administrative Team: Provide administrative support to Sustainable Carolina and all project teams.

Table 2.1
(Continued)

Resource Teams
• Campus Food Team: Promote research, education, and action on sustainable food systems.
• Recycling Team: Promote, research, education, and action on recycling and freecycling.
• Transportation and Energy Team: Promote research, education, and action on sustainable transportation and energy systems.
• Built Environment Team: Promote research, education, and action on sustainable landscaping, sustainable design, and green building technology.

now host their weekly meetings in our lounge and work with their leadership to collaborate on events and initiatives. Some of the more active SAGE members generally become student interns and undergraduate staff assistants for Sustainable Carolina, which greatly improves collaboration.

The second part of our strategy to create a critical mass of activist students was the creation of a Green Learning Community, which began in the fall of 2007. The Green Learning Community was designed to cultivate a smaller group of students living in the Green Quad, with the intention that the programming developed by and for them will energize students in the rest of the Green Quad. Today, in 2012, the Green Learning Community has thirty students, selected from over a hundred applicants and representative of a broad spectrum of majors throughout the university (everything from Business and Engineering to English and Anthropology). Community members all live on the same floor in the Green Quad and create and participate in special programs: an organic garden, occasional community meals, informal meetings with faculty members and visiting scholars and activists, on-going activist and research projects, and field trips to places and events of interest (such as an organic farm, an ecovillage, and student conferences). To coordinate these activities, community members meet for an hour each week, as part of the one-credit course that gives them credit for their community activities.

Creating a course on Green Explorations for first-year students, with the support of a grant from the Dean of the College of Arts and Sciences, was the third part of our strategy. The academic rationale for the course was to provide an interdisciplinary experience for first-year students that would strengthen offerings in environmental studies as well as create a structure within which faculty could collaborate on teaching and research. Our strategic rationale was that it would attract a set of first-year students already passionate about environmental issues and would also provide an opportunity to invite faculty from a wide range of disciplines to come to the Learning Center and interact with our students. The course itself encouraged students new to the university to expand their horizons in four different ways: (1) explore the community, by taking weekly field trips into the local environment, learning about the geography and the social and natural history of the region; (2) explore the disciplines, by learning about what the concepts of "green" and "environment" mean in a broad range of academic disciplines, from humanities and social sciences to the professional schools; (3) explore themselves, by regularly recording in a journal their own individual reflections about the relationship between humans and the environment; and (4) explore action, by engaging in opportunities to respond to the problems identified during the semester.

As a critical mass of activist students has evolved over the past five years, our programs have served as a catalyst for further sources of activism, and we have attempted to support new groups that have emerged. A few years ago we worked with the Residence Hall Association to create an Eco-Rep program to promote and expand sustainable living practices in on-campus student housing, and the first two students to lead that program were members of our Green Learning Community. A year later, the Student Body President first appointed a Secretary for Environmental Affairs, and the Student Senate first created an Environment Committee, and most of the students leading those organizations had been previously or currently participants in our programs. Sustainable Carolina now supports the Student Sustainability Coalition, an umbrella group made up of representatives from all sustainability-related student organizations. One of our most successful programs to support our activist students has been to send them to conferences to meet peers and spend time with national organizers. Recently we have been sending fifty to sixty students each year to conferences such as Power Shift and the Southeast Student Renewable Energy Conference.

Making Connections

Making connections was somewhat foreign to me. I had spent many years as a faculty member retreating into my office. I enjoyed interactions with students, but I also valued the ability to spend long periods of time alone in my office doing my research. Fortunately, as Faculty Principal my very first hire was Jason Craig, who is a master connector. As the Assistant

Director of the Learning Center, he prodded me to become aware of the multitude of connections and collaborations possible on campus. Many of these connections were with offices within Student Affairs, which I had been only vaguely aware of previously, including the Study Abroad Office, Undergraduate Research Office, Community Service Office, Carolina Leadership Initiative, and First-Year Reading Experience.

My attitude was initially one of reluctance, partly based on my faculty style and partly based on wanting not to lose control of our programs. But what followed in the early years was a push to make ourselves open, to accommodate and cultivate diverse constituencies. We opened ourselves to the community, hosting the annual meeting of Conservation Voters of South Carolina and monthly meetings of the local chapters of the Green Building Council, Trout Unlimited, and the Sierra Club. We opened ourselves to other campus departments, hosting academic classes and meetings of the Environmental Advisory Committee. Abandoning the normal faculty skepticism, we began to take advantage of each new campus initiative, whether it was integrative learning or the Quality Enhancement Plan or the Carolina Leadership Initiative. We became a gateway for student involvement in service-learning projects linked to sustainability and the environment, including projects in conjunction with community environmental groups and local organic farms. In our search for connections, some avenues were fruitful and some were not, but our general stance was being open to collaboration and experimentation.

Of course the fruit that we were seeking, in making connections, was in part the resources we needed to pursue our programs. Our connection making took on an entrepreneurial spirit as we sought resources from our collaborators. The Housing Department funded a graduate assistantship for us to promote sustainability within the residence halls. The Environment and Sustainability Program funded a graduate assistantship to promote campus-wide planning. The Provost's Office funded a graduate assistantship to promote campus-wide programming and the First-Year Reading Experience (during the year that the assigned book was Colin Beavan's *No Impact Man*). The Landscaping Department provided equipment and personnel to assist with our desires to tear up lawns and build organic gardens, orchards, and bioswales.

Growing a Green Organization

While creating energy and making connections were necessary for our success, the essential component was maintaining our green values as we grew and evolved into an organization incorporating a grassroots, decentralized, non-hierarchical structure. At the start we did not realize the full implication of these values. For the first two years we had a relatively traditional structure, with the Faculty Principal, the assistant director of the Learning Center, a graduate assistant, and an increasing number of interns and undergraduate assistants. But as we grew, that hierarchical structure began to be an inhibiting factor. Our efforts at making connections increased the number of graduate students, from one to three, thanks to the Housing Department and the Environment and Sustainability Program. At the same time we were attracting more and more undergraduate interns. Jason and I initially approached the situation with a sense of scarcity—how many graduate students and interns could we "handle," if we were to adequately "direct" them.

Then, in the spring of 2010, we made the crucial decision. Why not replace scarcity with abundance? Why not just accept everyone who wanted to be an intern, and see what happened? Why not create a radically decentralized and non-hierarchical structure, with graduate students and advanced undergraduates leading project teams that would accomplish our goals? This restructuring turned out to be the crucial decision that has led to everything else. The following fall we incorporated into that structure the Residence Life Coordinator of the Green Quad (along with the student resident mentors he directed). We also attracted the involvement of Michael Koman, the newly designated director of the Office of Sustainability (and previously the Sustainability Coordinator who left when I first started), when the mutually beneficial nature of the relationship became clear. At the time, the director had the title and access to the administration, and we had the students and the resources needed to work toward the campus sustainability goals.

Our structure has taken clearer shape over the past two years. In the spring of 2010, with the crucial support of the director of the Office of Sustainability, we decided to call ourselves "Sustainable Carolina," merging the Green Quad, the Learning Center for Sustainable Futures, and the Office of Sustainability. Maintaining a decentralized and non-hierarchical structure has been very challenging, and we have elaborated our structure in response to various problems that have arisen. Project teams now begin each semester with a set of goals, a history of their previous activities, a list of the Sustainability Tracking, Assessment, & Rating System (STARS) criteria related to their goals, and explicit guidance about the consensus decision-making process that should guide their operations. The Green Leadership Team provides training in our style of leadership and decision making through orientation and professional development workshops for all staff members. And the Assessment Team has emerged as the central accountability mechanism in the structure, monitoring both the performance of teams and the performance of individuals.

Once a month the entire staff assembles in a Green Council meeting, where project teams exchange updates on what they are doing and the Green Leadership Team usually provides training related to whatever organizational problems have developed. Between Green Council meetings, the Coordinating Council meets weekly to approve, through a consensus process, all project, policy, and funding proposals from the project teams. Two aspects of the council are notable for the overall success of Sustainable Carolina. First, the Coordinating Council is made up of all the stakeholders in the organization, including our graduate assistants and all the full-time staff either directly or indirectly associated with us. What this means is that, once a week, our currently nine graduate assistants assemble with the director of the Office of Sustainability, the Sustainability Coordinator for the Housing Department, the campus Recycling Coordinator, the Sustainability Coordinator for the Facilities Department, the Residence Life Coordinator for the Green Quad, and the Learning Center staff. Second, as part of the program approval process, the Coordinating Council makes all funding decisions (except for graduate student hiring, which is done by full-time staff), even though officially the resources available to the organization are controlled by the Faculty Principal and the director of the Office of Sustainability. Allowing the Coordinating Council to control the funding has been a key component of decentralizing control and empowering everyone.

I remember teaching my classes in American government about the structural principles of the founders, and about how they hoped to create an autonomous governmental "machine" by tinkering with the components—carefully balancing the three branches of government, creating an elaborate system of checks and balances. But, as James Madison put it, the machine needed the "great mechanical power" of representation to provide its energy. In our green structure, the crucial source of energy comes from the empowerment of students. From participating and leading the project teams, to being part of a consensus decision-making process in the Coordinating Council, the operations of Sustainable Carolina are student-run to a surprising degree. Empowering students requires sometimes tolerating a significant amount of chaos, but the benefit is to produce students skilled in a style of leadership that the university and the world needs. One exceptional example was in 2010, when two students became totally obsessed with documenting our programs for the Great Power Race, an international competition sponsored by Bill McKibben's 350.org organization, whose goal is to reduce the carbon dioxide level in the atmosphere to below the scientific consensus of a safe 350 parts per million. Through their energetic efforts, we amassed the highest point total of any university in China, India, and the United States. The competition was not something I personally would have advocated spending staff time on, but when the two winning universities for each country were announced, imagine how proud our students were that the University of South Carolina was able to share the stage with the University of California, Berkeley!

Concluding Reflections

My role in the creation of Sustainable Carolina over the past five years has been a time of great professional and personal satisfaction for me. I have been intrigued to see how "green values" can be successfully implemented in the real world, and how a grassroots, decentralized organization can be tolerated and even embraced by a classic hierarchical university structure. But most intriguing and satisfying to me has been the ability to help create and be part of a community—the first time I have felt part of a real community on a university campus. Some have perhaps found this more easily in their academic life, but in my experience it is relatively rare. Being part of a community has certainly re-energized me, providing me a work environment that is fulfilling and even inspiring.

What I have been arguing in the past several years at academic conferences on sustainability is that traditional leadership models and organizational structures are an impediment to the full realization of the mission of campus sustainability offices. "Greening the campus" must go beyond transforming the curriculum and the daily personal habits of students, faculty, and staff. Our recent efforts have focused on transforming the leadership, decision making, and culture of our campus sustainability organizations, following green principles of decentralization and grassroots democracy, and incorporating an extensive leadership training program based on the "social change model" of leadership (Komives and Wagner 2009).

But what is implicit in this argument, and what is clearer to me now, is that it is not just campus sustainability organizations that need to be changed. The same traditional leadership models and organizational structures that inhibit campus sustainability organizations are an impediment to the entire university community. Universities are a microcosm reflecting a global phenomenon—our over-reliance on huge top-down structures to dominate decision making. Instead, a "green structure" provides a model for the kind of leadership and organizational culture ultimately necessary for a sustainable future.

Acknowledgments

As should be clear from this chapter, it is somewhat uncomfortable to focus on my individual role in the development of Sustainable Carolina when our success has resulted from an extremely collaborative effort. The other key actors in its development were Jason Craig, Gene Luna, Michael Koman, Carter Cox, and numerous graduate and undergraduate students.

References

Komives, Susan, and Wendy Wagner, eds. 2009. *Leadership for a Better World: Understanding the Social Change Model of Leadership Development*. San Francisco, CA: Jossey-Bass.

Schmidt, Michael, Alan Elzerman, Bruce Coull, and Patricia Jerman. 2004. South Carolina Sustainable Universities Initiative. In *Sustainability on Campus: Stories and Strategies for Change*, ed. Peggy F. Barlett and Geoffrey W. Chase, 243–258. Cambridge, MA: MIT Press.

3

Science and Technology Leaders for a Sustainable Future

Richard D. Schulterbrandt Gragg III, LaRae Donnellan, Ryan Mitchell, Clayton J. Clark II, and Viniece Jennings

Florida Agricultural and Mechanical University (Florida A&M University, or FAMU), an 1890 land-grant institution of 12,000 students, is dedicated to the advancement of knowledge, resolution of complex issues, and the empowerment of citizens and communities. The main campus is located in Tallahassee midway between Jacksonville and Pensacola; the College of Law is in Orlando.

Florida A&M University (FAMU) has been nationally ranked among the top twenty academic institutions awarding science and engineering degrees to African Americans from 2006 to 2010, (Committee on Underrepresented Groups and the Expansion of the Science and Engineering Workforce Pipeline et al. 2011), and was among the top twenty-five baccalaureate origin institutions of African American doctorates in the natural sciences and engineering from 2002 to 2006 (National Science Foundation 2011);. As such, FAMU has made educating its students in STEM disciplines (science, technology, engineering, and mathematics) a high priority. Over the last six years, our STEM commitment has been combined with a new priority to integrate sustainability and environmental issues, not only into the curriculum and research, but also into campus operations and student engagement. This chapter recounts how the five of us have connected in this work and have been, ourselves, inspired by the goal to prepare sustainability-literate, engaged STEM professionals.

This work is especially important because research shows us that African Americans and other minority populations are facing greater socioeconomic, environmental, and health risks than others (Hicken, Schulterbrandt Gragg, and Hu 2011; Horner and Robinson 2008). Problem-solving teams with diverse voices, life experiences, and perspectives will be essential as we move forward to research, develop, and implement sustainable community solutions (Jennings, Gaither, and Schulterbrandt Gragg 2012; Hicken, Schulterbrandt Gragg, and Hu 2011; Duxbury and Gillette 2007). The FAMU commitment to sustainability literacy across the curriculum for STEM and other students thus encourages many kinds of diversity for the science and technology professions.

Expanding STEM

Clayton J. Clark

We were convinced that FAMU's STEM education must expand to include ecological and environmental dimensions of earth systems, global human population policy, and multicultural literacy. In 2010, I designed a new course on Environmental Engineering Sustainability for the Civil and Environmental Engineering Department of FAMU. As part of the joint College of Engineering with Florida State University, this course provides foundational perspectives for environmental sustainability and green engineering, the first such course at an HBCU (Historically Black Colleges and Universities). We hoped FAMU's role as lead institution in this endeavor would attract students traditionally underrepresented in the STEM fields, thereby improving the diversity of those participating in sustainability and the engineering workforce as a whole (Clark and Schulterbrandt Gragg III 2011).

The class had nineteen students in its first iteration and sixteen the year after, more than 55 percent being graduate students. The course required students in groups to select a project related to environmental sustainability, evaluate this process holistically, and compare these factors to traditional methods. A couple of examples included comparing sustainable energy sources such as solar power to petroleum- and coal-produced energy, and the use of bamboo as opposed to steel to reinforce concrete. Student response was a strong rating of 4.5 out of 5.0, and all of them said they would recommend the course to other students. The breadth of sustainability as a topic surprised more than half of the class, which showed that my efforts to draw diverse fields and topics into their engineering curriculum had been successful (Clark and Schulterbrandt Gragg III 2011).

Richard D. Schulterbrandt Gragg

Sustainability and environmental issues have become emphasized in numerous areas across campus. Some entities include agriculture, allied and public health sciences, architecture, engineering, business, law, and journalism. The faculty added a module on environmental literacy to the mandatory Freshman Experience course in 2011. In fall 2012, Professor LaRae Donnellan will teach a new course titled Special Topics in Public Relations: Global Climate Crisis, which is open to all students. This year, the School of the Environment is considering expanding its programs to include an undergraduate degree in environmental studies, environmental health, and sustainability science. These curricula are intended for students who are primarily concerned with designing integrated social, economic, and biophysical processes that will help to maintain a healthy environment. These tracks also require my upper-level courses on environmental justice and environmental toxicology and human health, whose key learning objectives include a systematic understanding of and sustainable solutions for the social, economic, and environmental health inequities that burden minority and low-income communities (Jennings, Gaither, and Schulterbrandt Gragg 2012; Hicken, Schulterbrandt Gragg, and Hu 2011; Bullard et al. 2008). As of 2013, the School of Business and Industry and the School of Architecture are collaborating to offer an undergraduate degree in facilities management.

Moving from Curriculum to Engagement

LaRae Donnellan

I worked in public relations and was a communications department head for more than thirty years before I turned to teaching journalism and public relations full time. Working in my own academic silo at FAMU, I was able to introduce issues about the climate crisis as writing assignments or class projects, and my colleagues in journalism were patient with my repeated suggestions to "go green" and "teach green." In 2006, I volunteered to serve as the Journalism Division's representative to the Faculty Senate with one goal in mind: to create a "green committee" on campus, using the Senate as the springboard. The Senate president agreed to appoint the committee, and as it often happens when someone advocates the formulation of a committee, I was named the chair. I had hoped to put together a faculty, staff, and student group that would work with the administration to promote environmentally sustainable initiatives within the greater campus community. Our major campus-wide student sustainability group, the FAMU Green Coalition, emerged by December 2006. Our early actions involved aluminum can recycling, compact fluorescent lamp distribution in predominantly low- to moderate-income communities near the campus, and support for campus environmental awareness through workshops and movie nights. FAMU students learned how to become leaders in the sustainability movement at the 2009 and 2011 Power Shift conferences in Washington, DC. In 2010, we got more than a thousand members of the campus community to sign pledges to cut their carbon footprints.

Another major effort led by the Green Coalition and the Environmental Sciences Student Organization (ESSO) was hosting the 2008 National Teach-In sponsored by Focus the Nation. The teach-in was part of a strong national campaign to highlight climate change and the political action needed to address its ramifications. We organized more than twenty-five seminars on such topics as the "greening" of Florida; energy alternatives for the campus community; and the impacts of climate change on food, water, and environmental justice. "We are excited to be a part of this initiative," said President James Ammons. "It represents the enormous power that young people have when they use their education to create positive change in the world." Faculty, staff, and students were also active participants in the national webcast featuring Stanford climate scientist Stephen Schneider, green jobs pioneer Van Jones, sustainability expert Hunter Lovins, and actor and clean-energy advocate Edward Norton. These were powerful role models for how STEM fields were contributing to urgent national issues.

The National Teach-In fostered collaboration across academic disciplines and departments and with our community partners. We realized that we had a national voice that could and should address the science and public policy issues. Another impact was the collective realization that the FAMU community had many members already aware, interested, and involved in environmental and climate issues and was already implementing many sustainability-related initiatives across the campus.

The teach-in also set the stage for deeper engagement with sustainability at FAMU, as President Ammons, in the presence of the mayor of Tallahassee and other dignitaries, announced the formation of the Environment and Sustainability Council "to develop and implement an integrated strategic plan, interdisciplinary in scope, to make FAMU a well-recognized green and sustainable campus." Our grassroots efforts had paid off with an official university commitment. In the following years, under Richard Gragg's leadership, sustainability was integrated into the framework of the new university Master Plan for campus development, and sustainability became a fundamental goal in the university-wide strategic plan for 2010–2020.

Supporting Our Efforts

Viniece Jennings

My research and campus service illustrate the FAMU commitment to both sustainability and engagement. I arrived in 2006 to pursue my doctoral degree in environmental science with a concentration in policy and management. Working with Professor Gragg, my dissertation focuses on the public health implications of greenspace and especially urban trees. I am the first person in my family to pursue a doctorate; however, with this journey, I am always reminded that scholarship and success are not solely dependent on personal achievement but also on acts of service that invest in our human potential and sense of community. As inaugural members of the Green Coalition and ESSO, Ryan Mitchell, LaRae Donnellan, and I learned to work together, connecting efforts to sustainability and translating information into practical steps on campus. We sacrificed spare time, energy, and occasionally money in order to keep the momentum going and maintain a space where students could be heard, included, and empowered. In testament to interdisciplinary and intergenerational unison, FAMU students have hosted and networked with dynamic sustainability leaders, including EPA Administrator Lisa Jackson and Reverend Lennox Yearwood Jr., president and CEO of the Hip Hop Caucus, allowing our campaigns and initiatives to have diverse perspectives and reach multiple audiences. Being involved in sustainability has framed the "big picture" portrait of my professional endeavors.

As a student in the midst of faculty politics, I saw how group dynamics throughout the chain of command sometimes hindered progress, and I learned how essential it is to hold onto our vision while tactfully resolving conflicts. Frustration with some of our roadblocks encouraged me to seek additional training in sustainability. In 2009, I was selected as a southeastern fellow of the Environmental Leadership Program. The following year, I joined thirty students from around the world in Switzerland for the Youth Encounter on Sustainability. This program was a personal and professional adventure of a lifetime and forced me to leave my comfort zone. "If you do not refresh your dreams daily, then you will fall into normality," shared one of my instructors during breakfast. I left challenged to fulfill my destiny in this lifetime and inspire the next generation to do the same in theirs (Jennings, Baud, Mahat, Demashqieh, Otieno, Mabrouk 2011).

Ryan Mitchell

There is a significant connection to be made between the theoretical dissemination of knowledge and its practical applications. As a graduate of the School of the Environment, I have a keen appreciation for the science of sustainability, and I am now in a position to influence campus decisions on our business operations and processes. I am a proponent of a student-centered sustainability movement facilitated by the administration, faculty, and staff. Almost immediately after joining the Plant Operations Team in Environmental Health & Safety, I began reaching out to students in ESSO and the FAMU Green Coalition and to graduate students in the School of Engineering, the School of Architecture, and other faculties to participate in our many projects. In October 2110, Viniece Jennings was one of the volunteers who helped FAMU implement a Home Depot grant to design and build a sustainable landscape irrigation project on campus. LaRae and I, along with Jacqueline Hightower, another FAMU Green Coalition adviser, oversaw the management of the grant and the execution of the project. Students were intimately involved in every aspect of the project from the landscape design in a School of Architecture classroom, to the design and selection of a solar-powered mechanical pump and 500-gallon rain barrel system, to the actual site preparation, tree planting, and final landscaping work. This project stands as an excellent example of the collaborative potential of the sustainability agenda here at FAMU.

Special Role for HBCUs in the Sustainability Dialogue

As we have worked together in a variety of settings, this journey has blossomed into a friendship that fuels our momentum to move forward. We are pleased with a recent breakthrough student vote to create a Student Green Energy Fund and our selection for the second year in a row to The Princeton Review's Guide to 322 Green Colleges (Princeton Review and the U.S. Green Building Council 2012). But for sustainability initiatives to be, well, sustainable at Florida A&M University, there must continue to be top-down and bottom-up commitment. We need to engage even more faculty, staff, students, and administrators in championing transdisciplinary collaboration and sustainability initiatives, especially as some of us graduate or retire. We are not there yet, but we are striving to embrace sustainability and a commitment to addressing the challenges of global climate change as the compass for an integrated teaching, research, and community service agenda at FAMU. With census projections that minorities will soon account for half of the nation's population, it is vital for minority-serving institutions to operate in the fullness of their purpose. In essence, we at FAMU are committed to producing a cadre of STEM scholars, social entrepreneurs, and workforce professionals who bring a diverse cultural lens to sustainable community solutions (Clark and Schulterbrandt Gragg 2011; Jennings 2011; Duxbury and Gillette 2007). This vision founded our existence, fuels us today, and will guide us in the future.

Acknowledgments

The authors wish to thank Joseph Bakker, Interim Vice President for Administrative and Financial Affairs and former Associate Vice President, Construction and Facilities Management, and Co-Chair of the FAMU Environment and Sustainability Council for his consultation in the preparation of this chapter.

References

Bullard, Robert D., Paul Mohai, Robin Saha, and Beverly Wright. 2008. Toxic Wastes and Race at Twenty: Why Race Still Matters after All of These Years. *Environmental Law (Northwestern School of Law)* 38 (2):371–411.

Clark, Clayton J. II, and Richard Schulterbrandt Gragg III. 2011. Evaluation of Initial Environmental Engineering Sustainability Course at a Minority Serving Institution. *Sustainability* 4 (6):297–302.

Committee on Underrepresented Groups and the Expansion of the Science and Engineering Workforce Pipeline, Committee on Science, Engineering, and Public Policy, Policy and Global Affairs, National Academy of Sciences, National Academy of Engineering, Institute of Medicine. 2011. "Appendix G: Baccalaureate Origins of Underrepresented Minority PhDs." In *Expanding Underrepresented Minority Participation: America's Science and Technology Talent at the Crossroads*. Washington, DC: The National Academies Press.

Duxbury, Nancy, and Eileen Gillette. 2007. *Culture as a Key Dimension of Sustainability: Exploring Concepts, Themes, and Models. Creative City Network of Canada*. Centre of Expertise on Culture and Communities.

Hicken, Maggie G., Richard Schulterbrandt Gragg, III, and Howard Hu. 2011. How Cummulative Risks Warrant a Shift in Our Approach to Racial Health Disparities: The Case of Lead, Stress, and Hypertension. *Health Affairs* 30 (10):1895–1901.

Horner, J. Andrew and Nia Robinson. 2008. *A Climate of Change: African Americans, Global Warming, and a Just Climate Policy in the U.S.* Environmental Justice and Cimate Change Initiative.

Jennings, Viniece L., Roger Baud, Jaya Mahat, Laila Demashqieh, David Otieno, and Ahmed Mabrouk. 2011. Engaging Multicultural Audiences in Sustainability Education. *Sustainability_ The Journal of Record* 4 (4):183–187.

Jennings, Viniece L., Cassandra J. Gaither and Richard Schulterbrandt Gragg III. 2012. Promoting Environmental Justice Through Urban Green Space Access: A Synopsis. *Environmental Justice* 5 (5):1–7.

National Science Foundation, Division of Science Resources Statistics. 2011. *Women, Minorities, and Persons with Disabilities in Science and Engineering: 2011*. Special Report NSF 11-309. Arlington, VA. http://www.nsf.gov/statistics/wmpd.

Princeton Review and the U.S. Green Building Council. 2012. *The Princeton Review's Guide to 322 Green Colleges, 2012 Edition.* Princeton, NJ: The Princeton Review, Inc.

4

Bowling Gutter Balls: My First Year as the Energy Conservation Committee Chair

Julie Snow

Opened in 1889 as a normal school limited to teacher education, Slippery Rock University is now one of fourteen state schools in Pennsylvania designed to provide Pennsylvania residents with an affordable option for college. Enrolling 8,800 students, Slippery Rock is located in rural western Pennsylvania, just north of Pittsburgh.

Have you ever gone bowling with small children and used bumper pads to keep their balls out of the gutter? You'd know then, no matter how erratically they bowl, the possibility of a strike always exists. That was how I lived my academic life for a long time, until I decided to chair the Energy Conservation Committee. That was when my bumper pads dropped and the gutters became wide open. As chair of the committee, I felt like I was bowling gutter balls for a year. Finally, our committee's ideas found their way to the pins and sustainability began to take shape. This is the story of how I learned to succeed without my bumper pads and, every once in a while, to enjoy a strike.

I found myself appointed to the Energy Conservation Committee my fourth year at Slippery Rock University. Before my first meeting as committee chair, I spent some time looking at what other universities in the Pennsylvania State system were doing and compared it to what *I* knew Slippery Rock University was doing. I went into that meeting all hot and bothered and somewhat on a tirade. I said, "Look, these other schools have already completed Energy Services Company audits, they've changed their lighting, they've hired sustainability directors . . ." and I went on and on. And then I was put in my place. The great folks on the committee said, "We've already gone through an audit, we've already started to change our lighting . . ." I was stunned. "How come I don't know about this?" I asked, feeling pretty stupid. I realized that I had just bowled my first gutter ball.

Slippery Rock University's Sustainability Secret

After that first meeting as chair of the Energy Conservation Committee, I knew environmental change was occurring at Slippery Rock University, but it was a broadly kept secret. There were also several other committees on campus working on environmental issues independently. We had groups working on environmental zoning, strategic planning, and sustainability, but there was a striking lack of structure and a rampant lack of communication that made creating campus-wide environmental change difficult. And we were *not* celebrating our successes. Nobody was communicating to each other or the campus community about environmental advancements.

This type of silence also created a sense of loneliness and frustration my first year as chair. My committee met every other Thursday at 9 a.m. in a third floor conference room with no windows. We met alone. We talked. We discussed. We recorded minutes. We posted them. *Nobody* read them. Or at least, that is how it felt. Who should be reading them? I didn't even have an answer to that. So the feeling that our hard work was not being recognized was a reality. The combination of striving for change when you feel like no one is listening is not a design for success, nor did it make the first year of chairing the Energy Conservation Committee anything close to ideal.

The lack of communication and the feeling of isolation often created what I call the "double whammy" effect, which is worse than the average gutter ball. My committee would work hard developing a great idea. For example, because residence halls on campus were metered for electrical use, we developed a proposal to connect those meters to building dashboards and project the energy usage to the users. This was not a new idea, but it took some work to write a proposal and get an organized plan together. About the same time I was finishing up the work on this project, I found out there was a similar proposal for building dashboards written by students and residential life staff. Part of me wanted to be thrilled; there were other people out there working hard on energy conservation. But part of me was beyond frustrated, feeling as if I had wasted my time and my committee's time duplicating someone else's work on campus. This proved to be a classic example of sustainability work being completed in silence, and I was as much to blame as anyone. Who knew what my committee was working on?

Over the first year as chair of the Energy Conservation Committee, bowling a strike was elusive. My committee worked diligently, striving for creative and new ideas to conserve energy. We had several objectives during that time such as reducing temperature set points, altering the heating and cooling schedule for buildings, requiring utility metering in all buildings on campus, and developing educational material to be distributed on campus. During that first year we were becoming a bowling team with a mission.

The Best Meeting on Campus

The Energy Conservation Committee is made up of leaders from important departments across campus. The committee was put together before I became chair and was well designed. It included representation from Facilities, the HVAC Technicians, Building Managers, Residential Life, Purchasing, Information Technology, President's Office, Campus Police, faculty from three different departments (Geography, Geology, and the Environment, Business, and Communications), and graduate students. These individuals provide everything from mechanical expertise to having the president's ear once a week. Not many changes have been made to the committee membership since 2008, and I feel that actually plays a key role in our success. Stability in membership! Working with the same folks over a period of years has allowed us to divide work according to expertise, interests, and strengths. We all maintain a historical knowledge of what we have been striving for, what has created our successes and failures, and what we hope for the future. This core knowledge creates a very strong team with members who know each other well and are incredibly supportive.

The hope this committee has for change is tempered, a necessity for success in the sustainable movement. If you are driven alone by the hope that *big* change will happen *tomorrow*, you will eventually lose that hope and then lose your drive to work for change. So we hold out hope for small change and with that comes a feeling of success, even if it is in small doses.

Humor is also a necessity. Not a meeting goes by that we do not laugh about something that has gone wrong. That is not to say we do not get frustrated and angered—but we also laugh and find humor in what we cannot control. This is important because it makes the meetings fun, and, more importantly, it puts failures into perspective. If we can laugh at our failures, it makes them less painful. And honestly, who cannot find humor in asking the president to pose for a photo performing the top energy-savings action, not realizing that the action you have suggested is taking a shorter shower. Whoops!

Sustainability on a $0 Budget

My committee drinks coffee. We have one tap water drinker, but the rest of us are into the heavy stuff. So we, as a group, are not running on empty, but our budget certainly is. On my first day as chair, number 4, section C of the agenda read: "Do we have a budget?" The minutes recorded, "It was determined that there is no money in any budget. However, we could write proposals."

As devastating as this news was, we forged ahead developing a list of projects that could save energy without costing the university any money (we actually hoped to save money). We divided into two groups: one focused on energy efficiency and one focused on education. We viewed both paths as equally important. From there, we pursued ideas that would have large impacts but cost virtually nothing. We went after the "low hanging fruit." Here's one such example, in which we mobilized undergraduate students to collect energy data.

One goal of the Energy Conservation Committee was to understand lighting utilization on campus. We had a gut feeling that lights were being left on all the time and we wanted to know if we were right. With no money in the budget, we utilized undergraduate students to conduct a simple light survey using student wages donated by one of our colleges. We also used this student job as an educational experience for the student workers themselves. We chose one academic building on campus and had our students walk the halls once every hour and record which rooms had lights on and if those rooms were occupied or unoccupied. We collected the data for several weeks and had our students organize and analyze the data. The results were not surprising (see figure 4.1).

There were many unoccupied rooms with the lights on throughout the day. But with the survey information, we actually identified one of the causes that occurred in the morning before classes started. Over 20 percent of the rooms in this building were unoccupied but had their lights on at 7 a.m., before classes even began. It did not take us long to realize that the custodians were using the lights as a way to signal each other that the room had already been cleaned. We used this discovery as an opportunity to educate the community and at the same time reduce our energy usage. The other problem time, we noted, was in the afternoon. This problem was attributed mostly to faculty leaving the lights on after class was finished, so we sent a memo to the president.

The lighting survey and subsequent educational efforts provided us with a look into the defiant human condition. Our memo resulted in

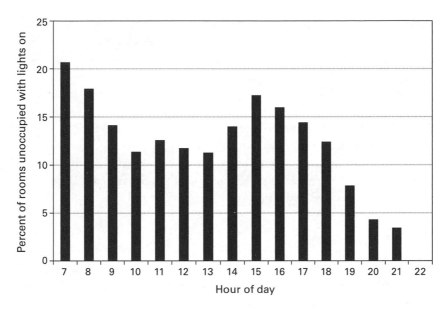

Figure 4.1
Light Use Survey in Advanced Technology and Science Hall (Slippery Rock University, Spring 2009).

campus members being asked to turn their lights off when not in use. Most folks took the message to heart and made an effort to shut their lights off, but not all. There was one colleague who took it upon himself to show everyone he could not be told what to do. We call him "The Man Who Turned on the Lights." Yes, he made sure every light in his building was burning on his way out the door. This was an important lesson for my committee; with every success, there will be failure, and finding humor in that failure helped us continue forward. This was not a strike, but we certainly knocked down a few pins.

Reorganizing for Success

After a year as chair of the Energy Conservation Committee and virtually no strikes to note, Slippery Rock University reorganized, and the bowling lane gleamed with opportunity. In November 2009, Slippery Rock's president, Robert Smith, signed the American College and University Presidents' Climate Commitment. This was the real changing point in forming an organized effort in sustainable initiatives. In signing the commitment, President Smith agreed to meet certain requirements that led to the need for an organized sustainability effort. The Energy Conservation Committee was thrilled, and many of us were present for the signing. Shortly after this event, President Smith formed the President's Commission on Sustainability.

Although the players were generally the same (the director of the Master's of Science in Sustainable Systems and the Strategic Plan, three other folks from the Energy Conservation Committee, a few new additions, and I), the formation of the commission gave us a formal pathway by which to create change and an organization through which to communicate. The Energy Conservation Committee immediately bowled our ideas right up to the commission. With the commission's endorsement, ideas were then presented to the President's Cabinet for approval.

A Strike!

In fall 2011, after several years of prep work, the Energy Conservation Committee launched an energy conservation campaign and pledge program called "Small Steps. Big Payoff."

The preparation for this campaign involved getting approval from the commission and then the cabinet, creating a slogan and artwork, creating a website and curriculum material, working with residential life to coordinate with move-in weekend, and above all else, building a public relations campaign. Given the make-up of my committee, these types of actions were well outside of our expertise. So we called in help. We worked with a professor from the Public Relations Department who created a class project to develop a slogan and artwork for the campaign. Her students conducted research to find out what slogan resonated with our community and what artwork would elicit a response. We worked with another professor in Environmental Education who prompted graduate students to create a set of curricular products that are available for all professors teaching freshman orientation classes. The products can be downloaded from the web or D2L (our online classroom software) and provide in-class activities and lecture materials that link directly to the "Small Steps. Big Payoff." campaign. Our Master's of Science in Sustainable Systems student went right to the folks who organize our move-in weekend and worked hard with them to create a campaign that fit their needs and got our message out to freshman.

Community members can take a simple pledge to help conserve energy on campus. We ask individuals to commit to three energy saving actions from a list of ten, which we posted on an energy pledge page: http://www.sru.edu/president/Sustainability/Pages/SRUEnergyPledge.aspx.

Has our campaign been successful? Yes and no. Yes, because the group we really wanted to reach was the freshmen, and we successfully did that. We have estimated that it will take at least five years to see an impact—in that time every class will have been exposed to the campaign during their freshman year. We have been less successful with upper classmen, staff, and faculty. We are not so concerned about the upper classmen, but the lack of support from staff and faculty has been disheartening. This is a community group that is ever present and is key to creating a cultural shift. We are working hard on getting "buy-in" from these members. The most common response I get from this group when I ask them to take the energy pledge is, "I already do all those things, so why should I take the pledge?" I explain that I see taking the pledge as a way to celebrate their efforts and our success as a community. Most colleagues understand that, but there are the stubborn few who refuse to participate.

Don't Be Chilly, Wear a Hoodie

On the heels of our successful "Small Steps. Big Payoff." campaign, we planned to initiate another program the first week of the spring semester 2012: "Wear your sweater or hoodie to work day." This is another simple idea that other universities have implemented; every Thursday night instead of Friday night, temperatures in all academic buildings will be brought down to their "weekend" modes. The new structure that was put in place makes initiating this idea straightforward. The communication lines that have opened are also extremely helpful in garnering support and not duplicating efforts. We really want to avoid those double whammies.

So our proposal went forward to the President's Commission on Sustainability and we were thrilled to hear that it was accepted, although slightly revised. The commission approved turning down the heat at noon on Friday but starting with only one academic building to "see how it goes." OK, so thrilled might not describe exactly how we felt, but we made progress.

Now here comes the interesting and tricky question. No one was told that the heat was being turned down on Fridays at noon in the Advanced Technology and Science Building. It has been a month and still no one has been told, *but* no one is complaining either. Should we keep quiet and slowly begin altering weekend set points in stealth mode across campus or should we boldly ask all faculty, students, and staff to wear their sweater or hoodie to work on Fridays to accommodate the small decrease in temperatures they might feel in the buildings? We have been debating the question ever since. Keep quiet and save energy like some stealth environmental group, or take this as an opportunity to educate our community? The discussion continues. I think when we get approval to reduce Friday temperatures across all academic buildings, we will do it with a campaign that contains a large educational component. Energy awareness and conservation education are, after all, part of our mission.

Hope Dissolves: Love Prevails

Recently, the Master's of Science in Sustainable Systems Program at Slippery Rock University has been placed on moratorium and will not be accepting future graduate students due to budgetary constraints. This was a huge blow to the Energy Conservation Committee's efforts, the work of other campus leaders, and to our students, both current and alumni.

Tensions ran high at our Energy Conservation Committee meeting as we heard of this development. I considered throwing my bowling bowl down the hall and marching right on out of there. But I was reminded at that meeting that I love to work on sustainability initiatives. I love creating a world that will be better for my young daughter. I love making a difference using my skills and passion. So I decided to stay, to continue to hope for small changes, and continue to do what I love—to work hard for sustainable initiatives. And while, for the moment, we dwell in the gutter, I am confident that another sustainability strike is in our future.

My committee remains strong, committed to each other and to energy conservation at Slippery Rock University. We are still meeting Thursday mornings, still laughing, and we are still interested in bowling, even into the gutter. We are strengthening our existing campaigns and hope to further enhance the educational components; an area we feel needs more attention. We are still supported by the President's Commission on Sustainability, and we still have a pathway for change. What we are *not* is silent. We are a joyful, singing bowling team, and we are hopeful those who want to share what we share will tune in.

II

Curricular Transformation

5

Curriculum for the Bioregion: Putting Communities and Ideas in Place

Jean MacGregor

The Curriculum for the Bioregion is an initiative of the Washington Center for Improving the Quality of Undergraduate Education, a public service center of The Evergreen State College. Established in 1985, the Washington Center collaborates with colleges and universities in Washington State and beyond to strengthen teaching, learning, and educational reform.

This is the story of building Curriculum for the Bioregion, a regional sustainability-across-the-curriculum initiative. In seven years, it has grown to involve fifty colleges and universities and close to a thousand faculty and staff members and their students, and equally important, dozens of community experts in agencies, non-governmental organizations, and tribes. When I was thinking about starting this initiative in 2004, many ingredients were already in place for getting under way. However, a happenstance propelled me forward and crystallized the approach I would take.

It happened at the Seattle airport on a rainy night in the fall of 2004. Returning from a conference, I landed, got my luggage, and took a shuttle van to the car park. I stepped up to the brightly lit glass payment booth and presented my ticket and credit card. The young woman on the other side of the window looked at the card, looked at me, and brightened. "Wow, I know you!"

"Really? How so?"

"Yes, you visited our class!"

"Well," I said, "In my job, I visit a great many classes. Which class was it and where?"

"At Bellevue Community College. Don't you remember, The Power of Place?"

Of course I remembered. An imaginatively designed learning community, The Power of Place involved a humanities class (Americans and their Landscape) linked with an English composition class. Built around Winifred Gallagher's book of the same title, The Power of Place was offered as a team-taught program. Beginning with the idea that we all are, to some degree, "placed," the program began with American Manifest Destiny and the American transcendentalists and culminated with James Howard Kunstler's *The Geography of Nowhere*. Field trips examined suburban sprawl east of Seattle and new urbanist designs in the fashionable Redmond Town Square shopping center. I had visited the class twice while doing research for a book on learning communities and, indeed, it was a "happening class"—intensely engaging teachers and students alike. As the young woman was running my credit card, she kept shaking her head. "I'll just never forget that class! It was so interesting. I will never forget *the ideas* in that class."

"Tell me your name," I said, "I'll email your teachers to tell them I ran into you. And tell me, what are you doing now?"

"Jodi. I'm still in school. I study in between flights. Just tell them I'll never forget those ideas!"

As I headed onto the highway for the dark, rainy drive home, I puzzled out that the Power of Place had taken place seven years earlier. "Gosh," I thought to myself, "Isn't that what we all want in our teaching? To have the ideas we teach still be alive for our students, years into the future? Maybe for their whole lives?" The ideas meant something to this class—the students' engagement was palpable. That both the historical and contemporary ideas were grounded in the local surround gave them particular tangibility and meaning. The Power of Place was, in actuality, the embodiment of the *power of place*.

Although the *power of place* concept has always nourished me, it took on new meaning as I created the Curriculum for the Bioregion initiative. Working with colleagues on sustainability's "big ideas" grounded in place-based teaching and learning, we have been building this sustainability-across-the-curriculum project in the Puget Sound bioregion and more recently on the Columbia Plateau. This chapter describes the foundational inquiry that shaped the initiative, the curriculum integration approach we developed, and the importance of ongoing communities for tackling the huge adaptive challenges that sustainability presents. Ours is a regional, multi-institutional, vision of change.

Getting Started

My perch at The Evergreen State College is in a public service center, the Washington Center for Improving the Quality of Undergraduate Education. I also teach in Evergreen's Master of Environmental Studies program.

In the fall of 2004, after an eight-year run of leading national projects on learning communities in higher education, I was considering next steps. My two decades of learning community work, visiting campuses with lively learning community initiatives and meeting their creative leaders, was exciting. Seeing campuses taking up new approaches to curriculum and teaching was gratifying. Yet only a handful of these campuses appeared to be seriously addressing the problems that, to me, would become prominent in the twenty-first century. At the time, I was reading the first edition of *Plan B* by Lester Brown (2003) and Jane Lubchenco's 1998 American Association for the Advancement of Science (AAAS) Presidential address on "a new social contract for science." Both challenged us to mobilize all our energy and talent to move toward a more sustainable biosphere. I felt impelled to engage faculty in inventing curriculum to better prepare students for the century at hand.

First, I had to determine whether the Washington Center's co-directors and Evergreen's provost would support this new initiative. Seeing the obvious connections between this vision and the Washington Center's focus on curriculum integration in its learning community initiatives, as well as a resonance with the college's strategic plans related to sustainability, they were enthusiastic. However, because the Washington Center had only modest institutional money to support its small staff, I would have to secure my own funding. The best way to get started, I thought, would be with local funding. The Russell Family Foundation, a regional foundation with interests in restoring Puget Sound and in environmental and sustainability education immediately came to mind. I visited the foundation's principal program officer to describe my vision of a region-wide, multi-year, sustainability-across-the-curriculum initiative and asked if the foundation would consider funding an initial project with a first set of partner-institutions. The answer was positive.

As I began to craft my first grant proposal, I struggled to find a distinctive name for this new project. "Education for Sustainable Communities," "Environment, Community, and Education," "A Curriculum for the Future"—no particular phrase resonated. I was fretting over these phrases with one of the Washington Center co-directors, Gillies Malnarich. "Well," she said, "Talk to me. Tell me what you want this to look like."

"Curriculum. We need to signal that this project won't duplicate emerging networks in the region focusing on campus operations. More to the point, we need new curricula that make sustainability meaningful to students. This has to have meaning where they live, to help them relate the global to the local and vice versa. We need to help them see how their

campuses and communities function and how people in all kinds of organizations are at work trying to make these communities healthy places—a
curriculum that has tangibility and meaning in their bioregion."

"Wait, you just said it!" Gillies exclaimed.

"Said what?"

"Curriculum for the Bioregion!"

Listening and Direction Setting

Curriculum for the Bioregion began as all initiatives begin in the Washington Center, with listening. As we plan any new initiative, we visit campuses to interview interested faculty and administrative leaders to identify
aspirations, assets, needs, and challenges. Then, drawing on what we have
gleaned, we shape a project, often in collaboration with partners from
those campuses.

Early in 2005, I recruited a steering committee, drawn from nine community colleges and nine four-year institutions in the Puget Sound region,
some regional non-governmental organizations involved in environmental and civic education, and our Russell Foundation program officer.
These individuals became crucial intellectual partners, critical advisers,
and co-leaders of many Curriculum for the Bioregion faculty communities. Many have assumed important leadership roles on their campuses
and in the bioregion. For many years now, we have been working collectively on the local and systemic level. The steering committee continues to
meet twice a year; in the intervening months, I consult this group through
email and conference calls.

At our first meeting, the steering committee decided that our initial listening exercise be called an "Inquiry and Planning Phase" to underscore
our intent to use our findings to shape the initiative. Each person on a
college or university campus agreed to coordinate a two-day visit for me
to his or her campus, a visit that would include a briefing of either the
president's or the academic vice president's leadership team. The steering
committee also suggested that we set up online surveys so that the faculty,
staff, or students whom we met on our visits could give us additional
advice if they wanted to.

In the spring and fall of 2005, I visited the eighteen campuses with a
steering committee member serving as host and fellow listener. One hundred and forty faculty members provided additional information online
and, in a separate student survey, over five hundred responded. At every
campus, we found interested faculty, imaginative curriculum ideas, and

campus- and community-based projects—most of them little known and unrecognized, even on the campuses where they took place. We learned that sustainability efforts were not coordinated, nor were they well communicated to the wider campus. Sustainability in campus operations was nascent but developing. Few campuses had a formal sustainability committee or task force. With respect to curriculum, we found sustainability content—as we suspected we would—in environmental and global studies. However, we also found sustainability content in a range of disciplines—art, business, mathematics, philosophy, sociology, and more.

At the same time, our inquiry, with its focus on the local community or bioregion, raised questions and concerns. Faculty would ask me what I meant by "bioregion" and to which specific bioregion I was referring. On almost every campus visit, those who led any form of field study bemoaned their students' lack of general knowledge about the region—the very region in which most of them had grown up. At one community college, a marine science instructor recounted that, "Of my classes of thirty-five students, only three or four on average have ever set foot on a Puget Sound beach, even though our community borders the Sound itself. Their experience of Puget Sound is just what they see out their car windows."

At several universities, the conversation turned to whether regional, sustainability-related research garners support, status, and rewards. "Is research of the local valued?" some wondered. One person declared the state of current research to be nothing less than "the glorification of the exotic." Today, universities take pride in their internationally connected faculty and globally significant research. Agreeing, a doctoral student described his dissertation research with a renowned ornithologist whose work concerns birds in urban and suburban habitats; but then, he said, "I love doing research on birds that thrive in the midst of human settlement. Yet, I do worry that it might be a career-ender."

At universities and community colleges and in the region's museums, Indian tribes, and state agencies, I actually found significant numbers of researchers doing research in the region, on issues ranging from Puget Sound's marine dead zones to urban growth policies, from the toxic legacy of Tacoma's American Smelting and Refining Corporation's smelter site to climate change's predicted effects on regional economies. Notably, a number of faculty members engaged their students or involved community members as partners in participatory research. On every campus, I discovered keepers of rich and important local information. But where this information was shared—and especially how it was shared among teachers in the region—was less clear.

The status of the local emerged in a different but telling way during a visit to a community college. The president there had an interest in sustainability. He convened his vice presidents, unit heads, and department chairs for my briefing. I had the privilege to speak to these twenty-five campus leaders for half an hour. First, I asked them to find the campus on a large bioregional map of the area. This map had no political boundaries, nor any place-names: it was simply a LandSat land use map. Then I said, "You're a community college. What are the most pressing issues in *this* community that every student should be at least somewhat conversant with?" The answers came without hesitation: first, the issues associated with immigration and settlement of migrant farm workers from Latin America and the tensions that this rapidly changing demographic were bringing to all the county's systems, and second, the ongoing conflicts over urban growth management and land use as agricultural land was being converted to housing developments—essentially, unregulated "rural sprawl." "Okay," I said, "so where are these community issues being taken up in classes here at this college?" No response. Everyone looked around the room. "*Any* classes?" I asked. Dead silence.

Our campus visits revealed exciting ideas and, more importantly, a large company of new colleagues and potential partners. Still, we wanted to take this "Inquiry and Planning" phase a step further, with a community-building and consensus-building moment. Early in 2006, we held a one-day think-tank for a hundred participants: teams from the eighteen participating institutions and twenty representatives of regional initiatives addressing land use planning, sustainability, environmental justice, and green business practices. First, we shared our findings from students: across a wide range of classes from freshman to seniors, students indicated strong levels of concern about environmental quality in the region. We noted that their concern intensified from freshman to senior year. At the same time, these students indicated that their knowledge of the region, its systems, and its problems was quite limited. Those reporting modest knowledge told us that they had acquired it from family experiences or, tellingly, experiences in elementary school. Only a handful of students could identify high school experiences that helped them learn more about the places or cultures or politics where they lived. When asked about sustainability, most students admitted to a lack of familiarity with the term. When asked what kinds of learning experiences they would suggest, students overwhelmingly recommended community-based learning experiences that would translate "classroom knowledge" to "real-world knowledge."

We then shared our findings from faculty members. Through our interviews and surveys, faculty told us that efforts to build sustainability into coursework were "still at an infancy stage" and that faculty themselves wanted to learn about sustainability. They wanted ideas for bringing not only conceptual material but also *local applications* into their courses. They needed opportunities for disciplinary *and* interdisciplinary curriculum development related to sustainability outcomes. And, they needed time and contacts to develop more extensive relationships with regional organizations involved in sustainability issues and practices—the very people we had in the room.

As often happens in participatory processes, the think-tank participants' brainstorming generated dozens of expansive ideas for strengthening sustainability education. Still, the consensus was not to mount narrowly defined projects, but rather to create opportunities for large numbers of students to learn about sustainability in introductory courses or those in general education. To accomplish this, the participants recommended weaving sustainability content into many courses and featuring place-based examples. They also wanted to see bioregional learning opportunities for faculty, especially for those new to the area. Everyone agreed that campuses should become learning laboratories so students could both study and contribute to sustainable campus practices. Finally, they said a clearinghouse was needed for sharing teaching approaches and resources. The think-tank and the report (Washington Center 2006) that emerged from it provided the data, credibility, and momentum to secure a series of grants to implement these recommendations.

Creating Faculty Learning Communities

Since the Washington Center was established in 1985, our various initiatives have involved the development of inter-institutional groups of faculty members, or intra-institutional faculty-and-staff leadership teams, who come together to support one another's learning and also to create common products. These various communities have developed learning community initiatives, campus diversity plans, curriculum collections and teaching cases, strategies for student and program assessment, and even monographs and book-length works. As the steering committee and I wrestled with what kinds of faculty learning communities to convene in order to create our potential curriculum for the bioregion, we all were drawn to the inherently interdisciplinary nature of sustainability concepts as well as of any public issue. Many on our steering committee were teaching at campuses with strong commitments to interdisciplinary teaching and learning. However, one of us, Daniel Sherman of University of Puget Sound, argued, "If we are to make any progress, sustainability has to have meaning and resonance in *all* of our disciplines. It can't remain on the margins in interdisciplinary courses or in certain electives. We won't change the academy unless every discipline sees the relevance of sustainability ideas."

We realized that Sherman was right. We agreed that our focus should begin with inter-institutional, discipline-based faculty learning communities in liberal arts disciplines. Over the past five years, we have convened faculty communities in nine disciplines and it is our plan to convene several more in the future. Each community, about twenty-four faculty members, has been recruited from two- or four-year programs in both public and private institutions; in most instances, faculty teaching in the same field and teaching in the same region are meeting many colleagues for the first time. They agree to meet over several months. With supportive colleagues serving as resource faculty, each community draws on the sustainability literature to identify concepts and topics that resonate with their discipline as well as regional issues that might illuminate course concepts. Then, with one another's support, each participant fully develops a "teaching and learning activity" for one of his or her courses; the activities are ultimately published in the Curriculum for the Bioregion's online curriculum collection.

Besides convening these disciplinary communities, we convened communities with a variety of other foci. We learned over the years that through offering a number of different entry points at different times of year, both on campuses and at locations in the community and field, we have broadened our audience. Figure 5.1 summarizes the foci around which we have built faculty learning communities, workshops, and field courses. Crucial to these communities have been resource faculty—experts drawn not only from our campuses but also from regional organizations and agencies. With their up-to-date knowledge and insight, these individuals have not only enriched our work, they have expanded our understanding of what it means to learn *in* community.

Also crucial to all these communities is their face-to-face nature. Learning in the company of interested others, often in retreat settings, with enough time and space to explore issues and questions, has been just as important as generating ideas for classroom teaching. Listservs and online workspaces have been useful, but our evaluations reveal that the direct experience of a supportive community engaged in common purpose—whether it has been an inter-institutional network or an intra-institutional one—is what has made this approach the most meaningful.

Figure 5.1

The foci of the Curriculum for the Bioregion Strategy

Our geography has helped: for the thirty-two colleges and universities in the Puget Sound bioregion, no one has to travel more than 90 miles to a meeting. However, in rural eastern Washington where we have begun offering introductory workshops and conferences, the distances among campuses are greater, and developing comparable regional communities has been more challenging.

Integrating "Big Ideas"

If the goal is to situate sustainability content and concepts in a broad array of undergraduate courses, this content must be significant and have staying power for faculty and students alike. If our courses can be visualized as trees (composed of knowledge and skills and habits of mind), sustainability content needs to become part of the trunk, holding up and nourishing the whole tree. If sustainability material just sits out on one twig or another, will students take it seriously? As teachers, we are all too familiar with those moments in class when students, sensing a twig-sized tangent or byway, let their attentions drift.

Integrating new material into our courses is no small endeavor when, in every discipline, we struggle with perceived curriculum scarcity: When there is so much essential material to cover in limited time, how can we add more? The way we have learned to address this issue is to ask our faculty communities to work directly with the "tree trunk" of their course—its most essential content. We ask faculty members to identify the "big ideas" (the most important ideas and skills) that compose the "tree trunk" of a specific, chosen course. Then we ask them to create a teaching-and-learning activity that would not only engage students with one of the big ideas but *also* to place it in a sustainability context and/or integrate it with a sustainability concept. Additionally, we encourage faculty to choose issues that help students gain deeper understanding of this bioregion. Finally, since *assignments* are what represent student learning as well as what students often take most seriously in a course, we ask faculty to create an assignment in which students can apply concepts and deepen their understanding of them. Here are some examples.

• In her Introductory Biology course for majors at University of Washington Tacoma, Erica Cline has developed a lab called "Catching Cheaters." Her larger module on molecular biology includes labs that teach the principles and techniques of gel electrophoresis, DNA sequencing, and phylogenetic analysis—the big idea is genetic expression. In this exercise, students use these techniques to analyze salmon samples collected from local stores and restaurants to see if farmed Atlantic salmon are mislabeled as wild Pacific salmon—a relatively frequent occurrence in the region. (Another big idea, consumer fraud, emerges here too!) Erica's lab then scaffolds a research assignment that challenges students to find out why farmed salmon is so controversial in the Pacific Northwest. Students explore the environmental consequences of industrial salmon farming on the Pacific coast and issues related to the conservation of wild salmon populations, both in terms of genetic integrity and habitat health.

• In his introductory ethics courses at The Evergreen State College, philosophy instructor Stephen Beck teaches a range of ethical frameworks.

He has developed a series of homework assignments and in-class conceptual workshops that link the big idea of virtue ethics with climate change. To gain a beginning understanding of virtues, students list and discuss attributes of people they most admire. Then, after reading selections from Aristotle's *Nicomachean Ethics*, students compare Aristotle's list of virtues with their own lists. Subsequently, students move to explorations of climate change through the film *An Inconvenient Truth*, additional reading, and selected website resources. A culminating essay assignment asks students, "What virtues does our society need to foster in people in order for us to be able to respond appropriately to climate change?" The essay is an opportunity for students to display their understanding of virtue concepts in detail as well as what role they play in living an ethical life.

• In his geology courses at Centralia College, Patrick Pringle teaches a module on the hazards of debris flows (lahars) from the Mount Rainier volcano. His big idea in geoscience is the immense power of lahars to move long distances, bury and reshape river valleys, and cause dramatic landscape changes; his sustainability ideas involve land use planning and risk management. Using maps and historical accounts of historical volcanic eruptions from Mount Rainier and other volcanoes, students evaluate the implications of this information on traditional, historic, and current land uses and users. Then they explore current land use planning decisions, property-rights issues, and risk-management efforts in the known risk zones in the probable paths of future lahars in our region.

• In an environmental studies course focusing on environmental health at The Evergreen State College, sociologist Lin Nelson interweaves ideas of toxic exposure and "just sustainability." She uses a recent court case, the 2009 federal criminal trial of the W. R. Grace Corporation for its role in the massive asbestos exposure of the community of Libby, Montana, The students use the lens of "just sustainability" to examine the way in which communities face differential risk and seek remedies for health and environmental damages. Students study the evidence surrounding the trial, develop argumentation skills, and explore different perspectives and knowledge systems—environmental science, law, journalism, and community—in order to discern how sustainability and justice are linked in complex ways.

Facing Challenges

Just as important as this curriculum formation is the *faculty formation* that also occurs. Through teaching big ideas and activities in which students can practice them, and through extending their teaching into the interdisciplinary territory that sustainability requires, I believe that faculty members cross thresholds. Many are embracing and teaching the key ideas behind sustainability, and more importantly they are beginning to see their own discipline in a new light. Ideally, they will have the confidence and curiosity to keep learning, to keep reforming their classes, and ultimately to see the centrality of sustainability concepts in their disciplines. However, we need *thousands* of faculty members and *whole institutions* to cross thresholds, a thousand-fold more than the faculty we have engaged so far. What keeps me awake at night is recognizing how slow this change work is. As my colleague David Blockstein[1] often laments, "The glaciers are melting faster than the curriculum is changing."

At the same time, sustainable, robust, and stable funding is the Achilles' heel of all inter-institutional initiatives in higher education. Few such initiatives find their way onto hard money. While the Curriculum for the Bioregion has benefitted from a variety of grants from regional and national public and private foundations, it remains a continuing challenge to find funders with interests not only in sustainability education but also the capacity to support multi-institutional, multi-year work. Most of us involved in the work of educational change know that meaningful reform requires "initiative thinking," that is, the long-term commitment necessary to start, scale up, and then sustain a change effort. Yet most funders operate with "project thinking," structuring their grants around short-term windows of just one, two, or three years. Moreover, seed money for new projects often takes precedence over support of long-term initiatives. I do not see an easy path through these challenges; these funding patterns are also changing much too slowly to stimulate deep and lasting reform. Until campuses make major investments in curriculum transformation, this is the philanthropic environment within which we will have to build momentum—and build the case for investment on a larger scale.

Sustainability-across-the-Curriculum as Adaptive Work

In our steering committee meetings, we often talk about sustainability as the ultimate adaptive challenge. Our colleague Sharon Daloz Parks (2005) introduced us to this powerful idea in her insightful book on how Ronald Heifetz teaches leadership at Harvard's Kennedy School of Government. Drawing on the work of both Heifetz and James MacGregor Burns, Parks makes an important distinction between adaptive challenges and technical problems. Technical problems, while complex, are solvable with known information and expertise. The solution, or goal, is often tangible—like "putting a man on the moon." By contrast, adaptive challenges are problems whose solutions are often elusive because the problems themselves are so complex and so continuously evolving. Facing and addressing these challenges throw into question our taken-for-granted habits and values. Adaptive challenges require continuous learning at all levels of organizations because the needed knowledge to address the problem—or just improve the situation—does not yet exist or must be drawn from disparate quarters. That is not to say that sustainability problems do not require technical expertise: obviously, they do. But much more is required—"changes in values, belief, and behavior," as Heifetz (1994, 22) would say.

Like the work of sustainability in general, creating a curriculum to embrace twenty-first-century imperatives is itself an adaptive challenge. Mobilizing higher education to make sustainability a core emphasis is an adaptive challenge. This requires nothing less than rebuilding the ship while we are at sea—without much in the way of blueprints. While the prospect is daunting, it can be—must be—inspiring, the way it feels when we hear of exciting citizen science projects, "chill-out" climate campaigns, grass-roots food initiatives, or "transition towns." It is inspiring also when we realize that we can be the creators of communities where, in the company of supportive colleagues, we begin to shift our courses and our disciplines and ultimately take leadership in our colleges and universities. If we do not take up this work, who will? As both Parks and Heifetz point out, adaptive work is not just about coping. It is about creating change.

Acknowledgments

My abundant thanks to the Curriculum for the Bioregion steering committee both for their inspiration and leadership along the way, and special gratitude to these individuals for their helpful suggestions for this chapter: Rebecca Chamberlain, Erica Cline, Kate Davies, Diane Douglas, Lynn Dunlap, Mike Gillespie, Marie Eaton, Karen Harding, Holly Hughes, Roberta Matthews, John McLain, Kim McNamara, Lin Nelson, Sharon Daloz Parks, Daniel Sherman, Barbara Leigh Smith, Claus Svendsen, Matthew Teorey, and Judy Walton.

Notes

1. David Blockstein directs the Council of Environmental Deans and Directors at the National Council on Science and the Environment.

References

Brown, Lester. 2003. *Plan B: Rescuing a Planet under Stress and a Civilization in Trouble*. Washington, DC: Earth Policy Institute.

Daloz Parks, Sharon. 2005. *Leadership Can Be Taught: A Bold Approach for a Complex World*. Boston, MA: Harvard Business School Publishing.

Heifetz, Ronald. 1994. *Leadership without Easy Answers*. Cambridge, MA: Belknap Press.

Lubchenco, Jane. 1998. Entering the Century of the Environment: A New Social Contract for Science. *Science* 279:491–497.

Washington Center for Improving the Quality of Undergraduate Education. 2006. *Curriculum for the Bioregion: Connecting What We Learn to Where We Live*. A Report on the Inquiry and Planning Phase of a New Initiative of the Washington Center for Improving the Quality of Undergraduate Education. Jean MacGregor, ed. Olympia, WA: The Evergreen State College.

6

From Environmental Advocates to Sustainability Entrepreneurs: Rethinking a Sustainability-Focused General Education Program

William Throop

Green Mountain College is a private liberal arts college founded in Poultney, Vermont, in 1834. The college takes social and environmental sustainability as themes that unify the curriculum and define the campus culture. All students take part in the college's signature Environmental Liberal Arts (ELA) curriculum.

When we started re-envisioning Green Mountain College, we had little idea where it would lead. In 1995, a group of faculty and a new president decided to create coherence in a liberal arts education by taking the natural and social environment as the unifying theme for the curriculum and the co-curriculum. Soon thereafter the board of trustees changed the mission to reflect this environmental theme. Within four years, we developed a new Environmental Liberal Arts (ELA) general education program, the environmental studies major had blossomed, and a wave of faculty departures made room for hiring a cadre of faculty who came for the new mission.

These beginnings are almost ancient history now. For more than 70 percent of the current faculty, they represent only stories told by others, no more salient than those of earlier periods in our 175 year history. But the way we crafted the environmental orientation of the college has shaped our current approach to sustainability and developed a powerful culture, parts of which we treasure and others we struggle to overcome. In this chapter, I describe our shift from a focus on the environment to a broader emphasis on sustainability and our efforts to cultivate entrepreneurial skills, as a way to integrate social and ecological dimensions of sustainability across the curriculum. I will outline some of our successes and also the challenges we must still meet.

Becoming an Environmental Liberal Arts College

Most schools started addressing sustainability through facilities and operations, but initially we had little funding for such changes and insufficient support from students. Thus we began with the curriculum. This had the advantage of moving greening directly to the heart of the college and of being relatively inexpensive. The college had a strong orientation to service learning and a hands-on approach to education before adopting the environmental theme. Senior faculty were familiar with using the bioregion as a learning laboratory; as a result, the transition to the environmental theme had some continuity with past curricular practice and did not appear as transformative as it turned out to be.

The new general education program involved four core courses taught by faculty across the college. First year seminars, Images of Nature and Voices of Community, emphasized written and oral communications skills, while introducing the two poles of our theme: relations with our ecological communities and with our human communities. A sophomore-level history of scientific visions of nature, Dimensions of Nature, and a capstone seminar, A Delicate Balance, were supplemented with seven distribution requirements. The four core courses created a shared dialog between students and faculty around texts that almost all students and faculty read, texts like Aldo Leopold's *A Sand County Almanac* and Francis Bacon's *The Great Instauration*. They also built a strong campus culture, grounded in shared values and focused on social critique and lifestyle change.

The environmental liberal arts program attracted a new breed of faculty interested in teaching interdisciplinary courses, which affected both campus culture and operations. Since the strong values-based campus culture helped the college to grow, we had an opportunity to hire a significant number of new faculty members. We also systematically rewarded contributions to interdisciplinary general education in contract renewal and promotion. In turn, the faculty commitment to the college and the region grew stronger because of the place-based nature of our environmental curriculum. This beneficial feedback loop created more pressure to green the campus as faculty focused more course projects on campus facilities and operations. This pressure enabled us to retrofit almost all of the lighting and plumbing, replace windows in most of the residence halls, and eventually build a biomass-based heat and power plant to replace the fuel oil that we had burned to heat the campus.

As these changes gained momentum, the quality and size of the student body increased further. Those faculty members who were out of step with the new orientation resigned, and the new mission was realized at a depth much greater than its originators had imagined. I came to Green Mountain the year following the mission change. I chaired the environmental studies program, became dean of humanities, arts, and natural sciences, and then, in 2002, provost. During this time, I became increasingly concerned about an emerging tension between our emphasis on the environment and our identity as a liberal arts college. Our success in developing a systematic environmental education across the curriculum brought an increasingly homogenous, environmentally oriented student body, which began to compromise the diversity of views necessary for a robust liberal arts education. We often talked of balancing the environment and the liberal arts, but this was misleading because our approach was to fully integrate these educational ideals. As students began to represent a narrower set of interests and to enforce an environmentalist ideology, we needed to make a special effort to attract faculty who focused on the social environment and brought diverse political and ethnic perspectives.

Transitioning from the Environment to Sustainability

Despite our consistent emphasis that the environment meant all of our surroundings, including the social and built environment, both internal and external audiences took us to be focusing on nature. Our location in a rural area and the research interests of faculty contributed to this perception. It seemed promising to address this issue by revising the general education program to focus on the broader concept of sustainability. While we were concerned that sustainability did not have the strong emotional resonance of "the environment," we saw tremendous opportunity in aligning our innovative core curriculum more closely to the growing campus sustainability movement.

In any event, we needed to more clearly articulate the program's learning outcomes and to design a stronger assessment program. In 2008, we secured a generous grant from the Davis Educational Foundation to support the development of an assessment system for a revised Environmental Liberal Arts program focused on sustainability. We began the process with an all-faculty workshop devoted to one question: What liberal arts skills, knowledge and dispositions must all students possess if they are to help create more sustainable organizations and communities? We asked the faculty to bracket concerns about how such an inquiry would affect the current program and to engage in the intellectual exercise of imagining anew what students should learn.

That May, after three days of intense discussion, the faculty converged on six broad principles, each supported by four or five specific learning outcomes. A small group then refined the outcomes and addressed objections, but avoided determining exactly how they would be implemented. By November the faculty unanimously approved the eighteen new learning outcomes and launched a three-year process of revising the general education core and distribution requirements in light of those goals. (See http://www.greenmtn.edu/academics/ela/ela_goals.aspx for Green Mountain's sustainability-themed college-wide learning outcomes.)

By the following March, the faculty had fundamentally revised the distribution categories for the Environmental Liberal Arts program, focusing on systems thinking rather than disciplinary breadth, and embarked on the process of developing new courses to meet the outcomes. The range of courses became broader and the social dimensions of sustainability became as salient as the environmental dimensions. Now with thirty-one new courses that systematically address the sustainability learning outcomes, we are moving from teaching about our environments to cultivating sustainability virtues.

The new curriculum, with its richer treatment of poverty and diversity issues, has significantly broadened our approach to campus sustainability. More faculty members are working on social projects on and off campus. We are attracting a somewhat more diverse student body, though political diversity is still a challenge. That challenge is magnified by a campus culture in which environmental advocacy is a daily affair.

The Legacy of Environmental Advocacy

For a generation, all of our students have been learning how to become powerful advocates for social change, but belatedly we have realized that few of them deeply understand *how* to actually work together to make change in complex systems. Our students saw themselves as change agents, but they interpreted this in terms of analyzing the ills of contemporary society and defending radical environmental and economic views. They showed relatively little ability to move groups except against a common foe and little inclination to work within structures to accomplish goals.

Our student-administered greening fund provides a catalog of the challenges students faced in making change. The students' ideas for projects have been very strong, and they have been effectively promoted, receiving broad support from other students and ample funding. With some exceptions, however, the project management has been problematic. It begins with the process of acquiring feedback and approval from the campus offices that a project affects. Surprisingly for a small campus, students understand very little about how these offices function and how to work with them. Then the challenges of setting a realistic timeline, managing volunteers, and changing plans during implementation often reduce engagement with the project. Other work interferes with meeting deadlines; projects drag on. Sometimes a group of students will graduate having made no serious attempt to hand off a partially completed project to returning students. Lastly the management of project funds is often an after-thought and the initial budgets no more of a guide than a hasty outline for a late term paper.

The advocacy orientation is associated with a developmental stage in which young people often see issues in terms of polarized oppositions. Problems on and off campus are typically understood as clashes between the forces of light and the forces of darkness—the latter characterized by gross ignorance, evil intent, or at best, incompetence and lack of concern. This tendency is powerfully reinforced by our political culture. Sustainability education has the potential to counteract such cultural influences and to advance moral development because it utilizes a complex systems oriented approach to issues. But the countervailing forces are strong. Even when "the administration" actively supports student sustainability projects and builds student support for those projects we initiate, we have to come to terms with a student culture which reflexively identifies us a shadowy "they" who stand in the way of real progress.

The students' tendency toward abstract advocacy fits naturally with the traditional approach to critical thinking still prevalent among our faculty and with the academic tradition of intellectual sparring. We talk about teaching students how to solve real world problems, but faculty are largely trained how to summarize extant research on a topic and defend a thesis. Much introductory college writing follows a similar form. The tension between teaching how to actually make change in a context and teaching how to advocate for change crystallized for me during a campus talk by Robert Costanza, the renowned ecological economist who now heads Portland State University's Institute for Sustainable Solutions; he argued that we need to change the way academics are trained to approach problem solving. The students are unlikely learn what their role models do not visibly practice.

In response to such observations, I started trying to reframe large portions of our curriculum and co-curriculum as cultivating social sustainability virtues—the dispositions that enable effective cooperative problem solving at multiple scales. Living in a residence hall provides a tremendous opportunity to develop such dispositions, though it is one rarely engaged in the classroom. Suppose that faculty and staff emphasized teaching the following dispositions as much as they focused on cultivating critical thinking:

• Dispositions to address problems through group action: an awareness of responsibility to a community, an understanding of the common good, and a sense of empowerment.

• Dispositions to effectively facilitate intra- and inter-group communication: charity in the interpretation of others, graciousness in disagreement and confrontation, sensitivity to audience and context.

• Dispositions to effectively address group conflict: fairness and empathy.

• Dispositions to persevere in the face of roadblocks: patience, adaptability, and optimism.

   Suppose faculty explicitly designed group projects to evaluate student progress in developing these dispositions, and engaged issues from residence life as they arose. Suppose the administration modeled these virtues in word and deed. (It is harder than it sounds sometimes.) Would our graduates be better able to help communities and organizations become more sustainable? I think so. But it has been a tough sell among faculty, many of whom do not want to think of themselves as cultivating virtue in their students. They express concern that such a goal is both presumptuous and invasive, though I often point out that similar things could be said about cultivating the disposition to think critically. As a result of such concern, I have been shifting my language toward cultivating entrepreneurial spirit.

The Development of Sustainability Entrepreneurs

In the last few years, the issues of affordability, access, and the value of liberal arts degrees have shifted what our students and their parents want from a college. Even our faculty members are beginning to realize that providing high quality liberal arts majors coupled with sustainability knowledge may not warrant taking on the debt that many students must carry. Most of our students are not interested in joining the corporate world. They are unlikely to make the kind of salaries that would enable them to rapidly pay down their educational debts. We need to provide students with the skills they need to navigate this economic environment without compromising our shared values.

   Even as we have lifted up the social dimensions of sustainability in the Environmental Liberal Arts program, our treatment of the economic dimensions has remained limited. Most students learn about standard critiques of classical economics. They can speak credibly about internalizing externalities and building strong local economies. They are less familiar, however, with how to use economic analysis to leverage change, and they are surprising naïve about the economic aspects of organizations like colleges. Many want to join small non-profits or start their own businesses, though most have little desire to take standard business courses. By combining more effective education regarding economic sustainability with teaching entrepreneurial skills across the curriculum, we should cultivate most of the social sustainability virtues identified above *and* provide students better prospects of finding or creating jobs that express their values. We will also be developing more effective sustainability change agents.

As we moved through a new strategic planning process, the importance of helping students develop entrepreneurial skills was a recurrent theme. If we are to embed this theme in the ELA program, then a wider range of faculty need to understand the economic dimensions of sustainability and be able to explicitly engage entrepreneurial skills in their courses. The idea that entrepreneurialism extends far beyond business is already well accepted in public discourse, but our faculty will need to highlight those elements of entrepreneurial activity that apply to their areas of study. Some may focus on the creativity involved in innovative solutions to sustainability problems; others may emphasize the courage and persistence necessary to achieve a long-term goal. Many will need to help students develop the financial acumen necessary to evaluate the economic impacts of their decisions. Fortunately most of our faculty members *are* quite entrepreneurial, though they might not describe themselves as such.

One way to cultivate faculty and student entrepreneurial skills is to open the college's financial books and use college decision making as a curriculum. At small schools where faculty and students can participate meaningfully in governance, we have an opportunity to expand the teaching of sustainability to include the economic health of the institution. As an experiment last year, the chief financial officer and I met with each section of the first year seminar, Voices of Community, to explain how the tuition is spent and how decisions are made. We were surprised about the myths that students had about the college's operations: for example, that we were making a profit on them, that student concerns did not really matter to us, and that they had no input on budgetary decisions. We were also gratified by their response to open, respectful discussion of college issues. The sessions were a tremendous success, and they are now firmly embedded in the curriculum. If we are doing place-based education, then all students need to understand the economic dimensions of their community. Of course we heard the students' thoughts about how the college is functioning as a complex social, economic, and environmental system. We were able to explain our economic constraints and explore how these could be modified.

We have already instituted other ways of engaging students with the economic dimensions of the college. Students sit on the college's budget advisory committee and the socially responsible investing committee. A quarter of our work-study jobs are now green jobs, where students are trained to use triple bottom line analysis to improve work performance. Our next task will be to expand such learning opportunities and integrate them more systematically into the education of all students. In May 2012, the board of trustees, faculty, staff, and students approved a new strategic plan, organized in terms of the three dimensions of sustainability and emphasizing the entrepreneurial skills our students are developing. Our young alumni already include many role models for them to follow, like Heather McDermott, who started Vermont Salad and Herb Company, or Andy Farmer's highly successful Northeast Vine Supply. The next iteration of the Environmental Liberal Arts program will help students to channel their activism into collaborations that can advance sustainability in some enterprise. In doing so, we think that students will be better able to translate the skills they are learning into jobs they love.

7

From Soybeans and Silos to the Prairie Project: The Journey to Restorative Global Sustainability Education at Central College

Jim Zaffiro

Central College is a private liberal arts college enrolling 1,650 students drawn mainly from across Iowa. Located in Pella, Iowa, (population 10,000), the campus is about 45 minutes south of Des Moines, in corn and soybean country.

Central College has been native to central Iowa since 1853, born as a tiny, church-affiliated school in Straw Town (now Pella), where the prairie grasses were said to be so high that one could barely see a rider sitting on a horse above them. Things changed rapidly. More and more settlers came to farm these rich acres and soon the old name—as well as its significance—faded away. As an institution, we grew up at a time and in ways that today place us squarely in the middle of the most environmentally altered state in the country. Few of us as teachers and almost none of our students are aware of what central Iowa used to look like, or that 99.9 percent of our original tall grass prairie ecosystem has been lost to human settlement and industrial agriculture. To most people, Iowa looks like it "always" has. And so, decade after decade, and especially since the end of World War II, we lived, learned, and did liberal arts education in a land of silos, agricultural and academic, growing, storing, and selling our corn-soybean and academic-disciplinary monocultures to Cargill, Archer Daniels Midland (ADM), and generations of college students.

This chapter shares our faculty's journey toward personal and curricular transformation, pointing out some landmarks and pitfalls, while conveying a measure of hope and an offer of support to colleagues at other institutions. Looking back over Central's sustainability education journey, the single most important factor was finding workable ways, within the context of this campus culture and ethos, to create, nurture, and sustain transdisciplinary faculty development opportunities. After significant successes—like establishing a sustainability core requirement and providing professional development for nearly one-fifth of our faculty—we find our community of around a hundred faculty moving closer to consensus about expanding global sustainability curriculum, investing in faculty development, and making sustainability a major institutional strategic planning goal.

Central's Journey to Global Sustainability Education

As a faculty, we have been at this now for about ten years. A larger-than-expected initial challenge was simply finding ways to communicate effectively and help colleagues to understand what sustainability *was*, particularly that it was more encompassing than environmental studies. Another unanticipated challenge was demonstrating that it was not the new buzzword for politically correct environmentalism. Once we experienced success with these perceptions it became possible to start discussing why and how sustainability education might be important enough to build into the curriculum. For the first several years, faculty buy-in was somewhat slow. It really helped to have a small group of advocates to keep each other's spirits and hopes up. I was too pushy and, I am sure my friends will agree, too impatient for the first few years; success was ultimately as much about me learning about myself and how I come across as it was about the power and validity of the message itself. Over time, we learned that patience, persistence, and building personal relationships with colleagues helped convey relevance, raised awareness, and generated interest.

Before the Prairie Project got underway in 2009, the ground had already been well prepared and the seeds of change were, in many cases, already planted, sprouting, flourishing—and generating new seeds. The most significant sustainability curriculum decision we made ten years earlier, in 2002, was to establish Intersections, a new first-year course for all incoming freshmen. Our choice of an inaugural common theme also proved momentous in ways we did not fully appreciate at the time: "The Human Place in the Global Environment." Intersections was designed to be very interdisciplinary; as Mary Stark, our fearless leader, told us, Intersections teachers would need to get out of our professional and disciplinary comfort zones, modeling interdisciplinary learning—walking the walk—for our students. And with 450 new freshmen, we needed enough professors to teach 25 sections of 18–20 students each—one-quarter of the faculty.

Over the years we have had a lot of fun and steadily more and more of us have taken a turn teaching Intersections. By now, as we approach the ten-year anniversary of the program, even with new colleagues coming in, easily half of us have participated. Participating in summer training workshops—now affectionately referred to by Peggy Fitch, Intersections Coordinator, as "Play-Shops"—and taking on the challenge of teaching Intersections, primed more and more of us to experience and embrace the value of nurturing a faculty learning community dedicated to infusing interdisciplinarity across the curriculum.

Intersections not only made us better teachers and learners; by nudging us out from behind our disciplinary and departmental partitions, it also made us better colleagues. Out of our common experience a shared vision emerged for Global Sustainability Education. We started using this language in 2007, and it soon became interwoven into our ongoing liberal studies general education core renewal process. In November 2008, Global Sustainability became a general education core graduation requirement; and get this: we passed it unanimously! But this is not the end of the story.

Empowering and Supporting Faculty

This transdisciplinary, integrative approach also defines how and why the Prairie Project, our place-based, faculty/professional training and curriculum development learning community, was conceived. Participants commit to helping each other develop, implement, share and evaluate strategies and activities for infusing global sustainability across the undergraduate curriculum, by developing new courses, transforming existing ones, and testing new assignments and pedagogy.

We see sustainability education and community-based service learning as "two sides of the same coin." Our goal is to model environmental stewardship and sustainability and to connect these directly into academic programs, community outreach, and bioregion-wide teacher training and development workshops and service opportunities for faculty and students. The Prairie Project is now engaged in training, connecting, and supporting transdisciplinary learning communities of faculty members and support staff. As the Coordinator of Global Sustainability Education, I work in a close collaboration with Cheri Doane, director of our nationally recognized Center for Community-Based Learning. In fact, we have moved our offices to be physically closer to promote spontaneous brainstorms and planning sessions.

This approach benefits students and builds community among faculty members. It also generates significant positive, community-wide multiplier effects. Faculty and students learn and teach ecological, economic, and social sustainability and help to design solutions for real problems in local, national, and international communities, based on the expressed needs of community partners themselves. Such benefits are likely to spread to other communities and will continue to have a positive influence on attitudes and behaviors well into their adult lives.

One good example is Jenny Heseltine, a 2005 graduate, who carried her interest in Central's organic garden into her work for the Pella City Administrator. Last fall, Jenny persuaded the city to create a community garden in Caldwell Park. Recently I shared her success with another former student working on similar plans for residents of Bondurant, Iowa, and they now collaborate. Tangible benefits of this approach to teaching and learning are rippling out, sometimes even before our courses end and our students graduate. Last spring, Ted and Chris, two community-based learning students working at the Des Moines Catholic Worker House, took along their passion for campus sustainability by building compost bins, installing rain barrels, and convincing residents to go organic in their garden.

Sustainability Education Extends Globally

In framing our commitment to sustainability across—and beyond—the curriculum, we have deliberately chosen to characterize our efforts at Central as *Global* Sustainability Education. Partly this reflects our academic heritage. As an institutional pioneer in undergraduate study abroad programming (we opened our first abroad programs in Paris in 1965 and in London in 1966), and with an ongoing, active commitment to global experiential learning today, we are equally committed to fostering and connecting local and *global* sustainability education. Central is actively pursuing more ways to connect and infuse our abroad programs with credit-bearing and service-based opportunities for global sustainability education. Particularly exciting are current developments with community partners in agriculture, global public health, and sustainability education, in the city of Merida and the village of Tinum, through our program in Yucatan, Mexico.

As a core goal for student learning, we seek to foster intercultural and intergenerational perspectives that nurture empathy, global awareness, and respect. Among our representative student learning outcomes we include:

• Discover and empathize with other cultural perspectives on sustainability, especially indigenous cultures.

• Examine how cultural values, beliefs, and practices correspond to environmental and social problems.

• Articulate the relationship between poverty, social justice, and environmental degradation in different cultural contexts.

• Recognize issues of intergenerational responsibility and be able to articulate a positive vision for a just and sustainable society.

For Transformation, Support Community Building

Sustainable communities foster connections based on trust and characterized by deep bonds of respect and care. They are dynamic, welcoming environments, with different people contributing gifts of time, talent, experience, ideas, and resources. One important variety is a learning community. This is not an easy thing to create and nurture in an academic setting.

In May 2010, we successfully launched the Prairie Project with an intensive three-day workshop, modeled after AASHE's Sustainability across the Curriculum Leadership Training Workshops, and fostered a sustainability education learning community. I had originally anticipated twelve to fifteen participants, but demand exceeded expectations. To ensure that no one was left out, participants decided by consensus to reduce stipends (funded by the president's office) in order to accommodate everybody. Ultimately, twenty-one colleagues—nearly one-fifth of Central's faculty, representing a dozen different academic programs and departments—joined the Prairie Project community.

During the workshop, Prairie Project participants worked in collaborative pairs and small groups, sharing assignments, pedagogy, and resources. We discussed ideas, participated in hands-on curriculum design activities, and forged ongoing partnerships with colleagues. By the end of the workshop, participants were already well on their way to finding new models for teaching and learning about sustainability within existing courses or through new curricular offerings. Participants developed and shared new assignments and learning activities. They also made new connections with community partners interested in helping them incorporate sustainability into the curriculum through community-based service learning and place-based, hands-on "learning by doing."

With the importance of place-based communities in mind, I opened the first day of the workshop by asking participants to reflect upon two questions:

- How is a liberal arts college like a prairie?
- How is sustainability education like prairie restoration?

The responses were creative and even profound. Participants examined how global and local communities of all varieties are connected, and how every place has intellectual, spiritual, social, and cultural dimensions that define its role within ecological communities (Zaffiro 2011, 11).

Facilitating Personal and Curricular Transformations

This work has been transformative for me personally, as I continue to make the transition from "recovering" academic specialist to interdisciplinary teacher-learner, and for all of us together as a faculty community. One example that was personally transformative for me came out of a presentation by Ellie Du Pre, biology colleague, who shared positive experiences facilitating student involvement in campus microcredit lending. At her invitation, we formed ourselves into lending teams and ended up making our own microloans on the KIVA.org site as a workshop activity. A few months later, I decided to work this up into a new assignment, while participating in an Associated Colleges of the Midwest (ACM) interdisciplinary faculty collaboration on Integrating Sustainability into the Undergraduate Curriculum: "Global Economic Inequalities: Microcredit Lending" (http://serc.carleton.edu/index.html)[1] I now incorporate it into my freshman level Intro to International Politics course as part of a unit on the politics of global economic relations.

One of the most valuable outcomes of this project is the ongoing conversation between faculty from diverse disciplines about how they have incorporated sustainability into their teaching and how their students and colleagues are responding. Participants reconnected for a half-day follow-up workshop before the start of fall classes in late August, and again in December in front of a roaring fire and a table full of homemade desserts. In March 2011, the group gathered to discuss a common reading, James Farrell's *The Nature of College* (Farrell 2010). These lively discussions and collaborations are continuing well beyond the official end of the first Prairie Project in May 2011.

As a result of the project, Central has gained several new courses in various disciplines, including Germany and the Environment (modern languages), Biomimicry (biology), Literature of Peace and Social Justice (English), Environmental Chemistry (chemistry), Economics of Sustainability (economics), Elementary Science Methods (education), Sustainability in

Chinese and Japanese Cultures (history and Asian studies), Community, Consumer, and Global Health (exercise science), and Doctrines and Ministry (religion). More courses with a sustainability focus were rolled out during the 2011–12 academic year. Many participants, including myself, have willingly gone well beyond our original entry-level commitment to transform or create one course, as the momentum and support of the learning community encourages the sharing and integration of creative ways to transform and infuse additional standard courses and assignments with global sustainability emphasis.

Looking toward the Future

Making and successfully fulfilling an institutional commitment to infusing global sustainability education across the curriculum is like restoring a prairie: a long-term journey. Transformation takes time, resources, vision, leadership, and most of all, the strong, clear-eyed long-term commitment to building a trusting campus-wide community of teachers and learners, not all of whom are professors (Zaffiro 2010, 42) Indeed, transformational change in something as entrenched (and with as many moving parts) as a liberal arts curriculum is rarely the original intent.

As the seeds planted by the Prairie Project sprout and put down roots, our commitment to restorative global sustainability education is expanding beyond the formal curriculum and traditional academic programs, thanks to committed and visionary friends and colleagues, including ecologist Dr. Pauline Drobney at the Neil Smith National Wildlife Refuge near Prairie City, Iowa, who is supervising the restoration of North America's largest tall grass prairie; Central English professor Dr. Mary Stark, who works on developing sustainability curricula with elementary and middle school teachers; and Central's field biologist Dr. Russ Benedict's Prairies for Agriculture Project. The Prairie Project has joined forces with Professor Cheri Doane, Central's Director of Community Based Learning, allowing us to connect our sustainability teaching, learning, and service with over ninety community partners across central Iowa. As more learning communities are created and connected over time, higher education can lead—as it must—in addressing the challenges of creating a more sustainable future.

In 2011 we approved a new interdisciplinary minor in global sustainability with a community-based learning requirement, the first school in Iowa to do so. Pauline and Mary, Cheri and Russ, and I still feel like we have only just begun our transformative journey, as we think now about expanding the entire concept of what a curriculum is and what should "count" as for-credit teaching and learning. We are aiming for the AASHE target of 10 percent of our courses with sustainability content or emphasis. This will take us way beyond content, toward more personally and collectively demanding professional development to create and embrace pedagogies that foster transformative teaching and learning. All of this speaks to the power of getting outside of our monoculture, disciplinary silos, in terms of our thinking—and acting—when it comes to what is important to have in our curriculum.

Notes

1. Students in an introductory international politics class study and learn about problems associated with globalization and structural global economic inequalities and working in teams then make actual microcredit loans to prospective borrowers on the KIVA.org website. Full assignment is available at: http://serc. carleton.edu/acm_face/sustainability/activities/46334.html.

References

Farrell, James J. 2010. *The Nature of College: How a New Understanding of Campus Life Can Change the World*. Minneapolis: Milkweed Editions.

Zaffiro, Jim. 2010. Green Buildings across the Campus and Sustainability Education across the Curriculum: a Faculty Member's Perspective. *Climate Neutral Campus Report* 2:40–44.

Zaffiro, Jim. 2011. The Prairie Project: Faculty Development for Global Sustainability Education. *Diversity and Democracy* 14 (2):11–12.

8

Take-Home Messages that Transform Individuals and Institutions: The Student Leaders on Global Environmental Issues Program

John Cusick

Manoa is the flagship campus of the University of Hawai'i system with 20,000 students, and it holds the distinction of being a land-, sea-, and space-grant research institution. The East–West Center, established in 1960 by the US Congress, promotes better relations and understanding among the people of the Asia Pacific region.

The state of Hawai'i imports fossil fuels to meet over 90 percent of energy needs. While water tables drop on Oahu, due in part to increasing urbanization, agricultural lands are rezoned and paved for housing subdivisions. Estimates are that between several days' to two weeks' worth of food supply are available at any given time, and the islands have earned the title of "extinction capital of the planet" by accounting for nearly three-quarters of the species of plants and animals listed on the Endangered Species List.

In the island context of urban Honolulu where the University of Hawai'i at Manoa campus is located, sustainability is being championed by administration, faculty, staff, and students as a means to adapt and build resiliency in response to the realities of securing energy, water, food, and ecosystem services. The Vice Chancellor for Research and Graduate Education remarked in 2010 that the state is "functioning, on borrowed time, at a level that is not sustainable" and went on to suggest we "become the leader in addressing this need, particularly with an emphasis on addressing the associated pressing issues faced in Hawai'i and the Pacific Islands."

I participated in several campus sustainability initiatives, facilitating student participation through my role as adviser of the Environmental Studies undergraduate program (Cusick 2008a), and in 2009 was invited by a mutual colleague to meet with East–West Center Education Program staff members Scott MacLeod and Christina Monroe to discuss a request for proposals from the US Department of State. Our collaboration resulted in an experiential summer learning program to investigate the dynamic complexity of environmental stewardship.

The Student Leaders on Global Environmental Issues Program began in 2009 and by the end of 2012, 120 international students from nine countries have participated. These students are from Pacific Island and well as Southeast Asian and Southwest Asian nations, including Fiji, Papua New Guinea, Philippines, Singapore, Malaysia, Thailand, Myanmar, Jordan and Palestine. Although the program is only open to international students, we partner with universities in Hawai'i and the US mainland to involve US students as peer mentors. Program staff have developed partnerships and field site activities on the islands of Oahu, Maui and Hawai'i, the San Francisco and Monterey Bay areas, Boulder and the Colorado Rocky Mountains, and Washington, DC, and the Chesapeake Bay (Cusick et al. 2010). Beginning with the program's mission to cultivate participants' skill sets and knowledge to address challenges identified while on the program, this chapter will present examples of transformative impacts for participants, as well as for the neighboring University of Hawai'i at Manoa and East–West Center campuses.

How the Program Works

The program envisions a future network of young leaders capable of contributing innovative and positive solutions for twenty-first-century challenges. During the six-week summer programs, our goal is for participants to explore how a diverse range of people and institutions in American society collaborate to address topics ranging from natural resource management to sustainable tourism. A primary learning objective is to identify solutions that may be applied to home institutions, communities and countries.

Program participants investigate the following three questions:

1. What is happening in the environment and how are humans reacting and adapting to change?
2. What leadership actions are being taken and are needed to affect positive human and environmental change?
3. What learning outcomes can participants take home to create desired outcomes in their home communities?

The program provides opportunities to conduct research and consultations with a variety of stakeholders in locations representative of the United States. Pedagogically, we incorporate aspects of place-based and project-based learning to investigate place-specific problems, which in turn, inform small group projects. The program culminates with presentations of potential solutions in public forums, as well as in a debriefing session with State Department staff in Washington DC. Program staff member Lance Boyd received funding in 2010 through the Distinguished Fulbright Awards in Teaching program to learn how colleagues in Singapore use a project-based model, and their five-month collaboration investigating island communities with vulnerabilities to resource constraints such as those in Hawaiʻi and Singapore informs the program curriculum.

To facilitate the participants' orientation to the island of Oahu where the program is based for the first three weeks, peer mentors from the East–West Center Asia Pacific Leadership Program and the University of Hawaiʻi at Manoa Environmental Studies program directly engage with participants in outdoor activities. These include a ropes course to develop team-building skills, ocean kayaking to promote collective endurance and overcome individual fears, and landscaping activities to foster stewardship and sense of place. Homestay experiences provide additional insights into American society as nearly all participants are first-time visitors.

One pedagogical challenge has been to balance effectively the delivery of interdisciplinary content with adequate depth for a rigorous program of study. Many study abroad programs invoke images of edu-tourism, particularly in Hawaiʻi, where the "risk is that students return home with stereotypes reinforced" rather than achieving the desired learning objectives (Cusick 2008b, 805). This risk is a critical concern because international experience is increasingly valued as a component of students' educational experience, but it must go beyond simply visiting and seeing sights to fulfill its transformational capacity. Integration of intellectual content, multiple perspectives on complex local issues, and guided personal reflection are all valued components of an effective study abroad program. We rely on a combination of seminars and workshops with academic experts, environmental professionals and community organizations, a short selection of reading, written and oral assignments, and informal gatherings with key informants to provide adequate details for understanding field site conditions and current issues.

One roundtable discussion, for example, featured three business leaders, an organic farmer, a chef, and founder of a biodiesel company, in order to highlight the cradle-to-cradle concept (McDonough and Braungart 2002). The farmer grows vegetables for the chef's restaurant and the used cooking oil is converted to biodiesel that contributes to balance Hawaiʻi's energy portfolio. The conversation helps students recognize the closed loop system and learn how relationships can foster similar benefits among businesses in their home countries.

Through assessment and evaluation over the past four years, a project-based model developed as a means to nurture change agents among the participants. As noted earlier, a program objective is to develop a network of participants who collaborate across disciplinary boundaries. Many of them arrive with considerable academic information so we have deemphasized lectures from staff and/or experts toward outcomes that focus on nurturing interdisciplinary teams of students able to identify problems and propose solutions.

In California, participants learn about the environmental movement with site visits that introduce accomplishments of iconic individuals and institutions and their impacts on land and seascapes. These visits include Muir Woods National Monument in Marin County; Sierra Club headquarters in downtown San Francisco; LEED-certified buildings, including the David Brower Center in downtown Berkeley and the Jerry Yang and Akiko Yamazaki Environment and Energy Building on the Stanford University campus; Elkhorn Slough National Estuarine Research Reserve and Point Lobos State Reserve; and Monterey Bay Aquarium, Monterey Bay Aquarium Research Institute, California State University Moss Landing Marine Laboratory, and California State University Monterey Bay campus. These site visits highlight Muir and Brower as transformative leaders at key junctures in the budding environmental movement, and provide windows into roles institutions of higher education have in environmental research, instruction, and community service.

Our 2009 visit with California State University at Monterey Bay faculty happened the day of a chemical fire at a paint factory in the town of Salinas. We altered the itinerary to meet with fire department officials as the event unfolded and witnessed the coordinated efforts of county and state response teams that confined leakage and kept toxic materials from entering drainage canals that direct agricultural and stormwater runoff to the ocean. We were eyewitnesses to a prevented environmental disaster that demonstrated the role of collaborative action and reflected the university's founding history, as a decommissioned former military base. "This story should be known because it stands as an object lesson in these difficult times: Everything is possible when vision and commitment bloom within a community—and when leaders step forward to take personal responsibility. . . . Today, [our] students are being trained to be those leaders" (Wood 2005). The take-home messages for our participants that day were experiencing the tangible results of demilitarization in support of higher education and of effective environmental management.

One opportunity in Boulder, Colorado is learning about intentional communities, such as at the Colorado Chautauqua National Historic Landmark that President Theodore Roosevelt described as "typically American, in that it is typical of America at its best" (www.chautauqua. com). Chautauqua's dramatic backdrop of the Front Range of the Rocky Mountains provides a view of the greenbelt that surrounds Boulder. The community's decades-long efforts to purchase and maintain open space prevents the spread of suburbs north from Denver and creates a network of hundreds of miles of hiking, equestrian, and bike paths that represent a new form of urbanism.

Boulder's summer tourist scene in Pearl Street Mall was the location in 2011 for program participants' presentations as part of an event called Gallery of Solutions. Students designed interactive displays and competed for attention with street performers. Aware that program funding comes from US taxpayers, one participant called out to passersby "Hey, you paid for my trip so you should listen to what I have to say!" Although their messages focused on issues relevant to Boulder, including reduction of freshwater consumption by using gray water for irrigation, reuse of building materials to minimize the waste stream to landfills, and proper sorting of recyclable plastics, participants came to understand the critical importance of being well informed themselves so as to increase education and awareness among community members and decision makers.

All programs end in Washington, DC for a meeting at the Department of State Bureau of Educational and Cultural Affairs, the program's sponsoring agency through the Institutes for Student Leaders on Global Environmental Issues. The purpose of our visits to a variety of actors in the environmental movement throughout the program is to recognize the roles of government and non-governmental organizations in policy, regulation, enforcement, advocacy, and funding to meet national standards of environmental quality. Throughout the week, participants come to understand the complexity of a democratic process working to ensure clean air and water, sustainable economic development, and environmental safety and health provisions at national and state levels.

Impacts of the Program

The program's transformational potential has been considerable, involving a federal government unit, as well as multiple domestic and international institutions of higher education. The range of places, problems, and projects reflects participants' diverse academic backgrounds and interests. For example, engineers gravitated to challenges imposed by infrastructure, medical students made links between ecosystem integrity and human health, educators considered the importance of outdoor learning to counter nature deficit disorder among urban youth, and ecologists realized that natural resource management has a lot to do with managing human behaviors.

To illustrate the program's impact, one Fijian participant, Subhanshi Raj, secured funding within a few months of her return home to attend the 2009 United Nations Climate Change Conference in Copenhagen. She was recently a Fulbright scholar in Urban and Regional Planning at the University of Buffalo, State University of New York, and wrote a chapter for the book *The Next EcoWarriors* (Hunter 2011). She wrote her cohort that the chapter was "really a result of my time in [the program] . . . so this chapter is to all of you, my hardworking environmentalist friends!" Bill McKibben's review of the book suggests we "never say that today's young people are apathetic." Our experiences suggest a similar message. Far from apathetic, these empowered youth are acquiring knowledge and skills needed to navigate their futures. Since we remain in contact using social media, staff members are able to monitor, assess, and facilitate their continued engagement in program-related projects while we all work to expand the network of emerging leaders and partnerships.

In February 2012, staff members organized reunions in Singapore attended by eighteen alumni from five countries and another in Amman, Jordan. The purpose of these gatherings was to develop relationships with partners and meet in locations that exemplify the challenges and opportunities of the two distinct regions. Staff and alumni conducted public presentations attended by faculty and students of local universities, staff from US embassies, and environmental groups, all of who made commitments to promote the future development of the environmental leadership program. Program alumni presented learning outcomes from projects initiated in the United States and applied to their local context, including a bike share program, coral reef conservation, green building innovations, and waste management strategies. Staff noted that alumni were eager to report how their program participation has contributed to increased environmental education and awareness in their home communities, and program staff have returned from these reunions with quantitative and qualitative measures of the program's impact on individuals and institutions of higher education.

Prior to and during the program, program staff have reflected on opportunities to infuse sustainability into the operations of the East–West Center and University of Hawai'i at Manoa. Collectively, we have organized, hosted, and attended a number of events in support of efforts at both institutions to undertake a collective responsibility of becoming models for sustainability. The recognition of geographic reality has been key, as it was to pre-European contact Hawaiians, which dictates prudence in matters associated with energy, water, and food security.

In summary, individual learning outcomes are a collective benefit for the Asia Pacific region. Serious challenges to present and future generations are still evident, and our environmental leadership program alone will not turn the tide on these trends. Nonetheless, the program provides international students glimpses of various localities in the United States where creative responses to a range of challenges and opportunities can be observed and considered when confronting similar situations upon their return home. The East-West Center and University of Hawai'i at Manoa have certainly benefited from the opportunity to host these emerging environmental leaders, thus reinforcing the significant role that institutions of higher education can play in providing the stories and strategies for transformation toward a sustainable future.

Acknowledgments

The author is grateful to Scott MacLeod and Christina Monroe of the East–West Center Education Program, and Lance Boyd and Brian Kastl.

References

Cusick, John. 2008a. Operationalizing Sustainability Education at the University of Hawai'i at Manoa. *International Journal of Sustainability in Higher Education* 9 (3):246–256.

Cusick, John. 2008b. Study Abroad in Support of Education for Sustainability: A New Zealand Case Study. *Environment, Development and Sustainability* 11 (4):801–813.

Cusick, John, Christina Monroe, Scott MacLeod, and Nicholas Barker. 2010. Sustainability Education and Public Diplomacy: A Case Study of the United States Institute on the Environment. *Environmental Practice* 12 (1):8–17.

History of the Colorado Chautauqua. 2012, February 29. *The Colorado Chautauqua National Historic Landmark Home Page*, http://www.chautauqua.com/

Hunter, Emily. 2011. *The Next Eco-Warriors*. San Francisco: Red Wheel/Weiser.

McDonough, William, and Michael Braungart. 2002. *Cradle to Cradle: Remaking the Way We Make Things*. New York: North Point Press.

Wood, Lori. 2005. To Future Generations. California State University Monterey Bay. http://about.csumb.edu/founding-csumb/future-generations.

9

Learning Sustainability in a Tribal College Context

William Van Lopik

The College of Menominee Nation is a tribal college in northeast Wisconsin. It was established in 1993 and chartered by the Menominee Indian Tribe. There are 720 students who attend either the Keshena campus located on the Menominee Indian Reservation or Green Bay campus located on the Oneida Indian Reservation.

When students enter my classroom at the beginning of the semester they always skeptically ask me: "What kind of job can I get learning about sustainable development?" I know they ask me this question because they have never seen a job in the classified ads that calls for a person with a degree in sustainability. However, my response to them is always the same: "I cannot think of a job that does not require a student to be familiar with the values of sustainability." I have taught courses on sustainable development for the past ten years and every year the students start with the same question: "Why do I have to take this course?" Ten years may sound like a considerable amount of time to be teaching on this topic, but it is nothing compared to the 10,000 years that my employers have been practicing sustainability. I work at the College of Menominee Nation, which is a tribal college chartered in 1993 by the Menominee Indian Tribe of Wisconsin. However, long before we started offering courses on sustainability at the college the tribe was practicing the values of sustainability in northeast Wisconsin. These values are based on the vision of the Menominee leaders of respectful, responsible, and kinship stewardship of our mother earth for future generations' survival and gift of life.[1]

For more than 150 years, sustainable forestry has been practiced on the reservation. Timber- and wood-processing operations have run continuously for that same period of time. As a result, the elements of sustainability are spirituality, ethics, government, business and resource management, and the Menominee way of life. Chief Oshkosh, an early tribal chief, proposed the idea of harvesting timber across the reservation at such a rate that there would always be timber ready to cut. This value of never taking more than you need is pervasive among the Menominee and exemplifies the essence of sustainability.

Mindful of my students and the culture they bring, I teach a course at our college entitled Introduction to Sustainable Development. I have taught this course since 2003 and have had about 500 students come through it. This is certainly not a lot of students compared to large state universities, but in terms of a college of 700 students with only 659 alumni, it represents a significant number. Students at the college generally fit a non-traditional student profile. Their average age at graduation is thirty-three; 72 percent are Native American and 76 percent are female. This is a general education course and therefore is required of all degree-seeking students (a decision made by the administration in 2005). The content covered in the course is as broad as our understanding or interpretation of sustainable development. The course follows the theoretical framework, developed by community members, tribal leaders, and academics when the college was first established, of the college's Sustainable Development Institute and offers six interactive dynamic dimensions upon which sustainable development depends. The model draws on a historical reflection and analysis of how the Menominee people have survived and sustained themselves in northern Wisconsin over the past centuries. (See figure 9.1 and table 9.1.)

The strength of this class lies in the fact that it is a general education requirement. Therefore, students come with various interests, majors, and backgrounds; there are students majoring in nursing, teacher education, business, accounting, physical science, and even in sustainable development. They all wonder what relevance this class holds for them. However, post-semester student evaluations indicate that all students come to realize the relevance of sustainability to their personal and career lives. The main assessment tool used in the class to determine the level of comprehension and acceptance of sustainability is a final reflection paper, five to six pages, explaining how the concepts of sustainable development directly apply to them. This practical application may be at the personal, academic, or vocational level and includes an analysis of the interface between at least two components of the Menominee Sustainable Development Model as they relate to a specific issue. The learning outcomes for the class are:

• Define sustainability in terms of its past, present and future initiatives.

• Explain how environmental, social, and economic systems in the Menominee model of sustainable development are interrelated.

• Utilize knowledge of sustainability to systematically analyze problems and think critically about daily actions and consumer mentality.

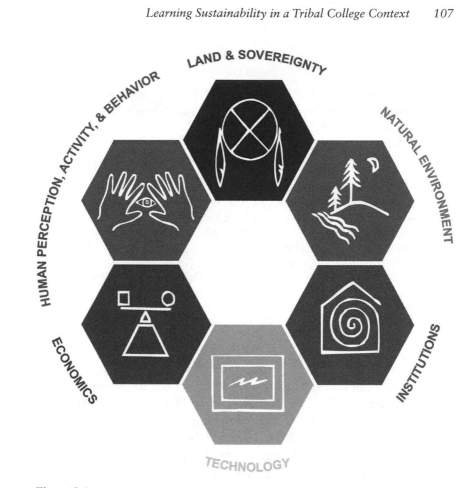

Figure 9.1

An illustration of the Sustainable Development Institute's six interactive dynamic dimensions

• Demonstrate a commitment to sustainability by actively applying knowledge of sustainability to personal lives, professions, and societies.

• Apply concepts of sustainability to campus and community as global citizens.

• Explain the relevance of sustainability to personal lives and values, and how actions impact sustainability outcomes.

• Demonstrate change-agent skills so that the students can implement viable solutions to shift the organizational, societal, or cultural practices and policies toward sustainability.

Table 9.1
Introduction to Sustainable Development

Part 1: Human Behavior/Culture	Part II: Land and Sovereignty
Population scales and monitoring	Indigenous land rights
Demographic distribution	Human rights
Population growth patterns	Global resource extraction
Global economic inequities	Economic globalization
Part III: Technology	Part IV: Economics
Appropriate and alternative technologies	Triple bottom-line accounting
Renewable energy	Green economics
Global communication technologies	Sustainable career options
Part V: Natural Environment	Part VI: Institutional Development
Global environmental threats	Non-profit institutions
Climate change	Resource development
Permaculture	Social activism

Over the past ten years of teaching, these 500-plus final papers have offered me insight and clarity about students' engagement with sustainable development. The students have prompted me to realize that the subject matter is so much broader than energy efficiency and renewable energy; it includes issues related to human rights, poverty, social entrepreneurship, population control, and cultural preservation. Importantly, the student reflection papers effectively contextualize and synthesize sustainability within the Native American cultural context. Through teaching this class my students constantly challenge me to realize that teaching about sustainability is not just an academic or cognitive exercise; it is a value system founded on the notion that we as humans have a relationship with the earth based on respect and mutual sharing.

Personal Sustainability Practices within the Local Tribal Context

The topic of sustainable development and how it relates to the cultural history and forest management practices of Menominee people consistently attracts the attention of the greatest number of students. This is not surprising considering the number of Menominee students in the class and their sense of pride and familiarity with the history of natural resource management on the reservation. There is no lack of appropriate topics for the students to choose from when they look around the community.

Many students have family members who are involved in sustainable forest management on the reservation and have grown up with the value of caring for the forest. They are concerned about sustaining their culture, their land, their language and traditional sources of food. Sustainability becomes very personal to people who have tried for so many years to preserve the uniqueness of who they are. They are concerned about native land rights, tribal sovereignty, and the adherence to treaty rights. They are also concerned about sustaining native culture amid the constant threat of forced assimilation by the dominant culture. Sustainability often becomes synonymous with survive-ability.

These values are also very much prevalent among the Oneida students who choose to write about the Oneida Indian tribe, often with a focus on food and economic systems. These students choose to write about the sustainable agricultural methods that are practiced in a very deliberate way by the tribe through the Oneida Community Integrated Food Systems. Student Mike Thundercloud illustrated the cultural connections as he quoted the Oneida Nation mission statement in his final paper: ". . . to sustain a strong Oneida Nation by preserving our heritage through the 7th generation. The Oneida family will be strengthened through the values of our Oneida identity by providing housing, promoting education, protecting the land, and preserving the environment. Our Oneida Nation provides for the quality of life where the people come together for the common good."[2] This is very much a statement of sustainability without actually mentioning the word. It is basically a value statement based upon balance, harmony, and only taking what you need from the earth.

This value of native rights spills over for many students to the story of the Ogoni people who live along the Niger Delta in Nigeria and their struggle for recognition and survival. We talk about this situation in class through the showing of the video *Delta Force* (the story of the nonviolent efforts of Nigerian writer and human rights activist Ken Saro-Wiwa) and a reading in the book *Resource Rebels* (Ellis 1998, Gedicks 2001). This case study undoubtedly strikes a strong cord with some students who choose to explore the situation further. They write about how oil mining, poverty, environmental degradation, and exploitation of human rights are all interrelated in this case. They are fascinated with the Movement for the Survival of the Ogoni People and how they went toe to toe with the Nigerian government and multinational oil corporations. They are disturbed by the direct connection they see between their tank of gas and the extreme suffering of native brothers and sisters in other parts of the world. This is a connection that very few previously envisioned, and it certainly resonates strongly with them.

Many of the students who take the course are business majors. They are interested in sustainable development as it pertains to a business position they are currently in or desire to start. They do an exercise in class that requires them to explore Green America's *Green Pages*. They are asked to pick a business from this list that they find interesting and to talk about it in class. The following is a list of some of the more fascinating business ventures that they have chosen to write about:

- Greening a grocery store
- Sustainability and the cosmetic industry
- Organic and sustainable breweries
- Fair trade products (coffee, chocolates, clothes)
- Greening of the military "Green Hawks"
- Socially responsible investments
- Green burials
- Starting a green auto repair shop
- Greening a golf course
- Hotel and casino maintenance and sustainability

The first time I saw this list, I was surprised by the inclusion of casinos. I grew up far from an established Indian reservation in a deeply religious and conservative community where casinos and gambling were definitely frowned upon, so I held a bias against the benefits of casinos. But because of the students, I have since adjusted my views on the positive attributes that these businesses can provide a tribal community. The student papers I have read have shown me how casinos contribute to the tribal sovereignty of Native American nations. Casinos provide direct benefits to the economic and social welfare of the community, offering jobs in economically depressed areas and creating business opportunities for vendors and suppliers. More importantly, they help fund tribal social programs like education, senior centers, historic preservation, public safety, and healthcare services. They are a major revenue generator and social safety net for local tribal communities that surround the college. Although casinos have their own recognized social problems, I have come to accept that they also empower tribes to tackle many other sustainability issues in their communities.

The majority of our student body is made up of non-traditional students who have children they are raising while they themselves attend college. These students choose to write about how sustainable development affects the way they live and think. They are most interested in bringing sustainability into their homes by teaching their children, changing their personal lifestyles, adapting their career paths, and leading by example. This change of behavior in the home is sometimes implemented by starting a family garden, eating only locally produced food, or actually becoming a vegetarian (which is very radical within a culture steeped in hunting and gathering). One student, Carlotta Perez, wrote:

This class has really opened my eyes to what goes on in the world and what needs to be done to keep our Earth healthy. I usually don't pay any attention to what goes on in the world because I get terribly stressed out, and I admit I was a bit worried when I started taking this class because I thought for sure it was going to put me over the edge. But sometime during the semester, it hit me . . . I'm a teacher! I have the power to make a difference in this world. Instead of stressing over it, do something about it. I can teach the children of our future how to care for the world, but first . . . I need to do before I can teach. So, let's start with my home life.

The students of our college have a strong connection to the land around them. Most grew up in the area and are avid lovers of the land. Much of this is tied to the rural nature of our college, but also to the Native American cultural value of land stewardship. The college is located in the Menominee Forest, which is world-renowned for its beauty. As Melinda Cook, a student and Menominee tribal member, wrote in her paper: "Menominee sustainability is more than just a promise to do good, it is built upon centuries of caring for the forest and the future. It is a point of sustaining not only the growing of the forest, but the people who are part of the forest." Students are understandably concerned about any threats to the environmental health of the area. They are interested in invasive species, water quality of surface waters, mining threats, species extinction, and environmental threats to human health.

Issues of climate change and how it will affect the local environment are also of special interest to students. They want to know the climatic changes that their elders have seen in their lives. They wonder about how it will affect wildlife, what mitigation and adaptation strategies are being discussed, and how it will affect local economies.

Another young woman who was a domestic abuse survivor wrote: "The Oglala Lakota people were very sustainable with everything for native plants and animals to housing. They took care of their families, their tribes, their animals, and their land. However, like many Native Americans they were forced from their land and could not avoid conflicts with the white man. After the coming of the white man, our people were forced to change many of their traditional ways of life. This was a drastic change that the Native people were not used to, brought on new corruption that the people were unable to handle. I believe this is where the abuse all started. Over time the abuse of alcohol lead [sic] into the abuse of one's self, family and all that surrounded them." This student showed me that sustainability is about sustaining one's culture. Just as we need biodiversity in the plant and animal world to ensure a healthy ecosystem, we also need diversity in the human cultural world to ensure the sustainability of a healthy planet for all.

The course is even required of all students enrolled in the nursing program, which is something that mystifies them during the first week of class. After a couple of weeks, they start seeing the connection between human health, social justice, and environmental sustainability. They often end up being the strongest advocates for sustainability and see clearly how it applies to their profession. The topics they choose to write about are ones that a few years ago I would never thought had any bearing on sustainable development. One is the sustainable use of the placenta after child birth. Some of these uses are medicinal, since the cord blood stem cells in the placenta can be used to treat diseases including leukemia, lymphoma, sickle cell anemia, and immune deficiency disorders. There are other more culturally based uses the students mention, such as burial (which adds nutrients to the soil) and companion tree planting (which celebrates the child's growth and is a sign that the child will always return home). There are many good uses of this essential life support system other than just putting it in a biohazard bag and disposing of it in a landfill.

Bricks and mortar will always be a key element of sustainable development as long as we continue to carry the word "development" with it. Our conceptualization of the term is very much grounded in the idea of building something. A sizeable portion of students is always drawn toward innovation, engineering, designing, and experimenting. They like to learn more about the concepts of Leadership in Energy and Environmental Design (LEED) certification, of developing alternative fuels and energy sources and of creating new types of building materials. They like to explore what is emerging in research and development that will positively impact our way of life. For Native students, this interest is tied to sovereignty and the poor housing conditions that are frequently found on reservations. They are fascinated to find that some of the most innovative housing projects in sustainability are coming out of Indian Country.

A significant number of students choose to write about renewable energy sources and their benefits to the environment, cutting fuel bills, and mitigating carbon emissions. They selected the common topical areas of wind, solar, biomass, methane gas, and geothermal power sources. However, one student who is a former cross-country truck driver wrote about how the trucking industry is researching the whole issue of fuel efficiency. In the paper she referred to aerodynamic devices on trucks, synthetic lubricants, Teflon fifth-wheel plates, wide-based tires, optimum shifting sensors, and LED lights. She made the point that the trucking industry itself is constantly adapting their equipment to minimize energy usage and increase efficiency. This was an area that I never seriously considered before when talking about sustainability. The example was a great case study of the linkages between the economy, environment, and technology in the trucking industry.

All of the responses that the students wrote in this class were greatly encouraging to me as far as the future of sustainability. One student came to me after class and said "I thought sustainable development was all about land, forest, and recycling. I realize it is more about all of the human aspects of life." Once students understand the interrelatedness of sustainability and how it impacts the total person, they then begin grasping one of the course learning outcomes of being a change agent.

Embracing Sustainable Living

What has this taught me? Students embrace the concepts of sustainable development when they realize their place in the world and how their actions can have a profoundly negative or positive influence. It is a concept that becomes more tangible, more practical, and more concrete when they can relate it to their home life, their job, their career aspirations, and their culture. This approach was initially a real challenge for me personally because I needed to put aside whatever assumptions I had that my academic training somehow made me the expert on sustainable development. It took me three years to learn to appreciate, admire, and acknowledge the fact that sustainability is so embedded in the place-based knowledge and indigenous ways of knowing that many of my students already possessed prior to entering the classroom. Second, the students have also taught me that the challenge of our whole academic institution needs to weave sustainability into the entire curriculum. This became so apparent to me in the broad tapestry of applications that they chose to write about. We need each student, faculty and staff person to realize that sustainability applies to them and that they individually and collectively can make a positive contribution to our terrestrial home.

Notes

1. See www.sustainabledevelopmentinstitute.org.
2. See www.oneidanation.org/culture.

References

Ellis, Glenn. 1998. *Delta Force*. VHS. Oxford, UK: Catma Films.

Gedicks, Al. 2001. *Resource Rebels: Native Challenges to Mining and Oil Corporations*. Cambridge, MA: South End Press.

III
Defining the Paradigm for Change

10

Driving Transformative Change by Empowering Student Sustainability Leaders at the University of Michigan

Mike Shriberg, Andrew J. Horning, Katherine Lund, John Callewaert, and Donald Scavia

The University of Michigan-Ann Arbor (U-M) is a large public university with a total campus population of over 80,000, including over 40,000 students. Founded in 1817, U-M's campus encompasses 3,153 acres with 571 major buildings. U-M's annual research expenditures top $1.25 billion, largest among public institutions.

At the University of Michigan, we employ an innovative strategy that directly involves students in fostering institutional change for sustainability. This chapter contains three interrelated examples of how the Graham Environmental Sustainability Institute channels student energy and creativity to effect sustainability transformations on campus, while simultaneously cultivating leadership and change management skills among our students. The first story focuses on the creation and implementation of an innovative collaborative co-curricular effort—the Student Sustainability Initiative. The second highlights the building of an operational campus sustainability master plan through an Integrated Assessment research process. The third story focuses on how the classroom can be used to spark sustainability projects while building student skills.

The Student Sustainability Initiative: Student Impact through Collaboration and Integration

In early 2008, three University of Michigan graduate students, representing our Engineering, Law, and Public Policy schools, came to our Graham Sustainability Institute offices with enthusiasm and frustration in their voices. They described how U-M had more than three dozen student groups with sustainability interests, but lamented that these groups rarely worked together and often competed for both recognition and resources. Engineering doctoral student Darshan Karwat noted that because the University of Michigan is such a large and decentralized institution, this lack of coordination held students back from effecting large-scale change.

During the meeting, Darshan and his collaborators, Melissa Forbes and Mark Shahinian, planted the seeds for a plan they thought would solve this complex problem. They laid out a concept to better organize and empower all U-M students around sustainability, while simultaneously making students more credible in the eyes of the administration. What they had in mind would ultimately transform the institution's sustainability efforts.

With guidance and support from U-M's Graham Sustainability Institute, a boundary organization (Guston 2001) that connects academics, policymakers, and practitioners by facilitating sustained and vibrant interactions to solve wicked sustainability problems, the Student Sustainability Initiative (SSI) was born. Developed with an innovative organizational structure and mission, the SSI did not seek to be *the* sustainability student group on campus, but rather to provide a mechanism to allow for more effective communication among like-minded students and the administration.

This structure empowers the SSI to chart its own course, while also providing the group with insights into the inner workings of U-M. The SSI's mission is not to advance a particular cause, but to actively engage sustainability-minded students across campus to identify common interests and pursue goals that large numbers of students and groups can rally behind. In the first year, the SSI board hit the ground running, hosting roundtable events and gathering student ideas to establish shared priorities. Original SSI board member and engineering undergraduate, Merry Walker, noted that in the early days, by leveraging social media and other broad networks, SSI was able to pass information to the student body at large and create a movement calling upon U-M's administration to make a commitment to sustainability.

Two Student Sustainability Goals

The SSI began its work by organizing, publicizing, and hosting several gatherings involving hundreds of students, which resulted in two aggressive goals for the students to pursue in the year ahead. First, they wanted U-M to establish an operations-oriented sustainability office to complement the academic role fulfilled by our institute. Second, they wanted U-M to make a binding commitment to Leadership in Energy and Environment Design (LEED) Silver certification for all new building construction.

Over the course of the next several months, the SSI continued to shape its strategy—benchmarking best practices at peer institutions and consulting with U-M leaders to assess receptivity and better understand institutional challenges. Finally, the SSI drafted a letter to U-M president Mary Sue Coleman, formally requesting that she endorse the group's priorities. This letter brought together a year's worth of student work and was supported by clear data and analysis, which made a strong business case for taking action.

The result? In 2009, President Coleman officially launched the U-M Office of Campus Sustainability and made a commitment that all new non-clinical U-M buildings with capital costs above $10 million would be LEED Silver certified. But she did not stop there. President Coleman also established the U-M Sustainability Executive Council, a policymaking body that she chairs comprising U-M's most senior leaders. She also named a Special Counsel to the President for Sustainability, and she declared that sustainability would be a top priority presidential initiative.

Could the SSI really have been responsible for all of this? The truth is that many forces—both internal and external—were at work here. For example, two of us worked closely with the SSI throughout the process, meeting with them regularly to provide insight and feedback on their strategy. These interactions helped the SSI to fine-tune their goals and messages so they aligned with other institutional priorities and resonated more clearly with U-M leaders. Our role, however, was to support the SSI in strengthening its own message and tactics. The reality is that the institutional shift would not have happened without the SSI's collaborative model, which was markedly different from prior student advocacy efforts on campus.

A New Approach
Since the 1960s, the University of Michigan has been renowned for student activism on issues ranging from civil rights to Vietnam to affirmative action. Advocacy is clearly in the DNA of our students, and the issue of sustainability is no exception. For more than a decade before the SSI existed, U-M students—either on their own or representing a student group—would regularly call on U-M leaders to advance various aspects of sustainability, with varying degrees of success. The problem was that many different, and sometimes conflicting, ideas were being voiced, greatly diluting the power of both the message and the messenger. To exacerbate the problem, messages and messengers changed regularly as students graduated or moved on to other priorities. This made it challenging for institutional leaders to prioritize and respond effectively to student requests.

The SSI alleviated these problems by establishing a clear mission, organizational structure, and succession strategy. This was critical because it allowed U-M officials to have a point of entry to discuss sustainability interests with the student body. According to Dashan Karwat, "the institutional memory of SSI sends a smoother, more coherent voice to the administrators and student groups. Each new group of SSI leaders is thoroughly briefed about the history of the group, its past failures and successes, as well as about effective ways of communicating with students as well as administrators."

The SSI has also been successful because its leaders have functioned as "tempered radicals," people who succeed in organizations without compromising their ideological beliefs (Meyerson 2001). By wearing two hats (student organizer and U-M student employee) SSI board members effectively employ critical strategies that allow tempered radicals to succeed. For example, they initiate conversations that create connections with others who have similar values, beliefs, and identities; they develop the discipline to manage heated emotions to effectively move the agenda forward; and they frame the agenda in language that has legitimacy among those in power.

Each year, by design, the SSI board membership changes as some students rotate out and others remain on to provide continuity and organizational memory. As new student leaders emerge, priorities developed in partnership with their peers evolve. What remains unchanged, however, is the overarching purpose of the organization: to continually build and empower the U-M student community around this all-important topic and to work in partnership with U-M leaders to find common ground in advancing sustainability.

The SSI has helped to transform U-M sustainability efforts and their efforts have been publicly lauded on multiple occasions. The group's accomplishments earned them the 2009 Oikos International Student Entrepreneurship Award, and its contributions were praised in a landmark speech given by President Coleman in 2011, who stated: "The Student Sustainability Initiative, in particular, has pulled together dozens of student groups working to make the University of Michigan a more sustainable place. They are formidable, they have pushed us as an institution, and we owe them our thanks."

Campus Sustainability Integrated Assessment: Shaping the Campus by Connecting Students, Faculty, and Staff

The seeds sown in the early days of the SSI continue to bear fruit as is illustrated by a subsequent two-year project investigating sustainability efforts on campus. Shortly after the President's Sustainability Executive

Council was established, its first action (in October 2009) was to endorse a comprehensive Campus Sustainability Integrated Assessment (CSIA). Integrated Assessment (IA) is a research framework we use at the Graham Institute to address particularly challenging topics by synthesizing natural, social, and economic information to help improve decision making. The CSIA was a comprehensive and open process to develop U-M's operational "master plan" for campus sustainability. This complex project combined the enthusiasm of students, expertise of faculty, and experience of staff to advance U-M campus sustainability. The project also provided an opportunity for students to continue pushing the needle toward sustainability.

From the beginning, students' interest and passion for the CSIA were clear—with nearly 300 undergraduate and graduate students applying for positions to work on the seven faculty-led analysis teams. Teams were eventually staffed by 77 student research assistants who completed over 10,000 hours of work. A significant benefit for students was the opportunity to be heard at the highest levels of the university. Ryan Smith, an engineering graduate student working on the Culture and Energy teams has observed that as his teams developed long lists of questions regarding U-M operations, staff members from the Office of Campus Sustainability were motivated and eager to serve as our source of data. In turn, "we were able to provide recommendations and analysis to help them improve their operations moving forward. We needed them and they needed us."

Ultimately, the CSIA led to an initial set of goals and actions under four themes (see table 10.1): Climate Action, Waste Prevention, Healthy Environments, and Community Awareness.[1] Each theme has both a guiding principle and a 2025 goal:

• Guiding Principles are broad philosophies guiding long-range strategies through changing circumstances.

• 2025 Goals are time-bound, quantifiable objectives aligned with each guiding principle where progress is measured from a *2006 baseline*.

Like the SSI, the CSIA project gave students an impactful way to deepen their commitment to sustainability—this time by using the campus as a living-learning lab to help develop the goals. Amy Braun was a member on the Purchasing and Recycling Team. She came to the project as a Master's student in Environmental Policy and Planning and after working as an intern at U-M's Waste Management Services Recycling Program. Her team, in particular, used the campus as a "lab" to craft recommendations that helped inform the Waste Prevention goal. When reflecting on

Table 10.1
University of Michigan Campus Sustainability Integrated Assessment Themes, Guiding Principles, and Goals

Theme	Guiding Principle	2025 Goals
Climate Action	We will pursue energy efficiency and fiscally responsible energy sourcing strategies to reduce greenhouse gas emissions toward long-term carbon neutrality.	Reduce greenhouse gas emissions (scopes 1&2) by 25%. Decrease carbon intensity of passenger trips on U-M transportation options by 30%.
Waste Prevention	We will pursue purchasing, reuse, recycling, and composting strategies toward long-term waste eradication.	Reduce waste tonnage diverted to disposal facilities by 40%.
Healthy Environments	We will pursue land and water management, built environment, and product-sourcing strategies toward improving the health of ecosystems and communities.	Purchase 20% of U-M food in accordance with U-M Sustainable Food Purchasing Guidelines. Protect Huron River water quality by reducing runoff from impervious surfaces and reducing the volume of land management chemicals used on campus by 40%.
Community Awareness	We will pursue stakeholder engagement, education, and evaluation strategies toward a campus-wide ethic of sustainability.	There is no explicit stretch goal for this theme. However, multiple actions will educate our community, track behavior, and report progress over time.

the assessment, Amy said, "Our team met with a variety of stakeholders, including a long list of staff with hands-on knowledge of U-M systems, and our recommendations were stronger as a result. We even started the project by getting our hands dirty (literally and figuratively) by sorting waste created by students."

While our goal for the CSIA was to advance institutional sustainability, it clearly promoted the growth and development of students as well as their understanding of sustainability, institutional change, and their roles as leaders. We anonymously surveyed students about their experience at the midpoint and conclusion of the project. At the midpoint, with enthusiasm still running high, nearly two-thirds of the students said they felt their individual efforts and the overall CSIA were making significant contributions to advance sustainability at U-M.

However, closer to the conclusion of the project student enthusiasm began to wane. Many student research assistants voiced concerns about whether their sustainability ideas generated through the CSIA would actually be implemented. Brennan Madden, the Transportation Team's student lead and a graduate student in the School of Natural Resources and Environment, commented that, "some decision makers were open to the overall motivation of our ideas but not supportive of some key specifics, which lowered our expectations of implementation."

In the second survey, staff at the Graham Institute found fewer than half of the students believed their efforts would make a meaningful contribution. Most of this decline could be explained by the students' realization that their detailed analyses were not wholly sufficient to bring about meaningful institutional change, nor implement specific projects, as noted in the following anonymous student comment: "The Integrated Assessment has significant potential to establish U-M sustainability leadership. However, its product is a framework for action that requires political will for its promise to be fulfilled. Success depends on whether that element is present."

When we discussed preliminary goals with the student research assistants, they voiced concerns that the CSIA's proposed targets were insufficient and did not reflect U-M's potential to show leadership. Kate Harris, a graduate student in the School of Education and the School of Natural Resources and Environment who served on the Purchasing and Recycling Team, along with other campus sustainability student leaders, drafted a letter to President Coleman calling for the U-M to "set the bar higher." The letter specifically called for stronger goals based on peer institution research and institutional knowledge gained as part of the CSIA experience. The letter was circulated among student research assistants from both phases of the CSIA and edited based on their feedback. Kate felt the letter "was necessary because the IA was supposed to set the bar for what we thought we could achieve, and I thought U-M really underestimated its ability to do great things."

Ultimately, the letter was endorsed by thirty-six of the student research assistants working on the project—many because they were disappointed that their teams' more ambitious recommendations were trumped by perceived limitations of the larger institution. The need to balance research teams' visioning and recommendations with views of operations staff was a challenge that we needed to address throughout the IA. The final goals were in many cases, stronger than some staff members were comfortable with and weaker than some of the students and faculty thought were possible.

While certainly not the first student letter the president received, the experience from the CSIA gave the students more confidence, a stronger voice, and positioned them as effective change agents to help advance the project's sustainability goals. The students' words clearly showed their passion, how well versed they had become in the campus sustainability movement, and how they were now empowered by the CSIA to speak directly to U-M leaders. As a result of student input like this and continued communications with campus operations and external advisers, most of the goals were revisited and some were even changed to address student concerns.

A significant step came in September 2011, when U-M president Mary Sue Coleman and her Sustainability Executive Council used the results and analysis of the CSIA to establish sustainability goals. She made it abundantly clear that sustainability is a deep, underlying theme that will guide U-M into the future. Importantly, given the student work that occurred, she also highlighted the essential role of students in defining U-M's sustainability path. "Students," she said, "shape the University of Michigan in unexpected and profound ways. They plant seeds of ideas, they forge new trails, and they take us in exciting new directions. We would not be here today if not for our students' persistence, their enthusiasm, and their deep concern about the future . . . sustainability defines the University of Michigan." Progress toward the goals is reported annually in the U-M Sustainability Report, and the goals will be revisited every five years to gauge success, review project ideas, and examine the need to make revisions.

The CSIA and the subsequent goal setting did not end with President Coleman's speech. Given the high degree of student involvement in the project, the CSIA continues to seed innovative student-focused sustainability initiatives. Key ideas identified through the CSIA include a new $50,000 annual Planet Blue Student Innovation Fund, which will be used to support the best and most innovative student-developed campus sustainability ideas and the new Planet Blue Ambassadors program. The ambassadors program, similar to successful peer-to-peer Eco-Rep initiatives on other campuses, is being implemented in dorms and other campus buildings as a partnership of the Graham Institute, University Housing, Office of Campus Sustainability, Student Sustainability Initiative, and the Voices of the Staff Environmental Stewardship Team.

Through her involvement in the CSIA, Kate Harris describes how she has learned to navigate the institution more easily: "Now, I walk into a meeting and speak the same language—being able to reference 'powerful' people in the organization, as well as offices, documents, and basic institutional knowledge has gotten me further than I could otherwise. The lesson there is that you have to know a system before you can change it."

Sustainability and the Campus: Building Leadership Skills through Campus-Based Projects

With students continuing to push for sustainability through the SSI, and new operational goals resulting from the CSIA, the Graham Institute felt an increasing need to engage students systematically and directly in campus sustainability efforts in a structured way, while simultaneously developing their leadership and change agent skills. The Sustainability & the Campus 3-credit, undergraduate course helps fill this need with a dual mission: 1) getting students' "hands dirty" through leading campus sustainability projects in conjunction with U-M staff sponsors; and 2) developing change management and sustainability leadership skills that move beyond the classroom into the professional arena. The intellectual framework for the course is derived from the organizational change and systems thinking for sustainability literature, with the core content derived from a deep study of U-M's sustainability efforts.

Housed in the U-M's Program in the Environment, the course focuses on student team-based projects sponsored by operational staff. Serving nearly eighty students per year, the course serves as a critical training arena for students and a venue for advancing projects that already have some level of operational support.

To assess the impact of the course on student development, the Graham Institute conducted surveys, interviews, and focus groups with twenty-eight students who took the course between 2001 and 2010, the forty-two students enrolled during the winter 2011 semester, and eleven staff project sponsors. The analysis focuses on the personal transformations and institutional changes the course engenders. One notable result is that Sustainability & the Campus students feel responsible for creating institutional change—they report an increase in leadership skills and empowerment even while battling bureaucracy. More importantly, the course helps forge connections and deeper understanding between students and operational staff through the creation of structured partnerships to manage the campus more sustainably.

While confidence and empowerment can lead to strong leadership skills, they come with a powerful but potentially confusing realization for students—change is far more complex than it appears. Almost inevitably, students begin their projects without understanding how it can take a team of four to seven students an entire semester to accomplish something that seems so basic. *Can't we just start planting the garden? We need to add recycling bins to the Union, so let's do it! Staff members don't know much about sustainability, so let's educate them!* As Lily Springsteen, a Residential College and Organizational Studies student who helped start the Planet Blue Student Innovation Fund through the course, has noted: "We learned that while an outcome seems really simple, there are so many avenues for reaching that goal, but there is always another way to look at it."

This complexity tends to hit students particularly hard at mid-semester, creating a challenge in terms of guidance. Students often find themselves falling behind initial timelines, unsure about where in the organization they should be seeking support or approval, and adjusting their project scope and ambition. At this point, co-learning with project sponsors begins in earnest. Sponsors often begin projects from the opposite perspective of the less experienced students: after years of navigating the bureaucracy of a large institution, they can sometimes overestimate barriers to progress. Students help broaden their perspectives, and as Andrew Berki, U-M Office of Campus Sustainability Manager, notes: "Students bring that level of enthusiasm and out-of-the-box thinking to projects that people on the operational side, may not have . . . because the students don't have those limits in the back of their mind, they just open it up and bring all kinds of cool ideas."

Students can open doors difficult for staff to open. Lindsey MacDonald, a project sponsor while working at U-M Outdoor Adventures program has noted: "Students have a different kind of leverage than I had as a staff person."

While students put many hours into projects, sponsors who enter the project with the idea that students will only provide free labor are quickly disavowed of that notion. What students ultimately provide is energy, creativity, and enthusiasm—in addition to the many hours of labor. Most sponsors say the projects were successful because of unique student perspectives and their ability to move sponsors out of typical modes of thinking.

The real learning and advancement for the institution and leadership development for the students in the course comes from the mutual understanding and complex interactions with staff. While difficult to quantify or assess directly, the most transformational elements appear to be the ambitions and personal transformations of students, as well as the co-learning opportunities with staff, which ultimately advance sustainability projects on campus.

Criticality of Student Empowerment

Empowering student sustainability leaders is a strategy with multiple benefits for a university. Students bring valuable ideas and energy to the institutional change process, but that force is not easily harnessed into approaches and actions that can be embraced by university leaders. This chapter highlights how empowerment is critical to advance institutional change within and beyond the classroom. Deep and meaningful student involvement leads to unexpected outcomes, broadened perspectives, and new partnerships that are critical to institutional transformation. Moreover, these efforts help develop a cadre of students who are not only "sustainability-literate" but are comfortable with complexity, organizational change, and developing relationships that span traditional boundaries.

Notes

1. The CSIA final report can be found at: http://www.graham.umich.edu/ia/campus.php.

References

Guston, David H. 2001. Boundary Organizations in Environmental Policy and Science: An Introduction. *Science, Technology & Human Values* 26 (4):399–408.

Meyerson, Debra. 2001. *Tempered Radicals: How People Use Difference to Inspire Change at Work*. Boston: Harvard Business School.

11

Metabolism and Resiliency: Key Concepts for Catalyzing Transformational Change

E. Christian Wells

The University of South Florida is a large, metropolitan, research institution, situated alongside Tampa Bay—Florida's largest open-water estuary. A relatively young institution (established 1956), the school has grown to become the eighth largest public university in the United States, enrolling nearly 50,000 students annually, most commuters from surrounding neighborhoods.

In March of 2008, the Sustainable Endowments Institute's College Sustainability Report Card informed my university, the University of South Florida (USF), that we had earned a D+ in our efforts to "go green." Within a month, our president signed the American College and University Presidents' Climate Commitment. In less than a year from the signing, we had a fully functional office of sustainability to oversee the commitment and, soon thereafter, a freshly minted school of global sustainability to overhaul the university's curriculum. How (and why) did this happen so fast? Was the administration moved to act because of one lousy grade? Were these rocket speed advances unbridled sparks of fleeting enthusiasm aimed at "keeping up with the Joneses," or was there something deeper taking root? In this chapter, I tell the story of transformational change at my university, where a culture of sustainability has begun to flourish. Initially convinced that sustainability was nothing more than a passing fancy, many groups on campus (representing the full spectrum of administration, faculty, staff, and students) have now begun volunteering their own strategies to show our students how their behaviors have global consequences, to help us understand the flows of resources and waste in the campus ecosystem, and to work collaboratively to build a more resilient university. In short, what began as a "going green" movement quickly morphed into a serious introspection that is fundamentally changing the campus climate.

Morphing (a term used in the animation industry to describe how one image seamlessly transitions into another image), rather than revolutionizing, helped expand our small core group of activists into a much larger and more diverse cadre of change agents. No one likes change, especially sudden change. That is why a seamless transition has been important to us for moving away from "business as usual" toward a new value system. Just as morphing requires serious editing of images that are sequenced in specific ways, the transformation at USF has been "edited" by several key individuals—among them, a student who never quit, a faculty member who refused to take "no" for an answer, and a top administrator who was willing to take a chance. This chapter features their stories of perseverance, united under two key concepts around which our office of sustainability organized its efforts: *urban metabolism* and *ecological resiliency*. This chapter reviews the application of these concepts to build a sustainable campus, with the greater goal of sharing chief lessons learned with other large universities.

Urban Metabolism

In 2008, a few months before learning about the D+ on my school's report card, I began teaching a new course that I developed called "Dirt." My interest in creating the class stemmed from my background in archaeology and a very supportive dean, who insisted that faculty in his college ought to teach what they are most passionate about. The class was very interdisciplinary, ranging from the physical and chemical structure of soils and sediments, to landscape art and pastoralist poetry, to the varying uses of clay by different cultures around the world. One of the key issues that emerged in our seminars was erosion, so I asked the students to study soil erosion on campus and to come up with some specific recommendations for our facilities management staff on how to deal with it.

The next time I taught the class, I included water as another core topic. After all, soil cannot exist without moisture (plus, this allowed us to make really cool mud sculptures, which was a great way to engage the class). For my third attempt at the course, I added air—another key component of soil—and began incorporating literature on environmental sustainability into the class, which helped students to realize the vital interconnections between soil, water, and air. Finally, by 2010, I had added all the components of soil—minerals, water, air, and organisms—and realized that I was teaching more about ecosystems than soil. I decided it was time to rename and reframe the class, so I chose the title "Campus Ecology" and proceeded to broaden the syllabus. I got the idea from Jim Farrell, a history professor at St. Olaf College, whom I heard speak at a national sustainability conference. Like Jim, I wanted to see if I could mix project-based learning with service learning to teach sustainability and make an impact on my campus at the same time (Farrell 2010). The premise seemed simple enough: we would read and discuss essential literature in sustainability studies and then apply what we were learning to enhance the integrity of the ecosystems that sustain us on campus.

From our readings, we learned that civil engineers, architects, and city planners often characterize urban infrastructure in terms of functional parts analogous to organs in the human body, and then proceed to map the inputs of energy, water, materials, and information as well as the outputs of people, products, and waste (Emmanuel 2005; Heynen, Kaika, and Swyngedouw 2006). This metabolic view of the city has been useful for modeling the flows of resources and wastes associated with metropolitan environments with respect to their sustainability as complex ecological systems (Acebillo 2012; Baccini and Brunner 2012). I decided to follow this approach in class. The students and I began by thinking of our campus as a living organism that consumes energy, food, and water, and excretes wastes of various kinds (garbage, carbon dioxide, and the like). As one student stated parsimoniously: "It's all about inputs and outputs." If this were true, I asked the students, then how might we reduce the inputs and outputs? If we reduced the inputs through, for instance, resource conservation, then what would happen to the outputs? And, perhaps most importantly, how would we measure our efforts and assess our progress?

The students formed small groups and set to work divvying up the campus into manageable parcels. Each group drew maps of their terrain, overlaying the built environment of buildings, sidewalks, roads, and such, on top of the surrounding "natural" environment of grasses, trees, shrubs, and so on. The next step was to complete an observational study of the life forms that used the space, including humans, squirrels, birds, butterflies, and insects. Some of the maps were amazing in their intricate detail, while others were just plain crummy. After all, it was challenging to get students to study the use of a particular space for an entire 24-hour period, especially when that space was difficult to access or marginal to the main campus. Once their maps were created, the students then began to analyze their plots in terms of inputs and outputs, making a careful list of each and identifying cross matches.

After some hand-holding with the mapping and analysis, I asked the students to devise a project designed to draw attention to their ratios of inputs to outputs and use the project to "make a lasting difference" on campus. One group of students decided to perform a food waste audit in the dining halls and then use that information as the basis for a pilot composting program. To conduct the audit, the students dressed conspicuously in white lab coats and wore dust masks and latex exam gloves. With clipboards in hand, they positioned themselves in front of the garbage cans in one of the dining halls and intercepted students as they approached. The student scientists carefully collected and weighed the food scraps headed for the trash and then posted the data on a giant white board in the cafeteria for all to see.

While I was tinkering with the Campus Ecology class, in 2009 I was invited to serve as the founding director of the university's Office of Sustainability (housed initially in the Provost's Office). My first task was to help create a new School of Global Sustainability to coordinate and expand our curriculum and serve as a permanent home for the office. Given the success of the Campus Ecology class, and to keep the momentum going, I decided that it was time to scale up the effort in the hope of getting others at the university to move toward this kind of systems thinking in their own classes. Working with twenty students each semester was impactful, but this work could have even greater reach if it could be amplified in some way.

Together with the global sustainability staff and facilities management, we dubbed the initiative our "campus metabolism mapping project," with the goal of analyzing how energy and resources move through the university's grids, pipelines, and streets. The underlying idea was that if we could identify how much of a given resource each part of the campus was consuming, then we might stand a better chance of reducing that consumption (through conservation or recovery efforts) and thereby optimize the efficiencies of the university's operations. At the time, we only had aggregate data for the entire university: for example, how much trash versus recycling the university produced per year or how much energy university buildings consumed monthly. As a result, we were unable to distinguish which building or built space was consuming how much of what resource. A detailed map of resources, energy, and waste could help us make decisions and could inform positive policy development.

Early on, we decided that this mapping project might best be facilitated with a GIS (geographic information system) database, and so we set out to collect basic spatial data about the university. This was easier said than done. At first, we found it challenging to convince some parts of our facilities management team to share information we needed. They were concerned about security issues if the information was leaked to the public. However, once we discussed with them that the data would be used only for modeling purposes, they relented. Another barrier was learning that not all buildings were separately metered for water, energy, or other resources. This is where our project stalled for almost a year. There simply was no funding in anyone's budget for energy- and water-monitoring equipment.

Along came the "student who never quit." Between 2008 and 2010, student environmental activists throughout the state of Florida were working to implement a new student fee to be used for campus sustainability projects. For USF, Karissa Gerhke, the president of the Student Environmental Association, was our advocate. She studied the fee process, spearheaded petitions and rallies on campus, drafted a very intelligent proposal, and argued her case all the way up to the state's Board of Governors (the entity that oversees public higher education in Florida). She encountered many bureaucratic and political roadblocks along the way, but never gave up. In the end, USF now has an annually recurring million-dollar Student Green Energy Fund, which provided us with just the kind of funding we needed for resource monitoring equipment for the metabolism mapping project.

After one full year, we had a detailed map of the campus and enough of the campus monitored so that we could begin to collect data to add to the map. Some of this work came easily. Physical Plant could report on building energy and water consumption, for example, while the Grounds Department could add information on water consumed for irrigation. However, there was a good deal more information we needed to gather to understand the total campus ecosystem fully. We needed to know how many and which species of trees we had, how many students used cars versus bicycles and at what times of day, how many lights remained on in unoccupied classroom buildings at night, and so forth. We decided that the most efficient way to collect this kind of data was to bring the campus into the classroom. We held a mini-workshop for faculty interested in incorporating sustainability into their courses, much like the Ponderosa Project (at Northern Arizona University) or the Piedmont Project (at Emory University in Atlanta), but with the specific objective of filling in our database with research on campus operations and activities that are otherwise not captured by normal business activities.

There have been several class projects that emerged from this effort, though far more are needed. For example, one project (for a civic leadership class) identified two student residence halls on campus that are identical in size, occupancy, and age. Water conservation devices (specifically, low-flow shower heads and faucet aerators generously donated to the university by the City of Tampa) were installed in one residence hall but not the other. Water use was then measured monthly to determine the capacity of the new technologies, and these data were then added to the mapping effort. The study recorded an average savings of 65 gallons of water per bathroom each month, a 10.2 percent savings. Given the success of the project, the university has decided to retrofit all 1,350 bathrooms in the on-campus residence halls, projecting an annual savings of nearly one million gallons of water!

Data from all of the projects are being entered into the campus metabolism database, which is available for students and faculty to use as a source of information for future class-based research. For example, an undergraduate student in an environmental engineering class studied the concentrations of heavy metals (lead and copper) in water sampled from new water bottle refilling stations compared to our older, traditional water fountains throughout campus. The goal of his project was to examine the differences between the water sources, with the hopes of communicating to the university community that both sources of water were equally safe, and that purchasing bottled water from the vending machines did not necessarily offer a better alternative for getting hydrated. His research showed no significant differences between the sources of tap water and is now being incorporated into an education campaign (Drink Local), which will include signs for the water fountains showing the results of his chemical analysis.

Ecological Resiliency

The work on the campus metabolism project suggested to many of us in the Office of Sustainability that we might be able to have a greater impact if we could find a way to scale up our efforts to the broader community outside the bounds of campus life. We did not realize it at the time, but an opportunity would soon emerge to do just this.

In 2005, Daniel Yeh, a new assistant professor in the Department of Civil and Environmental Engineering (who specialized in water management and sustainable infrastructure), created an undergraduate study abroad program that sent students to UNESCO-IHE's Institute for Water Education in Delft, the Netherlands. Over the years, collaborations and partnerships between IHE and USF deepened and, in 2009, Daniel invited one of the IHE faculty members to USF to give a lecture on water management in the Netherlands, which is physiographically similar to the Tampa Bay region. What could we learn from the Dutch, who had been dealing with sea level rise and storm surge since the twelfth century?

The day-long workshop drew larger-than-expected crowds, including a number of curious city and county officials, planners, and urban designers. Discussions about how to keep the conversation going ensued, and Daniel created an annual workshop that brought together knowledge experts from both institutions for in-depth meetings with community partners to explore strategies for incorporating resiliency principles into growth planning in the Tampa Bay region. In the first USF/IHE workshop, the audience was informed that resiliency—learning from the past and making positive changes so that future anticipated threats will not jeopardize social, economic, and environmental sustainability—refers to the adaptive capacity of a system (Chapin, Kofinas, and Folke 2009; Gunderson, Allen, and Holling 2010; Otto-Zimmermann 2012; Walker and Salt 2006). The workshop participants focused on water management resiliency, but considered other resources and services as well. The underlying premise was that coastal cities around the world face a range of dynamic regional and global pressures, which make them more vulnerable to urban flooding, storm surge, coastal erosion, and other challenges associated with sea level rise and climate change.

In 2011, the workshop ballooned into a three-day mini-conference called "Resilient Tampa Bay." For the conference, key stakeholders from the area, including regional planning councils and commissions, chambers of commerce, metropolitan planning organizations, and city and county governments, were contacted and asked to participate. No one responded. But Daniel would not give up. Through a bit of patience and persistence, he managed to convince a number of representatives from various governmental and non-governmental agencies about the importance of the effort and the powerful role that resiliency planning could play in the region. To help recruitment, he presented a "shock and awe" PowerPoint presentation at various meetings in the community, showing dramatic photos of the different scenarios that the Tampa Bay region would face if sea level rose one or two meters over the next century. The photos showed most of downtown Tampa underwater and several other inland areas vulnerable.

Once assembled, the stakeholders, who included faculty and staff from USF and IHE, self-organized into four geo-focal teams to identify vulnerabilities and make recommendations on resiliency strategies for four regions: Tampa Bay, City of Tampa, City of St. Petersburg, and Gulf Beach Communities. The stakeholder groups represented many different sectors of the community and, in the end, were composed of whoever our geo-focal teams could find with an interest to participate. The greatest challenge we faced was in bringing together such a large and diverse group of individuals and maintaining momentum, especially with our government partners who do not enjoy the same kind of flexibility in their work schedules as faculty members. We also found it difficult during election years, when the government sector experiences a lot of turnover, to sustain progress in many of the initiatives recommended by the group. On the other hand, working with the corporate community to develop public-private partnerships around some of these initiatives has enhanced our ability to integrate the university campus into the community and bridge the "town and gown" divide that has plagued the university community for many years.

The goal of the conference was to exchange ideas on developing interlinked resiliency plans for the Tampa Bay region. The challenge was to consider plans to protect vital infrastructure (such as the utilities), improve conditions for economic development (for example, tourism), and minimize the impact of hurricanes and other natural disasters on real estate. Workshop participants created a master plan for resiliency for the Tampa Bay region, which includes a vulnerability assessment and an adaptation strategy for each of the geo-focal areas. The groups are also working on a set of urban planning guidelines and building codes to improve resiliency, which is paving the way for a series of demonstration projects at USF that will take into account site-specific vulnerabilities (e.g., hospitals, public utilities, and food distribution systems).

For me, the meetings provided an important flashpoint for strategizing how to translate resiliency principles into urban design using the USF campus as a laboratory to experiment with different ideas. After the conference, the university's sustainability steering committee (many of whom participated in the conference) suggested that we find a way to apply the insights from the conference to our own campus. As luck would have it, at that time our facilities management team was involved in drafting its five-year update to the campus Master Plan, which outlines the campus growth strategy to guide future resource allocations. Since drafting the 2005 plan, the university has increasingly faced new challenges as energy consumption, transportation limitations, increasing state regulations, and decreasing operation and maintenance budgets have combined to change the ways and extent to which the university can expand over the coming decade. The steering committee proposed that the new Master Plan emphasize sustainable design strategies, including smart growth, energy system improvements, and transportation demand management. Moreover, they recommended a set of six basic principles for resiliency design planning that emerged through consensus from the conference and in consultation with an external consulting agency.

The campus steering committee convinced a top level USF administrator to take a chance, and incorporate a resiliency framework into the master planning process. The framework, outlined in Figure 11.1, features five dimensions: energy, land and water, social equity, buildings and waste, and transportation. In the illustration, each dimension is presented with a set of action items designed to help prioritize funding applied to the growth and development of the campus. Many action items focus on reducing carbon dependency and carbon emissions, while others deal specifically with enhancing infrastructure durability. To the extent possible, we have aimed to translate the resiliency principles discussed at the conference to specific planning efforts at the university.

How do you take a really great plan and move forward without a budget? At USF, we decided to leverage the power of status and prestige by asking the university's administration to commit to reporting requirements, not dollars (at least not directly). We witnessed the speedy transformation that took place on campus when our president signed the American College and University Presidents' Climate Commitment, which obligated the university to conduct and publicly report a greenhouse gas inventory and climate action plan. These requirements may have seemed fairly benign in the beginning, but ended up requiring investment in recurring human and financial resources to "make good" on the commitment. With this strategy in mind, we proactively sought awards, commitments, and other recognitions for the university that would bring attention to sustainability on campus while requiring the university—in the long run—to comply with the requirements of the various commendations, which overlapped with our Master Plan priorities.

For example, we applied for the Tree Campus USA designation from the Arbor Day Foundation, which requires the university to convene a campus tree advisory committee with input from the community, develop a tree care plan for the campus, report annual expenditures on the tree canopy, and host an annual Arbor Day celebratory event on campus. Having this designation has excited and engaged many people on campus, and has helped us meet several major goals of the Master Plan, specifically, to plant as many trees as possible, to conserve and protect natural areas, and to work toward turning the campus into a Florida-friendly garden with the addition of more native species. One

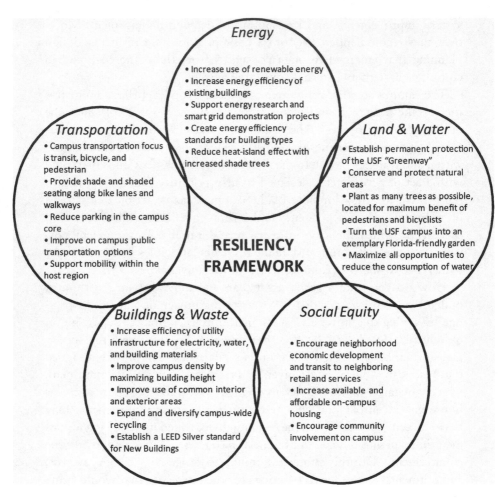

Energy

- Increase use of renewable energy
- Increase energy efficiency of existing buildings
- Support energy research and smart grid demonstration projects
- Create energy efficiency standards for building types
- Reduce heat-island effect with increased shade trees

Transportation

- Campus transportation focus is transit, bicycle, and pedestrian
- Provide shade and shaded seating along bike lanes and walkways
- Reduce parking in the campus core
- Improve on campus public transportation options
- Support mobility within the host region

Land & Water

- Establish permanent protection of the USF "Greenway"
- Conserve and protect natural areas
- Plant as many trees as possible, located for maximum benefit of pedestrians and bicyclists
- Turn the USF campus into an exemplary Florida-friendly garden
- Maximize all opportunities to reduce the consumption of water

RESILIENCY FRAMEWORK

Buildings & Waste

- Increase efficiency of utility infrastructure for electricity, water, and building materials
- Improve campus density by maximizing building height
- Improve use of common interior and exterior areas
- Expand and diversify campus-wide recycling
- Establish a LEED Silver standard for New Buildings

Social Equity

- Encourage neighborhood economic development and transit to neighboring retail and services
- Increase available and affordable on-campus housing
- Encourage community involvement on campus

Figure 11.1

Resiliency Framework for the 2010–2020 USF Tampa Campus Master Plan.

of the outcomes of this process has been the planting of over 1,000 live oak trees on campus since 2011, which moves us closer toward meeting our Master Plan goals.

Above all, we have found that obligating the university to comply with requirements of external evaluation agencies, awards, and other kinds of national or international recognition (and then working hard to advertise these with our friends in the media) has moved us closer to achieving the goals outlined in our Master Plan. The strategy works because it does not usually require any upfront capital, which is often the major stumbling block for getting these kinds of projects off the ground. Instead, it leverages small pots of funding and human energy from various departments and offices around the university that otherwise could not accomplish the goal by themselves. From these experiences, we have come to appreciate that sustainability is something meant to be shared widely. Whenever any single group or individual has attempted to "own" this or that initiative or success story, the significance and effectiveness of it has faded rapidly.

Lessons Learned

Over the years, I have been involved in a wide range of sustainability initiatives at USF. Some have succeeded in what they set out to do, some have failed, and many more have gone un- or under-assessed, mostly because of a lack of clear metrics for assessment. This has been our greatest lesson—structured assessment (whether quantitative, qualitative, or through a mixed-methods approach) is key to demonstrating success and attracting additional resources to move forward. Our efforts toward mapping the campus metabolism (with the greater goal of changing it) showed us that we cannot begin to understand how the university operates on a macroscale without understanding the microscale. Moreover, we were only able to convince administrators to invest in resource-saving technologies and policies by demonstrating their efficacy through specific empirical data. Assessment has also been the key driver for operationalizing our campus Master Plan. By engaging external evaluating agencies that require self-assessment, university offices are moved to comply.

Finally, we have also learned that sustainability initiatives work well when research, teaching, and practice go hand in hand, largely because those domains of university activity differentially involve contrasting stakeholder groups. In the case of our metabolism model, it was only when we brought the campus into the classroom that we succeeded in marrying research to practice in a curricular context. In the development and implementation of the resiliency framework for the Master Plan, we succeeded only when we involved multiple stakeholders and shared the initiatives—and the accolades—with the rest of the campus community. After all, sustainability is ultimately about recognizing our interconnections with the biophysical environment as well as the people and communities that inhabit it.

References

Acebillo, Josep. 2012. *A New Urban Metabolism*. Barcelona, Spain: Actar.

Baccini, Peter, and Paul H. Brunner. 2012. *Metabolism of the Anthroposphere*. 2nd ed. Cambridge, MA: MIT Press.

Chapin, F. Stuart, Gary P. Kofinas and Carol Folke, eds. 2009. *Principles of Ecosystem Stewardship: Resilience-Based Natural Resource Management in a Changing World*. New York: Springer-Verlag.

Emmanuel, M. Rohinton. 2005. *An Urban Approach to Climate Sensitive Design*. New York: Taylor and Frances.

Farrell, James J. 2010. *The Nature of College: How a New Understanding of Campus Life Can Change the World*. Minneapolis, MN: Milkweed Editions.

Gunderson, Lance H., Craig R. Allen, and C. S. Holling, eds. 2010. *Foundations of Ecological Resilience*. New York: Island Press.

Heynen, Nik, Maria Kaika, and Erik Swyngedouw, eds. 2006. *In the Nature of Cities: Urban Political Ecology and the Politics of Urban Metabolism*. New York: Routledge.

Otto-Zimmermann, Konrad, ed. 2012. *Resilient Cities 2: Cities and Adaptation to Climate Change—Proceedings of the Global Forum 2011*. New York: Springer.

Walker, Brian, and David Salt. 2006. *Resilience Thinking: Sustaining Ecosystems and People in a Changing World*. New York: Island Press.

12

Reimagining Professional Development: Collaborative Circles for Creative Change

Krista Hiser

On the slopes of Diamond Head, just minutes from Waikiki Beach, Kapiʻolani Community College is home to the Culinary Institute of the Pacific and programs in business, hospitality, health, legal education, and arts and sciences. The college has over 9,000 students representing Hawaiʻi's diverse resident population, international students, and students from the continental United States.

First came the freeze on faculty travel. Prior to 2008, Kapiʻolani Community College faculty could access a reasonably generous fund to support its development and professional leadership through attendance at conferences, mostly in the continental United States. As a community college in Hawaiʻi, maintaining a connection with national associations is important. But, as the most remote populated location on the planet, 2,500 miles of jet fuel away from the closest academic conference, perhaps this freeze was a harbinger, a jolt to encourage a new way of thinking about faculty development. The travel freeze was a purely economic mandate by the governor, followed by a 7 percent pay cut, all related to the fiscal woes that have challenged public colleges in every state. As a faculty member with a strong interest in both professional development and the sustainability movement in higher education, and acutely aware of our situation in Hawaiʻi, I turned my attention to a bigger issue: How could we think more creatively about professional development in a way that would be both environmentally sustainable (using our in-state and on-campus resources better, and leveraging technology more effectively) and that would be, to be honest, more effective?

The example of our travel freeze illustrates how considering sustainability (in both its economic and environmental dimensions) offers an opportunity for deep reexamination of what works in our organizations, and what could be reimagined. In my experience, sustainability curriculum flourishes on flexibility. It is about responding to student interests and faculty initiative, working with community organizations, and acknowledging expertise that may reside outside of faculty disciplines. Higher education, on the other hand, sometimes feels like it is heading in exactly the opposite direction. New accountability measures, performance-based funding, and a myopic emphasis on transfer and graduation as the only important measure of effectiveness appear to be contradictory to the culture of adaptation, innovation, and transdisciplinary collaboration that would support a true sustainability-across-the-curriculum movement. This chapter does not specifically describe our sustainability initiatives. Rather, it is about creating an underlying culture of transformative learning on campus through an organic, decentralized model of professional development. Such an approach to faculty development supports the idea that sustainability is not only about green initiatives, but also about the broader institutional cultures and connections that make up higher education.

The Metaphor

To use a current metaphor from the leadership literature, we can think of higher education as a spider and sustainability as a starfish. In *The Spider and the Starfish*, Ori Brafman and Rod Beckstrom (2006) describe leaderless organizations in the business domain, but the application to higher education is easy to see. Universities are large bureaucracies with hierarchical leadership—and in many ways there is nothing wrong with this system. Chancellors and presidents and deans and chairs make powerful decisions that support sustainability, and top-down leadership can be incredibly effective. It is not that administrators are "spiders," it is that traditional hierarchies are spiderlike. As Brafman and Beckstrom describe, "With a spider, what you see is pretty much what you get. A body's a body, a head's a head, and a leg's a leg. . . . It could maybe survive without a leg or two, and could possibly even stand to lose a couple of eyes, but it certainly wouldn't survive without its head" (2006, 34–35). Spiders represent the traditional organizational structure of institutions. After all, someone has to be in charge.

But on my campus at least, sustainability tends to be a faculty-driven initiative, and faculty, in this metaphor, organize themselves they way starfish do. "Starfish have an incredible quality to them: If you cut an arm off, most of these animals grow a new arm. . . . Instead of having a head, like a spider, the starfish functions as a decentralized network. Get this: for the starfish to move, one of the arms must convince the other arms that it is a good idea to do so. The arm starts moving, and then—in a process that no one fully understands—the other arms cooperate and move as well" (Brafman and Beckstrom 2006, 35). Sound familiar? On my campus, a starfish-style professional development initiative has learned to co-habit with a spider. The Collaborative Circle for Creative Change model, which we call C4ward, is creating a culture of facilitative leadership among the faculty. It is a non-hierarchical, leaderless model that empowers faculty members to follow their own interests and connect with colleagues who have similar needs and interests. Our college has some great sustainability initiatives: gardens, a worm bin, an ecology club. But the program described here is laying an essential groundwork for peer learning and new roles that support other transformations toward sustainability.

Planning the Model

After the travel freeze (which remains in effect at this writing in 2012), the next critical event in the transformation of our professional development programs occurred when my colleague, Leigh Dooley, participated in a Webinar in which it was said: "Professional development without followup is malpractice." She started repeating this phrase around campus, and we realized that our beloved workshops and institutes were, in fact, "mal-practice." As in, "not effective." Our professional development programs were preaching to the choir and creating a head-nodding type of enthusiasm for the initiative of the day, whether it was learning communities, writing across the curriculum, online learning or even . . . sustainability.

When I attended the Association for the Advancement of Sustainability in Higher Education (AASHE) sustainability curriculum training workshop in 2010, I especially loved the inclusion of quiet, reflective practice. This was the first professional development workshop where I was invited to sit by a tree and consider what I was learning. That sunk in. I was motivated to replicate the Piedmont and Ponderosa projects (from Emory University in Atlanta and Northern Arizona University, respectively) in Hawaii. I debated great Native Hawaiian tree names with myself: the *kukui* project, the *ohia* project. But, we had no funding to persuade attendees and no structure to really catalyze the enthusiasm for curriculum around sustainability. I knew I could draw the same ten or fifteen "green" faculty who were already driving campus sustainability initiatives. We had grown as much grass as a grassroots effort can grow. I knew I could create a successful workshop, but it felt a bit like . . . malpractice.

Working with a team of faculty responsible for professional development on campus, I started researching traditional alternatives, studying professional learning communities, apprenticeship models, and adult learning theory. I saw Etienne Wenger's Communities of Practice model as a synthesis of all these ways that professional adults learn. Wenger (1998) describes communities of practice as *organic*. The model assumes that, when adults want or need to learn something relevant to their work or life, they will naturally gravitate to others who share the interests and skills that support their goals. Very little research exists on implementing Communities of Practice (known as CoPs) in higher education, and we were initially stumped by the oxymoronic task of institutionalizing an organic model. However, communities of practice have been used to support doctoral students, and one program used the term *guardian supervisor* to describe a person who held these freely chosen, organic groups together and supported their goals (Shacham and Od-Cohen 2009). We came up with the title "Concierge," perhaps influenced by the proximity of Waikiki hotels. Just like a hotel concierge, this person would be there to help, direct, and recommend: he or she would schedule the meetings of the group, recruit members and make contacts, obtain resources, and generally broker the needs of the community of practice. These communities would form around the professional needs and personal interests of faculty to focus on a wide variety of topics and initiatives.

Since we did not like the sound of "CoP" as an acronym, we came up with a new program name, Collaborative Circle for Creative Change (C4ward). We insisted on the use of the term *circle* to differentiate these sessions from traditional meetings, committees, or task forces. We designed the C4ward pilot around existing loose networks on campus, each with different members, goals, and origins. Instead of leading workshops, our professional development leaders each became a concierge to one of these groups. Here is what happened.

Piloting the Model

One circle, focused on gaming, was not even officially part of the pilot; it was just a loose gathering of faculty and staff who were into *World of Warcraft*. They got together to talk about why they and some of their students loved gaming, and to play together. Instead of seeing themselves as "nerds," they named their group the Gathering of Gaming Gurus, and began to take their own ideas more seriously. Participant Keala Losch described the circle as "an intellectually safe space" that brought different sectors of the campus community together. Keala made the point that if teachers have a passion for something, there is bound to be a relevant academic connection, saying: "What is it that drives us, that gives us this passion? And how can we share it in a way that's relevant to our colleagues, relevant to the institution, that's going to help our students, ultimately?" Now in its third semester of collaboration, the group has studied the pedagogy of gaming and defined principles of engagement and play that translate directly into curriculum design. They play games at each session, and talk about what makes the game engaging. They even got the chancellor, for whom *engagement* has become very important concept, to play Apples to Apples with them.

The Hawaiian pedagogy circle (renamed by the group Miha Lanaau) was originally formed to fulfill a grant condition to research and apply effective learning techniques for Native Hawaiian students. The circle not only validated the shared knowledge and leadership of the original members, but expanded to include faculty who had not previously been involved in anything "Hawaiian." Participant Cheryl Souza said, "From the beginning, Miha Lanaau was real, and honest. We wiped the slate. We got into that, and it's one of the best things that's ever happened for me . . . and I've been teaching for a long time."

The e-portfolio circle, however, emerged out of a political quagmire. This group was basically getting together to complain about the institution's stagnation in a long-awaited e-portfolio system to help facilitate student learning and assessment. But a concierge was able to listen to the group and broker meetings with administrators and external software designers. The concierge helped to clear away some of the frustrating aspects of the project so that this group of passionate portfolio leaders could share with each other how they used portfolios and share with the campus what features needed to be implemented in the new system.

The Sustainability across the Curriculum circle, which I concierged, was a group that split off from the Sustainability Committee—which had a massive agenda already—to focus on one topic: curriculum. The circle created a place to share resources, speakers, and assignments about local food issues, environmental topics, and how to foster creativity and teach systems thinking. As a circle, the group has investigated sustainability learning outcomes, and is discussing how to create resilience and how to engage students in sustainability without using "shock-and-awe" techniques. As a participant in both the committee and the circle, I saw how the dialog of the circle created an environment of possibility, while the committee meetings often felt overwhelming.

Each of the pilots was different in its origin and its goal. The concierges learned how to shape the interests of the circle into a goal that included both faculty learning and a tangible product. We learned that, as Wenger had observed, the groups could have different timelines. One circle might exist only for three weeks, to get together to learn a new software program, for example, and then disperse. Another might continue each semester, renewing its membership and crafting a new goal.

We also learned that it was hard to be the concierge! In the case of the e-portfolio group, the concierge, who was herself an e-portfolio leader, felt emotionally embroiled, and spent a lot of time navigating campus politics and behind-the-scenes issues. Since the group had a lot of complaints, she had to distance herself from the topic in order to move the group forward. In the sustainability circle, I found myself, as concierge, wanting to drive my own agenda, while others in the group were more interested in talking about resources and assignments. We created another role to partner with the concierge: the host. The host is a member of the group who is a passionate driver for the group's agenda. We found it works better if the concierge remains more neutral to the topic of the group. For the concierge, the experience is about leadership and group dynamics, not about the agenda or the topic. Concierges are trained in creative facilitation techniques and receive a "card deck" of strategies designed to elicit participation and equalize group dynamics.

How the C4ward Model Is Transforming Campus Culture

Anyone who has endeavored to create a professional development program for sustainability curriculum knows that, once you have engaged the "green" contingent on your faculty, there is a wall that you hit, in terms of how to push sustainability deeper and wider, moving beyond environmental sustainability and into the political, social, and economic domains. This wall is created by traditional campus culture, which is often hierarchical, fragmented, and political. Sustainability is ultimately about creating deeper transformative change in the sociocultural context in which higher education operates, and that change needs to start with campus culture, not just classroom curricula. The C4ward model is demonstrating that faculty are ready for such a shift in campus culture and that they can create it by connecting with each other—starfish style—as well as by working through the "spider-like" hierarchy of the administration. In two years, our C4ward model has taken on its own life, with over one hundred faculty members participating, twenty-six trained concierges, twenty-four active circles, and over thirty topics on a "wait list" to become new C4ward circles. The initiative is changing the campus culture in fascinating ways that we did not predict or plan. Here's what faculty are saying about the program (all responses come from personal interviews):

• *Campus dynamics are friendlier and more holistic.* "Lecturers are talking about their own wellness as instructors and how that impacts their teaching." "This program allows us to explore passions from other parts of our lives that might not fit with what we teach."

• *Committees and meetings are more productive.* "There's a huge difference in the vibe, in the halls and in department meetings." "This makes me wonder how much more productive you can be when things are non-threatening."

• *Interdisciplinary dialog is happening.* "I was in a C4ward about social networking, and I walked out understanding more about the developmental studies department. I didn't intend to make that connection, but because of the people sitting in the room, there are all these hidden, unexpected turns that come out of the C4ward [model in practice] that really are professional development in a new and creative way."

• *New perspectives are emerging.* "People who are not normally involved in specific topic now have a place that they can come to knowing that they have been invited to the conversation in a way that perhaps they never have been invited before . . . we're getting these new ideas coming in."

• *Barriers are falling.* "C4ward cut across ranks and disciplines: instructor, CTE, arts, counselors. It's this flat structure, where nobody is there to look at who is there. We're all learning from each other."

Assessing the C4ward Model

Not surprisingly, the administration wanted the impact of the C4ward groups on student learning to be assessed and evaluated. Working with a very creative institutional researcher, we designed outcomes, measurements, and tracking mechanisms. In exchange for a course release to serve as a concierge, each concierge would be responsible for rigorously documenting and assessing his or her group using an online "concierge log" and a series of tools from SurveyMonkey. It was a good assessment plan, but it was also very tedious and not very much fun. So, when we encountered another round of funding cuts and some additional restrictions on course release time, eliminating the incentive of a course release for concierges, we said, "Okay, so no assessment, either." Instead of documenting every circle and centralizing the assessment, each circle creates a poster summarizing their goals and activities. These are shared at an end-of-semester celebration, and the institutional research department uses the posters as artifacts to assess the program. In the end, the starfish and the spiders agreed on an elegant assessment plan defining short-term, mid-term, and ultimate goals of the program. More information about the C4ward model and the concierge training can be found at: http://www2.hawaii.edu/~ofie/c4wardevaluation.htm.

Organic, Decentralized Professional Development

The organic nature of the C4wards model is important. Each step that veered away from decentralized leadership, free choice, and natural time has come to an obstacle. Each step that has followed the natural unfolding of the initiative has taken on its own life. The model holds its own integrity. Concierges receive nothing for their work, yet many people want to be a concierge. Not only does participating in C4ward demonstrate a commitment to professional development, but it also gives faculty a new opportunity to practice leadership that is not based on a role or a position in the campus hierarchy.

Today, we have phased out all one-shot workshops in order to commit to this transformative model. The most thriving C4ward groups include: iPad Users, Miha Lanaau (Hawaiian Pedagogy), Meditation and Stress Relief, Social Networking, Early STEM Faculty, and the Gathering of Gaming Gurus. The entire program is supported by one course release each for two coordinators. The only expense of the program is for food and supplies used in the poster session celebration each semester. The biggest obstacle that the program faces is scheduling, and solutions that are being devised include a designated campus C4ward activity period as well as use of online environments to extend the conversations and include more participants.

Effective faculty development can create a shift in campus culture that is fundamental to truly transformative sustainability initiatives. Individuals, then networks, then departments, campuses, and university systems need opportunities for transformative learning that invites them to see themselves as leaders and as learners, as whole people living and working in a fascinating period of intense change.

References

Brafman, Ori. and Beckstrom, Rod. 2006. *The Starfish and the Spider: The Unstoppable Power of Leaderless Organizations*. New York: Penguin.

Shacham, Miri., and Od-Cohen, Yehudit. 2009. Rethinking PhD Learning Incorporating Communities of Practice. *Innovations in Education and Teaching International* 46 (3):279–292.

Wenger, Etienne. 1998. Communities of Practice: Learning as a Social System. *The Systems Thinker* 9 (5).

IV

Institutional Mission and the Culture of Sustainability

13

The Journey to Green: Becoming Sustainable Spelman

Beverly Daniel Tatum

Founded in 1881, Spelman College is a private historically black college for women, known for academic excellence, leadership development, and community service. Located in an enclosed park-like setting, the 39-acre campus of 2,100 students is an urban oasis of historic buildings and flowering trees, just ten minutes from downtown Atlanta.

Spelman College, a historically black college and a global leader in the education of women of African descent, is dedicated to academic excellence in the liberal arts and sciences and the intellectual, creative, ethical, and leadership development of its students. Spelman empowers the whole person to engage the many cultures of the world and inspires a commitment to positive social change.
—Spelman College Mission Statement

The Spelman College mission statement is a powerful articulation of our community's values and aspirations, and is a source of inspiration to all members of our community. What does it have to do with sustainability? If I had been asked that question in 2002 when I assumed the role of president, I am not sure that I would have had a good answer. Ten years later, the answer is clear. How can we be a "global leader in the education of women of African descent" without paying attention to the global impact of our environmental choices? How can we foster "ethical leadership" without educating our students about environmental responsibility? How can we honestly "engage the many cultures" of the world without acknowledging the American over-use of the world's resources? How can we "inspire a commitment to positive social change" without setting a clear institutional example ourselves? These are the questions with which we are now engaged on our campus. How did this shift—our journey to "green"—happen?

Every journey has a beginning, and for me the journey began before I came to Spelman College. I lived in Northampton, Massachusetts, for twenty years and worked at Mount Holyoke College for thirteen of those years, before moving to Atlanta to serve as president at Spelman. Both at home and at work, recycling was a requirement. Also, during my tenure at Mount Holyoke, a large-scale construction project was underway for a new science facility, and I was privy to conversations about a donor who was willing to make a very large contribution to the project on the condition that it was designed as a green building, eligible for Leadership in Energy and Environmental Design (LEED) certification. So I brought two things with me from Massachusetts—the habit of recycling and the awareness that there was philanthropic interest in environmental sustainability.

When I arrived in Atlanta in 2002, and conscientiously separated my recyclables, as was my habit, I was dismayed to learn that there was no recycling program on campus, primarily because the city of Atlanta did not have a recycling program at the time in our area. Though this was disappointing to me, I turned my attention to other concerns at the college. One of those concerns was that our student population had grown significantly, and there was a great need for more housing. In 2004, we had the opportunity to acquire land adjacent to the campus and began planning for a new residence hall. The board had to be persuaded that this would be an affordable project, as we would have to issue a bond to finance the project, and they were reluctant to take on any additional debt. But the need was clear, and the project was approved.

As is often the case, the project turned out to be more expensive than originally planned. Apart from the basic construction of the building, there were decaying pipes underground that had to be replaced in order to support the heating and cooling systems. In addition, the start of our project was shortly after Hurricane Katrina had devastated the city of New Orleans and other areas along the Gulf Coast, and construction costs were rising rapidly due to scarcity of materials, as building supplies were redirected to rebuild New Orleans. My CFO, Danny Flanigan, was doing the best he could to ensure our project was on time and as close to on budget as possible. So when I suggested that we should make this a green project, his response was that it would be too expensive, suggesting that it would add millions to the cost. But I kept asking the question: "What would it take to make this a green building?" When it became clear that I was not going to give up on the idea, he investigated further, and the real number was about $1–$1.5 million on a $43 million project (or less than 5 percent more), not nearly as expensive as we might have feared.

Even though the additional upfront cost was a concern, it was clear to me that it was in the college's best interest to pursue the goal of LEED certification, and it did not take too long for Danny to become a convert to the idea. He was certainly aided in his thinking by our Director of Facilities Management Services, Art Frazier. An architect by training, Art had worked on other sustainability projects prior to his employment at Spelman, and was very enthusiastic about our green project. With Art's help we were able to work with construction partners who also brought LEED expertise to the task. And we were on our way!

Building for 100 Years

The founders of Spelman College, Harriet Giles and Sophia Packard, often said that they were "building for 100 years" and the quality of the buildings on our historic campus reflects that expectation of endurance. My office is the same one that every Spelman president before me has used, located in a building that was dedicated in 1886, just five years after the school opened on April 11, 1881, in the basement of a neighborhood church. So when we began planning for this new building, the first new construction on our campus in the twenty-first century, I too said, "We are building for 100 years." How could we build a building that we expected to last for a century and not make it environmentally sustainable? *How could it not be green?* At the opening of school in August 2006, I announced that our new residence hall would be designed to minimize its environmental impact in terms of energy use, water runoff, and other environmental factors, and in October 2006 we began construction.

Clearly it was the *right thing to do* for all the environmental reasons we know. *It was also the strategic thing to do.* We would be modeling social responsibility for our students, many of whom were already expressing interest in environmental causes in and out of the classroom. We would set an example for other institutions. We would generate long-term savings, particularly in terms of utility costs. And we would position the institution favorably with donors who valued green commitments (and I already knew of at least one generous donor who did.) Our new residence hall and dining complex, known as The Suites, opened in 2008—home to 300 students—and was awarded LEED Silver certification.

In operation since 2008, we estimate almost a 20 percent reduction in energy costs, and nearly 31 percent in total water use reduction as compared to a conventional building of the same size. In financial terms, that is a savings of about $200,000 a year in utility costs alone. In just five years, we will have saved the additional $1,000,000 we spent on its construction. Our 100-year building will have paid for its "green" cost but the savings will continue.

In fact, *all* of the benefits we anticipated materialized, and then some. Our students are excited about the building, the healthy environment it provides, and the commitment to sustainability it represents. Our alumnae take great pride in it as well, adding momentum to our efforts to increase alumnae support and engagement. In 2008 it generated great visibility for the College, including national coverage on CNN. Both Art Frazier and I were interviewed on local and national news programs about it, because it was one of the first green residence halls in Georgia, and certainly the first green building on an HBCU (Historically Black College or University) campus. The chief administrator of the Environmental Protection Agency in Washington DC saw the news item on CNN and paid us a special visit, which generated more favorable news coverage. Our new residence hall is a beautiful building with conference space in it, providing us an opportunity to showcase it frequently to visitors. And, as hoped, environmentally conscious donors have taken an interest.

In particular, we were well positioned to take advantage of the Grants to Green initiative of the Community Foundation of Atlanta in partnership with Southface Energy Institute and Enterprise Community Partners. We were first awarded an in-kind grant, which allowed us to do an audit of our carbon footprint at no cost to us. The report revealed that our Science Center was the biggest consumer of energy on the campus, and that there was a real opportunity to reduce energy consumption and save as much as $150,000 a year on utility costs if we made some changes in our heating and cooling systems in that building. The cost of making those changes was estimated to be about $150,000, but we could recover those costs in just one year with the increased efficiency. At the time, just after the collapse of the financial markets in 2008, external economic pressures were forcing us to cut our budget in lots of ways, and we were carefully watching all our expenditures. I knew that finding an extra $150,000 would not be easy. But after the audit was completed, we were able to apply to the Grants to Green program for an implementation grant, and we received $50,000 toward the cost, with a matching grant of $50,000 from Home Depot (a corporation also concerned about sustainability), and the rest we were able to budget ourselves.

And as we planned for renovation of our older residence halls, it has not taken any convincing to say that we need to get as close to LEED certification as we can with the renovations. It makes sense to do so, no matter how you look at it. In fact, in 2010, the Spelman College Board of Trustees approved a policy ensuring that all new construction and renovation projects will be completed to at least the U.S. Green Building Council's LEED Silver standard or equivalent. Establishing such a policy was important so that our commitment to sustainability is not dependent on any particular president or CFO, but is a permanent part of the institutional practice.

Living Green Everyday

In 2009 we completed a new strategic plan called "Strengthening the Core: The Spelman College Plan for 2015," and environmental sustainability was a key component. Efforts to put a plan in action had begun in fall 2007 with a Sustainability Focus Group made up of five students, five faculty members, and five staff members, all of whom played a key role. Having students involved was important because they have been actively engaged in this effort from the beginning. In winter 2008 we held a two-day strategic planning retreat at which we identified six campus priorities, and one of those priorities was focused on the campus infrastructure and learning environment. Integral to that work was the following sustainability objective:

To identify opportunities to improve Spelman's operating efficiency and at the same time, establish the college as a model academic institution dedicated to reducing its impact on the environment by developing and implementing sustainability initiatives to generate environmental action by students, faculty and administrators as an aspect of positive social change.

When the plan was completed and approved by the board in the fall of 2009, we established GOALS for each of our constituent groups—students, faculty, staff, alumnae, trustees, and community partners. GOALS is an acronym—its meaning varies slightly from one constituent group to another. For example, the "G" stands for *global perspectives*; for students it signifies that we expect every student will have a meaningful global experience before she graduates. For staff and administrators, "G" also stands for global perspectives, but in our campus context that means going "green" as we think globally and act locally. In March 2009 we launched, with Art Frazier's leadership, an energy management policy that provides guidelines for everyone on campus to encourage energy efficiency and conservation practices.

My focus here has been on our administrative actions, but our faculty members have done (and are doing) important work in the classroom.

For one of our newest majors, Environmental Studies, student interest is growing rapidly. We have two real champions: Professor Victor Ibaneusi, a biologist by training whose work is on water remediation, and who has patented a biological process for cleaning toxins from water; and Professor Fatemeh Shafiei, a political scientist who has been very involved in work related to Environmental Justice, and who has teamed with public school teachers and local community activists on environmental education projects of all kinds. Spelman alumna Na'Taki Osborne Jelks, raised in what is known as "Cancer Alley" in Louisiana and now a leading environmental activist at the National Wildlife Federation, is also teaching at Spelman, along with Jewell Harper, a visiting scholar from the EPA.

Signing the American College and University Presidents' Climate Commitment

Clearly the "journey to green" was well underway at Spelman by 2010, but we had not yet become a signatory to the American College and University Presidents' Climate Commitment. Though committed to the concept of environmental sustainability, I had been reluctant to sign the commitment as I was unsure that we could meet its obligations. However, in the summer of 2010, three things happened. The first was my attendance at the United Negro College Fund Building Green Institute held in San Antonio that June where Spelman was highlighted as a leader among HBCUs for our environmental responsibility. The second was my experience of watching helplessly for weeks that summer as gallon after gallon of crude oil bubbled up from a deep sea well into the Gulf of Mexico, polluting coastal fishing waters and marshlands. The third was reading Thomas Friedman's book, *Hot Flat and Crowded* (Friedman 2008). In particular, Friedman's words were catalytic, making clear that we need a greater sense of urgency about the environmental degradation that is taking place around us. And if we do not step up—and teach our students to do so—we will all regret it. He writes:

If we want to maintain . . . a habitable planet, rich with flora and fauna, leopards and lions, and human communities that can grow in a sustainable way—things will have to change around here, and fast (Friedman 2008, 7).

We are the first generation of Americans in the Energy-Climate Era. This is not about the whales anymore. It's about us. And what we do about the challenges of energy and climate, conservation and preservation, will tell our kids who we really are. (Friedman 2008, 412)

Moved to lead our community toward greater action, I launched the 2010–11 academic year with a speech entitled "Sustainable Spelman." Acknowledging the good work that had already been done and the recognition that we had received, I have challenged everyone at Spelman to do more. As one way of supporting this notion that we are all engaged in a sustainable Spelman, I signed the American College and University Presidents' Climate Commitment, joining more than 670 other college and university presidents who have signed. The Presidents' Climate Commitment requires us to create a long-term plan (perhaps as long as twenty or thirty years) for achieving climate neutrality, and to report publicly on our progress on a regular basis. We know that our efforts will be by necessity incremental, and our plan may be revised many times in the process, but we cannot in good conscience ignore the science that tells us we have to change our ways, and do it as quickly as we can.

We often hear the phrase "think globally, act locally," and indeed that is what attention to environmental sustainability requires us to do. The choices we make here at Spelman and in our daily lives have ripple effects not just at home but around the world. We must have an *ethic of conservation* on our campus.

Our mission statement talks about ethical development—but what are ethics? Friedman writes, "Ethics are not laws. They are not imposed by the state. Rather they are norms, values, beliefs, habits and attitudes that are embraced voluntarily—that we as a society impose on ourselves. Laws regulate behavior from the outside in. Ethics regulate behavior from the inside out. Ethics are something you carry with you wherever you go to guide whatever you do" (Friedman 2008, 192).

Or to say it differently, ethics are what you do even when no one else is watching. In *Hot, Flat and Crowded*, Thomas Friedman quotes Michael Sandel, a political philosopher at Harvard, who describes an ethic of conservation as "an ethic of restraint," understanding that we cannot just use our natural resources as though they were limitless. An ethic of conservation requires us to be good stewards of our resources now, so there will be resources available in the future, not only for us but for those who will come after us. Our sustainable Spelman policy requires all of us to adopt an ethic of conservation.

A couple of years ago we faced a severe drought in Atlanta—the reservoir was down so low that it was said there was a water supply of less than ninety days. At that time, we launched a water conservation campaign on campus, and the governor stood on the steps of the Capitol Building and publicly prayed for rain. It did eventually rain, and the reservoir filled back up, and some of us went back to our old habits. But the fact is that we still live in a place that has a limited water supply and a rapidly growing population. We have to have an ethic of conservation for our own sake, and for the sake of others.

Self-Care and Sustainability

Environmental sustainability is just one dimension. When I think about sustainable Spelman I also think about *sustainable people*—people who are demonstrating enough self-care to ensure their good health. Unfortunately, we African American women, as a group, have *not* been taking such good care of ourselves. But Spelman's mission statement says that the college empowers the *whole* person—mind, spirit, *and body.*

It has been said that the health status of African American women is a primary indication of the health status of blacks living in America. The historical context in which the experiences of black women have emerged has taught us to care for ourselves last—and often not to care for ourselves at all.

Although the pantheon of black women (s)heroes—from Sojourner Truth and Ida B. Wells to Rosa Parks, Maya Angelou, Marian Wright Edelman, Queen Latifah, First Lady Michelle Obama, and so many others known and unknown—testifies to our strength, fortitude, character, and resilience, in our story remains a theme that resonates truth: *we have not been taking care of ourselves.* We often prioritize the needs of others or have no priorities related to our care at all.

Taronda Spencer, the archivist of Spelman College, tells the story of a young woman who, in the college's early days, picked 1,000 pounds of cotton in 24 hours to get enough money to enter Spelman College. *A thousand pounds of cotton!* Can you imagine that? The story goes that upon her arrival she was admitted to the infirmary—and died before she could attend one class at the college. She had literally worked herself to death.

Her story may appear to be an extreme case. But, in many instances we *have* worked ourselves to death, *loved others* to our death, and *paid little attention to the cost of so much giving and so little care.* Our survival and the survival of our community requires that health and wellness become priorities in our lives. At Spelman, our attention to the topic of health disparities is critical, because we know that black women are dying much too soon. How can Spelman, the premier educator of women of African descent, stand idly by without doing what we can do to educate young women about these health issues?

We know what an impact the epidemic of HIV/AIDS is having on black women. According to the Centers for Disease Control and Prevention, HIV/AIDS is one of the leading causes of death for African American women between the ages of twenty-five and thirty-four. It is not always easy to talk about this epidemic, but our silence places our students and our community at risk, so we must break that silence. Our Women's Research and Resource Center has been leading the way for Spelman in a global dialog about the impact of HIV/AIDS in the lives of black women.

Right here on our own campus, we need to remember that if we believe our own health and well-being and the health and well-being of those around us is important, then we must behave as though that were true. Our beliefs and our behaviors have to match. If you believe that self-respect is an important value, then your behavior will reflect that. If you *respect* yourself, you will *protect* yourself, and you will do what you can to preserve your health.

But HIV/AIDS is not the only threat to our students' health and longevity. As experts at the CDC tell us: "Poor diet and physical inactivity (the foundation for obesity) is the leading and fastest-growing killer of Americans and will overtake tobacco-related deaths." In 2005, the Surgeon General predicted that today's young people will be the first generation that will be less healthy and have a shorter life expectancy than their parents. We don't have to just accept that though—we can do something about it. We can take charge of our health, take charge of our life choices, we can develop an *ethic of self-care.*

Chavonne Shorter, our Wellness Coordinator, has helped our community become more active, both students and employees. In the summer of 2010 we began offering on campus a fitness boot camp for employees at 7:15 every morning, aqua aerobics at the end of the day, and a walking program that encouraged participants to track their own walking activity (at least thirty minutes a day) throughout the summer. I received messages of appreciation from employees who participated. Here is an email testimonial I received from one of them:

I've consistently attended Boot Camp classes since last fall, started the Zumba class this past Wednesday and will join the Walk Around the AUC Program later this month. The benefits of having these classes on campus [are] tremendous! Not only is it very convenient, but the rewards are amazing! We have time to work out with each other, keep one another encouraged, share weight loss and get in shape tips, share recipes, have loads of fun and sweat a whole lot!!! And best of all, we all have a personal trainer, FREE of charge!!!

That is an ethic of self-care in action, and we need more of that to be a community of sustainable people.

As we move forward, I continue to think about the intersection of our commitments to sustainability of our environment, and our commitment to the sustainability of our people, the intersection of our commitment to the environment and our commitment to health and wellness.

We need to ask questions about the kind of food we find in our cafeteria—are we using organic and locally grown produce? What choices are we offering our students? What are we doing about the "food desert" that exists in our surrounding community? We have an epidemic of obesity and all the health issues related to it—diabetes, heart disease, cancer—all impacting the quality of life for students, faculty, and staff as well as impacting the cost of our health care benefits. As an educational institution, we can and should do something about that. That should also be part of what we mean when we say we want to be "sustainable Spelman," sustain the earth, sustain ourselves, and help our students to see their roles as change agents in the process.

If we have fulfilled our mission, our students should leave us *healthier* than when they arrived—with an understanding of what an ethic of self-care means. An ethic of conservation, an ethic of self-care, and an ethic of commitment to our mission: together these values will help ensure a sustainable Spelman—a Spelman College that endures, a college that thrives, and a college that delivers on its promises to its students.

At Spelman we have a slogan—we say that coming to Spelman is a choice to change the world, and I truly believe that it is. But I also say that a choice to change the world also means taking responsibility for the ways each of us is always changing the world—and not always for the better—through our excessive consumption of the world's resources. Understanding our own environmental impact and seeking to reduce it is a choice that all of us can make every day. At Spelman we are making that choice. Our journey is not finished, but we are on the way.

References

Friedman, Thomas L. 2008. *Hot, Flat and Crowded*. New York: Farrar, Straus and Giroux.

14

Weaving a Culture of Sustainability: Santa Clara University's Evolving Story

Sherry Booth, Lindsey Cromwell Kalkbrenner, Leslie Gray, and Amy Shachter

Santa Clara University is a leading Jesuit, Catholic institution that strives to cultivate knowledge and faith to build a more humane, just, and sustainable world. Founded in 1851, Santa Clara is California's oldest institution of higher learning. The university has over 8,000 students and is located in Silicon Valley.

Implementing a single component of sustainability on a college campus can happen easily and quickly—and can be the work of one or two interested individuals—but creating a culture of sustainability occurs only over a long period of time and requires the commitment of many members of the campus community. In 2009, Santa Clara University's twenty-eighth president, Michael Engh, SJ, announced in his inaugural speech that, "Santa Clara University is uniquely positioned to make a significant contribution to achieving a more just and sustainable future." He set as one of his priorities to pursue justice and sustainability across all aspects of the university:

We see with increasing clarity the fragility of our planet: the depletion of the soil, the destruction of its forests, and the pollution of air and water. Probing more deeply into these issues, we learn that the poorest of the poor suffer the most. They lack the resources and access to basic necessities when the natural world is so corrupted. And we might ask ourselves: Who hears the voice of the needy and listens to their concerns about exploited lands and economies? Who is the voice for the defense of the assaulted world? Who trains the leaders we need to understand the intricacies of biodiversity and who are also equipped to discern the ethical dimensions of their decisions? (Engh 2009)

President Engh's words crystallize the passion and the goals that have become ever more prevalent among our faculty, staff, students, and administrators.

Our story of how Santa Clara University (SCU) has moved toward a culture of sustainability brings together stories from our community's members to focus on four themes. The first theme illustrates the importance of linking grassroots efforts to top-down endeavors in making long-lasting institutional change. Amy Shachter is an associate professor of chemistry but has worn many administrative hats at Santa Clara University, including Director of the Environmental Studies Program, Senior Associate Dean, and Associate Provost. Each of these positions has allowed her to be both an active participant and observer of the many changes in campus culture over the years. Amy's section below reminds us how important it is to have collaboration between grassroots efforts and administrators to make long-lasting institutional change.

The second theme examines how and why coordination is crucial, particularly once multiple strands of sustainability emerge. Lindsey Cromwell Kalkbrenner, the director of the Office of Sustainability, describes how her first position was initiated as a partnership between several campus entities and only as a half-time position. Cobbling together financial support for this position was an important element of its success, giving many different units a stake. One of the most important moving pieces of Lindsey's effort is communication, as she meets sustainability champions and, in turn, champions their ideas.

The third theme highlights the power of validation in a community, examining the ways that giving both permission and platforms for individuals to join broader efforts allows for innovation in curriculum and faculty development. Sherry Booth, a senior lecturer in the English Department and co-director of a sustainability-themed residential learning community, describes the Penstemon Project for Sustainability across the Curriculum and the Sustainable Living Undergraduate Research Project (SLURP).

Finally, embedding sustainability into institutional mission and identity plays a pivotal role in moving the wider campus community toward sustainability. Leslie Gray, the Executive Director of the Environmental Studies Institute, describes how such an inclusion allowed the "critical masses" to adopt sustainability as part of their operating framework. Leadership from the presidential level has propelled us forward to institutionalizing our identity around sustainability.

Amy Shachter: Building Sustainability from the Grass Roots Up and from the Top Down

Over the past twenty years, the sustainability transformation at Santa Clara University has been advanced at key points where grassroots efforts combined with administrative priorities to create significant and lasting institutional change. Alignment with the fundamental Jesuit mission and values of the institution has been integral to our transformation. Examples of key tipping points include: launching our environmental resource assessment in the mid-1990s, developing a campus sustainability policy in 2003, founding an Office of Sustainability with a sustainability coordinator in 2006, and, most recently, integrating sustainability and justice into the vision and strategic plan of the university.

In the early 1990s, working closely with several colleagues and teaming with the student club, GrassRoots Environmental Efforts Now (GREEN!), I helped to develop our environmental studies program. Shortly thereafter, students within GREEN! initiated a campus environmental audit. Working with our Bannan Center for Jesuit Education, the students helped to bring to campus Father Al Fritsch, SJ, to conduct a preliminary Environmental Resource Assessment (ERA) in 1995. Though initiated as a student effort, the ERA project bridged to and engaged campus leadership particularly at the provost level. A key factor was bringing in a Jesuit scholar to conduct the initial assessment. As a Jesuit university, the influence of the Jesuit community is significant. At this time both the provost and president were Jesuits—at SCU the president is always a Jesuit. Bringing to campus a respected Jesuit colleague through the Bannan Center to conduct the initial environmental resource assessment was a brilliant decision by the GREEN! club and significantly accelerated campus change.

During the summer of 2003, I joined with an ad hoc task force to consider possible courses of action regarding sustainability. Creation of the task force was the result of the assistant vice president of University Operations approaching environmental studies faculty members and students to work collaboratively to request that the president establish such a task force. Confusing as that may sound, it worked within our culture and structure. We presented a proposal to the president to establish an ad hoc task force to report on next steps for sustainability. The task force concluded that a more coordinated and integrated approach would dramatically enhance the university's sustainability efforts and proposed establishing a comprehensive campus sustainability policy. As a result of work of the task force, the then president, Father Paul Locatelli, charged an expanded task force with developing a draft policy on sustainability for administrative review within three months, and the final policy was approved in early 2004. The rapid approval of the policy was, in many ways, due to intentional alignment with the SCU mission "to act as a voice of reason, conscience, and service to society" and our vision "to build a more humane and just world."

Since the policy was established, the faculty and students and various levels of the university administration have worked collaboratively to continue the transformation. A sustainability coordinator was hired to bridge university operations and academic and co-curricular programs; a Campus Sustainability Council was appointed in 2008 that now advises on achieving climate neutrality. Though change occurred rapidly after the policy was established, another key point where transformation was accelerated occurred when our current president gave his inaugural speech in 2009. President Engh held a series of coffees with the campus community shortly after he arrived and, influenced by these conversations, provided essential top-level support.

Lindsey Cromwell Kalkbrenner: The Role of Coordination in Transformation

For truly transformative change, we know that initiatives need coordination—a central hub to serve as a mechanism for sharing resources and best practices—as well a place for people new to the cause to congregate. The title sustainability coordinator is good and bad at the same time. The bad: the title seems to define the person in that role as the "do-er of sustainability." Realistically, sustainability is something everyone needs to contribute to. Alternatively, the title defines the role perfectly: this job is truly about coordinating—it implies a catalyst role, to foster a transformative reaction.

For most campuses, change is most widely accepted when it happens in small increments. Rather than hire a full-time permanent sustainability coordinator (which was such a new career, few knew what the job entailed), the co-chairs of the sustainability task force created a part-time, two-year pilot position. The salary was pieced together from two pools of money, from discretionary funds in the College of Arts and Sciences and from University Operations. The sustainability coordinator was housed within the Environmental Studies Institute. This was a noncommittal way to gain administrative approval to pilot test a new staff position. The fact that this position reported to two different areas of the university was an added benefit, as these relationships helped bridge the gap that often occurs between silos. I work daily with faculty and staff, and am accepted by both worlds.

Of course, the sustainability task force had every intention this position would end up as a full-time permanent position. That happened two years later, in 2008, when timing was right and we were able to prove sustainability could pay for itself. Our Operations division was experiencing savings associated with energy efficiency measures as well as more effective waste diversion and recycling programs. Now, the position reports directly to Joe Sugg, the assistant vice president of University Operations (driver of developing the campus sustainability policy five years earlier). Keeping ties with the College of Arts the Sciences, I am still physically located in the Environmental Studies Institute.

When I originally applied for the position, I had no idea what it entailed. Sure, I recycled and reused my traveling coffee mug. But I gained most of my knowledge about sustainability, climate change, and leadership on the job. Early on, I was encouraged to take an environmental leadership program that helped me understand regional and global environmental issues, as well as build a network of sustainability professionals in the area. I later earned my master's in business administration and developed my knowledge of leading people and organizations.

In 2006, my first assignment was to get to know the campus and meet the champions who had been leading our disparate programs. Like driftwood floating in an ocean, each person (with his or her projects) was floating along; most people I interviewed felt like they were the only ones out there. As I interviewed them, I shared others' stories, and this served to bind the driftwood together. Slowly, we gathered the initiatives into a small raft. As I got to know more of our campus's early adopters, I asked them to refer me to more of their colleagues. Soon, the small raft of sustainability initiatives and ideas became a bigger vessel, and we began navigating the sea of change toward sustainability.

As more champions were identified, more support was added to our raft. We soon realized our campus had a story to tell . . . multiple stories, in fact. I created a report to document our stakeholders' stories and suggestions for future projects and shared it with everyone I interviewed. Many were surprised how much was happening. Now, the challenge was how to share these stories with the broader campus, to begin moving beyond early adapters and into the critical majority.

One of the suggestions from those early interviews was to distribute a campus-wide monthly email with tips for sustainable living. After a few months, people began submitting their own stories, and we expanded the email to include not only sustainability projects, but also profiles of campus community members—sustainability champions—going out of their way to develop a culture of sustainability.

Now I work with our student sustainability interns to develop themes for each month's newsletter. These students develop articles based on stories they hear and interview campus stakeholders as they write the monthly articles. Recent profiles included a senior who worked with facilities staff members to install over twenty gooseneck water-filling stations on campus, a professor of modern languages who integrates sustainability into courses like Contemporary Latin America and Chicano/a Literature and Film, and a staff member who hosted a workshop teaching peers to create items from reused and salvaged materials.

Sustainability interns enjoy the empowerment that comes with their jobs. Each has a respective group on campus she or he works with, and therefore brings a certain skill set to the role, while acquiring different professional experiences. The intern for faculty and staff initiatives, for example, partners with Human Resources to create engaging workshops to draw participants from staff and faculty. The residence life intern engages resident staff, enabling them to spread sustainability to students where they spend the majority of their time—in their residence halls.

One of my favorite parts of the job is working with faculty to develop campus-based projects for their course assignments. I maintain a list of projects that need student help. The list is fed by ideas from facilities and operations directors, the housing office, student life, and students themselves. Students enjoy campus-based course assignments because they are able to make a visible contribution to the campus and community. In a course called Energy and the Environment, students worked with individual residence halls to promote energy conservation and conduct energy audits. This year, a group in a communications course is developing a marketing theme and materials to promote the Energy Challenge.

The skills and background knowledge I find most critical to this position are mostly soft skills—interpersonal relationships, communication, and flexibility. This position involves working on multiple projects at a time, facilitating and engaging new collaborators, and constant communication with stakeholders and multiple audiences. It is crucial for coordinators to have a deep understanding of how their university functions and to respect and get to know the people who make up the university. Also critical is an understanding that in this job you function as a catalyst. Success is measured by the transformation that happens around you, not necessarily the number of projects you complete.

Sherry Booth: Community, Validation, and Innovation

The heart of my academic work for the last seven years has been finding ways to help bring into being an ecological consciousness on our campus. One of the primary questions became how to engage, educate, and motivate the next generation to work toward sustainability—and thus affect a sea change in values and patterns of thinking and acting. I want to describe two sites of this work: our interdisciplinary workshop, the Penstemon Project, to help faculty embed sustainability across the curriculum, and our Sustainable Living Undergraduate Research Project (SLURP) where our young undergraduates conduct research into sustainability in residence life.

Like so many of my colleagues, I came to sustainability through a circuitous route. To me, trained in literary and gender studies, sustainability was a private passion and practice until my professional interests merged with the personal when I discovered ecofeminism. The confluence of gender roles as they connect with environmental issues gave me a focus and purpose I had been searching for, but as the only ecofeminst scholar in the English Department, my community was a textual and virtual one. The years 2006–2009 were not only watershed years for the university but for me as well; I took the training offered by the Association for the Advancement of Sustainability in Higher Education (AASHE) with four of my colleagues and became co-director of a Residential Learning Community with a theme of sustainability and the arts. Working with faculty in environmental studies, biology, and political science, we built on the AASHE training and designed the first Penstemon workshop for our campus.

Twenty faculty members from a variety of disciplines participated in the Penstemon project, and they committed to redesigning their syllabus, teaching the course with the new content, and then reporting back once they had taught the class. The hidden curriculum was the creation of a community among faculty with very different ideas about and approaches to sustainability. Every faculty member who attended had some form of previous commitment to sustainability, and we often heard comments like "I thought I was the only one doing this," or "I have been trying to get my department to offer a course with a sustainability focus," or "This is one place my teaching and research need to be." An English faculty member wrote me recently: "For years I was in the closet. I was an environmentalist, but I could not bring that into my first-year composition classroom. [Penstemon] empowered [me] to teach writing through a theme that means the world to me, about material that could mean the world to us all." Penstemon could not have happened without the foundation of the previous twenty years of quiet work by a few committed individuals, but it came at a moment when many endeavors across the campus were gaining ground: the Office of Sustainability, the Presidents'

Climate Commitment, and Santa Clara's entrance into the Solar Decathlon. In Penstemon, I found a community that validated my work—not necessarily my ecofeminist work, but the shared emphasis on environmental issues. Before Penstemon I sometimes felt as if I were sneaking in material that many did not believe belonged in English classes. Change can be individual, and often is, but when a group commits to a vision and then works to make it happen, each member's contribution is part of something much larger and thus energizing.

SLURP has become a different kind of experiment in teaching and learning over the last five years. Seen as part of a fairly recent trend in higher education, learning communities offer "an innovative approach to teaching and learning, provide environments for students to acquire common and disciplinary knowledge, and improve academic performance" (Zhu and Baylen 2005, 253). SLURP is housed in a residence hall with the theme of sustainability and the arts, and our challenge was to find ways to integrate student learning about sustainability with their living environment.

The project provided a mechanism for students to engage deeply with work on sustainability. We designed a directed research course through Environmental Studies for which the students receive credit and placed all of the SLURP students on the same floor—a floor chosen because it had a kitchen and we wanted food to be a part of their community building. The SLURP students undertake research into some aspect of sustainability on campus, projects that they are interested in pursuing as well as projects that emerge through consultation with other campus units. Since the students live together, their group projects make residence life and academic work indistinguishable, and because this cohort chooses to live in SLURP, they come in committed.

Student feedback on living and conducting research in SLURP indicates that it is, for many, a formative experience. One student said:

Little did I know at orientation when I decided to sign up for SLURP that it would be the best decision I made after choosing to attend Santa Clara University. Not only was SLURP a good opportunity to get more involved with sustainability on campus, but it provided an immediate community for me at school, making my dorm room not just a place to live, but a new home.

Themes that emerge in other comments from students include the sense of this community as a place where participants share a passion and get to work closely with professors on projects they care about, allowing them to get involved with different campus groups, learn about sustainability, and sometimes find a life path. As a four-year veteran wrote, "Every year

I learned something new that in many ways encouraged me to rethink the idea of sustainability and how I could incorporate it into my life at Santa Clara and beyond." The energy and commitment of the students has made this curricular work unmatched by any other I have done and gives me hope that this new generation of learners will indeed work to change the world.

Leslie Gray: Diffusing Sustainability from the Dedicated to the Critical Masses

As a culture of sustainability grew, we diffused sustainability to a wider audience, bringing in people who never saw sustainability as part of their job. By making sustainability into a defining feature of our mission and identity, university leaders broadened it from the dedicated core to the mainstream. Once there were so many sustainability initiatives around campus, we believe that university leadership felt compelled to get on board, and then other campus units that were not at the forefront of sustainability also felt impelled to act.

When did the university leadership come on board with sustainability in a strategic and sustained manner? Our past president, Paul Locatelli, SJ, made several commitments that signaled that sustainability had become important. One small but significant change was in our university vision statement: What was "education for a just and humane world" became "education for a just, humane, and sustainable world." This shift was made with little fanfare or public announcement but made a public statement that sustainability mattered to the university as a whole. This was at a time when we were garnering significant press, including high rankings in various sustainability polls, placing in the national Solar Decathlon despite being a primarily undergraduate institution, and receiving attention for some of the innovative research being undertaken by undergraduates. In 2007, Father Locatelli signed the American College and University Presidents' Climate Commitment and then created the Office of Sustainability and a Sustainability Council to implement the climate commitment.

Our new president Michael Engh, SJ, went even farther. I was in Washington, DC, at a National Science Foundation panel when a colleague emailed me, telling me to hold onto my hat. This colleague, an English professor, was astonished that Father Engh started his speech with a poem, "Song of the Builders," by Mary Oliver. In this poem, Oliver sits down to pray to God but then refocuses on a cricket "moving the grains of the hillside / this way and that way." President Engh related this shift from the all-encompassing idea of God to the small and insignificant actions of a cricket to pose the question of how we as a Jesuit Catholic institute can frame our relationship with the most needy members of society. He then went on to say how this sort of education is something that Santa Clara is uniquely poised to foster, and he wanted us to become a "major center for center for discussions of environmental justice and for examining the ethical dimensions of how we treat the physical world" (Engh 2009).

I think there was some surprise in his speech for the broader university community and even for those of us in environmental studies and other sustainability-related fields. But when we reflected on his words, it became apparent that he did not see this initiative as something new but as emanating from our long-term commitment to social justice.

Some of the tangible effects of Father Engh's inaugural address were a new sustainability and justice research initiative and a year-long set of sustainability programs that involved speakers, curriculum development workshops, and a campus-wide sustainability teach-in. The biggest shift, though, came when the president appointed a faculty group to rework the strategic plan to reflect the older priorities but also to integrate the new priority of justice and sustainability. I was one of the six faculty members in this group, and we had very different approaches. While the plan went through many iterations and revisions, justice and sustainability emerged as one of the five main priorities. Because of our history, we grounded sustainability in social justice, illustrating "connections among a healthy environment, just societies, and a vibrant economy that meet all people's fundamental needs, especially those of the global poor."

In 2011, the University Strategic Plan was approved to become the basis for the next fundraising campaign (Santa Clara University 2011). While it is too early to see fundraising results around justice and sustainability, those of us in the sustainability field noticed some subtle and not-so-subtle shifts. Many campus units that had previously not engaged sustainability explicitly now developed sustainability plans. One of the most impressive results was detailed in a report from the dean of Student Life. The report described paperless record keeping, the creation of certification for sustainable events, and programs to reduce energy use. The Career Center created a new program on green careers, and international programs came up with a sustainability policy for study abroad.

As we move forward with sustainability as a strategic priority, there are new opportunities and challenges for the future. One significant challenge will be enhancing and expanding our infrastructure to manage and sustain efforts. And with recent, strong top-down framing of sustainability, another challenge will be keeping the grassroots engaged. This is particularly crucial for faculty developing courses. Once initial changes have been made to a course, whether incorporating a component of sustainability into an existing course or designing a completely new one, the danger is inertia. The world is indeed fragile, and our work is grounded in the desire to help provide a "voice for the defense of the assaulted world" and train "the leaders we need to understand the intricacies of biodiversity and who are also equipped to discern the ethical dimensions of their decisions" (Engh 2009). Creating a culture of sustainability is an exercise in hope for ourselves, our students, and our world.

References

Association for the Advancement of Sustainability in Higher Education. 2012. STARS (Sustainability Tracking, Assessment, & Rating System). http://www.scu.edu/sustainability/commandpol/stars.cfm.

Engh, Michael. 2009. Inaugural Speech. April. http://www.scu.edu/president/inauguration/transcript/index.cfm.

Santa Clara University. 2004. A Comprehensive Policy on Sustainability at SCU. http://www.scu.edu/sustainability/commandpol/policy.cfm.

Santa Clara University. 2007. Climate Commitment. http://www.scu.edu/sustainability/commandpol/climatecommitment.cfm.

Santa Clara University. 2011. University Strategic Plan. http://www.scu.edu/sustainability/commandpol/strategicplan.cfm.

Zhu, Erping, and Danilo M. Baylen. 2005. From Learning Community to Community Learning: Pedagogy, Technology, and Interactivity. *Educational Media International* 42 (3):251–268.

15

Sustainability as Leadership Ethos

Margo Flood

Warren Wilson College, located near Asheville, North Carolina, is a private liberal arts college with a distinctive learning "Triad" comprising academics, work, and service. The 1,100-acre campus, with working farm and garden, inspires and engages 950 undergraduates and its low-residency MFA students in purposeful inquiry.

The universe does not exist "out there," independent of us. We are inescapably involved in bringing about that which appears to be happening. We are not only observers. We are participants.
—John Wheeler 1974, 689

With a fresh commitment to sustainability as the framework for institutional decision making, Warren Wilson College president Sandy Pfeiffer and his leadership team—the President's Advisory Council—departed for their summer retreat in 2007. Along with flip charts, tape, and pens they carried three baseball caps labeled "economic," "environment," and "community" to focus their discussion.

Introduction

Sustainability is woven into the fabric of Warren Wilson, grounded in a rich history of place and purpose, and embedded by generations of community members who have modeled an enduring commitment to connect values to action. Near Asheville, North Carolina, bordered by the Craggy Mountains and the Swannanoa River, the college's working farm and forest, organically managed garden, and Leadership in Energy and Environmental Design (LEED)–certified buildings of native stone and wood frame a cherished landscape. Upon this land, the practice of sustainability flows from the mission, which serves as a compass for responsible citizenship, and from Warren Wilson's unique liberal arts model of engaged learning.

In the past decade, faculty, students, and staff wrestled with a sustainability discourse and developed an articulation that draws from the college's lyrical narrative to frame a more specific, strategic relationship to the campus, the region, and the world beyond. Central to the adoption of sustainability as a working ethos is that leaders model what students come to learn as the parameters of responsible decision making. Sustainability viewed this way is not simply a useful term to corral Warren Wilson's legacy of commitments to social justice, economic resilience, cross-cultural understanding, and environmental responsibility; it is a dynamic process that knits these interdependent goals into a framework for institutional decision making and infuses best as a habit of mind.

Living Laboratory Frames Pedagogy

Warren Wilson educates for a life of responsible citizenship through its unique Triad of academics, work, and service. In addition to taking a liberal arts course of study, students work 15 hours a week on one of the more than 120 crews that support all campus operations, and they fulfill a service requirement for graduation. The campus itself—the 300-acre working farm, 6-acre garden, 700-acre managed forest, and riparian habitat—serves as a living laboratory for the engaged learning that has proven to be as relevant to citizenship in the nineteenth and twentieth centuries as the twenty-first.

For the student crews who dammed Bull Creek in 1910 to generate the school's first electricity and the undergrads in 2000 who helped to design and then build the LEED–Platinum EB EcoDorm, a "working education" grounded in strong academics remains the defining quality of the Warren Wilson experience. It serves as the framework for development of the critical-thinking skills required to address local and global challenges.

This world-as-living-laboratory pedagogy extends to the region and beyond. Students examine complex and chronic regional issues such as homelessness and domestic abuse through the lens of sustainability. They develop a broader conscience through hands-on study of diverse cultures where they learn, first-hand, a global context for their daily lifestyle choices. This dynamic immersion in study, synthesis, and application forges critical thinkers who know how to participate effectively in civic life because as undergraduates, they practice doing so . . . daily. They prepare for the citizenship challenge articulated in 2003 by the American Association of University Professors' Resolution on Liberal Learning: "A liberal education prepares responsible citizens who inform themselves about local, national, and global issues and participate actively in civic life. The critical thinking and the habits of careful inquiry developed through a liberal education are vital to these tasks."[1] Sustainability, for Warren Wilson's emerging citizen activists, offers a framework for interdisciplinary inquiry that enhances their participation in civic life.

Legacy Invokes Responsibility

The college's interpretation of sustainability as a leadership compass builds upon the legacy forged by generations of leaders who have shaped the college's educational approach to responsible citizenship. In 1927, when students were raising produce and livestock in order to feed the campus, the forerunner Asheville Farm School superintendent Henry S. Randolph proclaimed, "Give me the real teacher, and with a few directions, I shall expect him to discover and use the functional approach. I shall expect him to find in most every relation cultural and moral values." In 1952, Warren Wilson president Arthur Bannerman, deep in the folds of a segregated South and two years before *Brown v. Board of Education*, admitted an African American student to the college. In 1960, he established a service requirement.

In 1974, with support from the National Endowment for the Humanities, President Ben Holden led a general education revision, which the college called "Ways of Knowing," to achieve "an organization of knowledge that more adequately reflected the interconnectedness of human experience and the systematic nature of the world." During President Alf Canon's tenure in the late 1980s, the college established the Black Swan Center to foster sustainable business development in western North Carolina. And from 1991 to 2006, President Doug Orr established the Environmental Leadership Center, the iconic EcoDorm, and numerous campus greening initiatives.

Building upon this momentum, and steadfast to the college's mission and values, President Sandy Pfeiffer took several noteworthy steps that led to the adoption of sustainability as a framework for "responsible decision making" at the leadership table and its formalization as one of Warren Wilson's core values.

Campus Calls for Clarity

In 1990, Warren Wilson adopted architect Christopher Alexander's pattern language process to articulate principles for the built environment, land use, purchasing, biodiversity, and other college functions.² By 2001, several sets of principles, written by faculty, students, and staff and approved through the shared governance process, framed a broad scope of concern. They ranged from the general, "Everything at Warren Wilson must work for the common good. None of the land or its fruits should be neglected," to the more specific, "Purchasers must take into account the environmental and economic impact of their buying choices."

In 1997, the college approved a pivotal Environmental Commitment Statement that incorporated social justice, global responsibility, and economic conscience into its evolving environmental ethic: "We recognize the need to exercise wise use of the resources of the global commons, and, at the same time, the need for a deep, aesthetic, spiritually-based involvement with the community that extends beyond the human inhabitants of Warren Wilson. An essential goal of Warren Wilson College is to develop good environmental citizens who recognize and perform their duties and responsibilities as members of the larger human and ecological communities in which we live."³ The commitment to rigorous inquiry was implicit, for *how* the college would achieve this fine balance was not yet known. When Warren Wilson became a signatory of the Talloires Declaration in 2000 and pledged to "create an institutional culture of sustainability," it headed toward yet another unmapped destination.

In 2004, Warren Wilson was recognized by the National Wildlife Federation's "National Report Card on Environmental Performance and Sustainability in Higher Education" as one of the twenty-four leading US institutions with "students and staff working for a sustainable future." Warren Wilson alumna Olya Milenkaya spoke for many of these students when she said, "I came to Warren Wilson because I did not want to debate whether we have an environmental crisis; I wanted to debate how to fix it." Students like Olya quickly learned there was no easy fix. Problem solving a sustainable solution started with a required first step—disentangling the cluster of economic, scientific, spiritual, ethical, practical, environmental, social, cultural, and political strands that formed the issue.

According to Web pundits, 2006 was a banner year for sustainability. The term was employed as a synonym for "green," an adjective, a proper noun, an outcome, and a branding strategy. The confusion generated by the semantics alone fueled the fevered debate that accompanies the development of a new paradigm. Warren Wilson was distinguished by the Association for the Advancement of Sustainability in Higher Education (AASHE) in 2006 with a Campus Sustainability Award. While honored by this distinction, faculty, staff and students questioned the veracity of this new gold standard, "sustainable."

Across disciplines and throughout the Triad, the community said, "Define the terms." "Does sustainability really mean environmental stewardship?" "What relevance does it have to the humanities?" "Is it a product? A process?" At the Environmental Leadership Center, we began to investigate the full impact of the college's "green buildings," and to ask, "But how are they sustainable?" Faculty across disciplines sought to define their relationship to the concept. The Brundtland Commission's call for "intergenerational fairness" grounded the conversation in stewardship—a cherished Warren Wilson value. Sustainability began to take shape as a standard for accountability and a process of inquiry. As the vigorous campus dialog progressed, ranging from organic to orchestrated, it revealed Warren Wilson's cultural approach to change: principled debate, careful examination of semantics, congruence with legacy, grounding in moral imperatives, and ultimately, formal community commitments.

President Pfeiffer, who had come to the college in 2006, became a founding signatory of the American College and University Presidents Climate Commitment in 2007. This pledge to address climate change and sustainability education galvanized action to the degree that Warren Wilson was eventually distinguished in 2010 by Second Nature's award for Institutional Excellence in Climate Leadership. Pfeiffer created a cross-sector campus committee and we translated the challenge, from the start, into the emerging Warren Wilson sustainability vernacular:

Climate change poses one of the most daunting sustainability challenges of our time. Its projected impacts will affect environmental, economic, and social/cultural systems world-wide. Complex problem solvers, capable of synthesizing information across disciplines, will be required. Through the experiential engagement of the Triad, the community will participate in the interdisciplinary problem solving needed to address this formidable challenge.

In 2007, the Arthur Vining Davis Foundations invited President Pfeiffer to propose a curriculum initiative that would repurpose environmental literacy. Our team from Academic Affairs and the Environmental Leadership Center developed a grant request for an interdisciplinary, theme-based curriculum that used "full-cost accounting" as the conceptual tool to "encourage broad analysis of full environmental costs and diffuse the tendency to solve environmental problems from disciplinary silos" and to "assess the social, cultural, scientific, environmental, and economic cost of one pressing environmental issue each year, from a global and regional perspective. Central to this model, students will participate in community-based research to deepen their problem-solving skills."

Leadership Adopts New Paradigm

When we learned the grant was funded, we were elated . . . and terrified. Faculty would need to embark upon a steep learning curve to shape team teaching skills across disciplines and personalities and establish a replicable model for inquiry. Students would have to learn a new framework for analyzing complex community issues. And leaders of this institution, famed for "walking its talk," would come to question whether this new curriculum conferred an obligation to "deepen *their* problem-solving skills."

We took a lead role at the Environmental Leadership Center in championing sustainability as a decision-making framework. Drawing from the concept of "full-cost accounting," and with input from faculty sustainability experts, we developed a model for the president and his advisory council to pilot, along with a rationale steeped in the college's tradition of walking its talk.

Fundamental to this new decision-making process was asking many questions. Herman Daly, keynote at the college's 2009 Headwaters Gathering, invoked the physicist John Wheeler: "We make our world by the questions we ask. If we want to make a different world, we need to ask a different set of questions." The leadership team's adoption of sustainable decision making would mean asking new questions—a qualitative and quantitative change in business as usual.

In June 2007, the president and his advisory council formally adopted sustainability as the framework for institutional decision making and agreed that they would serve as the college's de facto Sustainability Committee.[4] They departed for their annual summer retreat with a daunting new challenge and the three baseball caps to assist the deans of Student Life, Academics, Work, Service and Admission; the vice presidents for Finance and Advancement; and the president with institutional planning. They were to make their case, for proposals ranging from new positions and capital expenses to division changes or degree tracks with a rationale that addressed the short- and long-term impacts represented by the triple bottom line caps. They struggled with the change. As one of the president's advisory council members recently recalled, "At first, the hats seemed too big for our various administrative heads and we were not sure which one to put on. Then the cold reality set in. We would each need to wear every hat . . . at the same time."

While the president and his council bridged the divide from formal adoption to practice—a process peppered with the challenges of shifting to a new paradigm in a fast-paced, decision-making environment—the Environmental Leadership Center introduced the model to the campus and to the region. Using GIS maps instead of baseball caps, the campus community, along with regional leaders, examined water quality issues through multiple filters for streams tainted, in part, by straight piping from manufactured housing. With sustainability as the framework for question asking, the water quality issue quickly reframed as a complex web of social justice, political, economic, and environmental impacts that called for a much wider slate of remedies. We posed the question, "Who, besides the water quality experts, must be present at the table to solve this complex problem?"

Faculty, staff, and students warmed to this interpretation of sustainability. It was inclusive and empowering. The process for arriving at a sustainable decision was equally relevant to students deliberating how to spend their Friday nights and work crews deciding whether to install paper towels or electric hand dryers in the bathrooms. It was as relevant to Work and Service as to Academics, where an interdisciplinary approach to problem solving had been brought into focus by the grant-funded curriculum.

Model Adapts to Realities

In July 2008, President Pfeiffer elevated sustainability to a seat at the leadership table with his official announcement of a new position, Chief Sustainability Official, noting that he had "asked the Executive Director of the Environmental Leadership Center to join the President's Advisory Council in the role of Chief Sustainability Official." Within a week, the president and his newly expanded advisory council were seated at their annual summer retreat with a question about enrollment growth on the table. In my new role, I was charged to "provide leadership for the assessment and the discussion of sustainable decision making." The right-sizing discussion for different enrollment scenarios provided me with an entry point for a sustainability analysis. The issue was loaded with specific, logical, cause-and-effect impacts that were easy to map and difficult to dismiss.

What environmental, economic, and community qualities define a right-sized, high-functioning institution? The discussion ranged from appropriate faculty/student ratio to adequate dining facilities, and from the practice of energy reduction measures throughout campus to sufficient wellness programs and financial aid to ensure a diverse community—and more. The sustainability analysis revealed the scope, the interdependence, and the extent of the variables that must be kept in balance to ensure a high-quality Warren Wilson experience, no matter the size of the student population.

In the months that followed, the president and the advisory council adapted the sustainability framework to their team style. Without a doubt, everyone at the table was committed in concept. Integrating sustainability as a working ethos, however, required a fundamental shift in orientation from the good of one's division to the common good; from calculating the benefit for the current year to the impact years down the road. It required extra time for broader analysis and for collaboration between divisions to accomplish interdependent goals. And implementing this shift to focus on long-term impacts in the midst of a gnawing, economic downturn tested the strength of the commitment.

To warrant investing precious extra time in this new decision logic, addressing sustainability's comprehensive scope of questions had to *prove* to result in better decisions for the college. The new protocol evolved from baseball caps and flow charts to a preference for less formal and more self-directed application—a habit of mind that was demonstrated time and again by the shift in the questions posed by the team to analyze the issues at hand.

Whereas room assignments for winter break program participants were previously based upon room availability throughout the array of residence halls, we now discussed the economic and environmental benefit of clustering participants in a few buildings, perhaps even the "green" ones, and setting back the heat in the others. Applying full-cost analysis to this operational decision revealed new, game-changing information. Slowly but steadily, the sustainability analysis began to penetrate the council's decision making, and when it did, it often resulted in an outcome that was better for the institution. We fondly coined this new decision-making process *sustainifying*.

Campus Adopts Working Ethos

Away from the table, however, the pace was altogether different. From 2008 to 2009, the translation of sustainability as a working ethos within each division proceeded rapidly. To name a few examples, Human Resources included sustainability as a metric in annual employee evaluations; Admission and Advancement integrated sustainable practices into their off-campus protocols; the Work Program included sustainability as a metric for student work-crew evaluations; Facilities Management incorporated sustainability as a core value in its service mission; faculty, students, and staff completed a preliminary review of sustainable practices using AASHE's first Sustainability Tracking, Assessment & Rating System (STARS) tool; the college adopted a Sustainable Vehicle Policy; and Student Life added a sustainability component to First-Year Student Orientation.

The Environmental Leadership Center hosted its second regional conference in 2008 to "promote sustainable community practices in the mountain region"; the President appointed a Sustainable Foods Task Force to guide dining services purchasing practices; we launched a cross-sector Sustainability Working Group; and the grant-funded sustainability curriculum embarked upon a semester-long pilot. Not surprisingly, an Admission survey indicated that more than 75 percent of Warren Wilson student applicants were "closely split among a wide range of features" in rating what is important to them. "Environmental awareness, community, sustainability, service learning, and cross-cultural understanding are the top five."

In spring 2009, Warren Wilson prepared to write a new, five-year strategic plan. Over the course of several surveys, sustainability, along with other values, was tested to determine its rank in the order of priorities. More than 85 percent of the Warren Wilson community agreed with this statement: "Provide leadership for the global community by continuing to integrate and model sustainable practices in all aspects of life at Warren Wilson College." The five-year strategic plan was completed and approved by the trustees in April 2010. "Sustainability—environmental responsibility, social and economic justice"—premiered as one of the college's five core values with the breadth of meaning gained through the robust discourse of the previous decade.

Leadership Commitment Renders Diverse Benefits

True to the college's tradition of a "working education," the president and his advisory council learned by doing. In advance of the college's formal articulation of a sustainability ethos, leadership put into play a working definition which provided fodder for the campus discourse and positive benefit to the community. To what degree their formal commitment to sustainable decision making influenced the cascade of actions that followed may be debated, but without a doubt it was influential. And with the right-sizing debate abuzz on campus, the decision-making commitment provided a measure of comfort. Sustainability practiced this way served as an accountability metric through which the leadership team's actions could be viewed, especially for sensitive issues like growth. Furthermore, sustainability was inclusive—relevant to every discipline and division.

The value of the decision-making model to the leadership team itself is significant. The first of Wendell Berry's seventeen rules for a sustainable economy speaks to the model's greatest value: "Always ask of any proposed change or innovation: What will this do to our community? How will this affect our common wealth?" (Berry 1994). To Herman Daly's point, we shape our college by the questions we ask. So first and foremost, decisions made this way are simply better long-term institutional decisions. Data gathered about the short- and long-term economic, environmental and social justice/community impacts of a proposed action—whether to add a new dorm or a new graduate level program—reveals unimagined costs down the road and options that will work best over time. Next, with the pace at which each division is incorporating sustainability into their practices, the hands-on use of the framework by the leadership team prepares them to lead the implementers. And finally, though the use of the model at the table is informal, the standard by which the decision will be judged by the community is not. The model serves to remind the team of the lens through which the campus will view their decisions.

Lessons Support Leadership Engagement

The adoption of sustainability as a working ethos at Warren Wilson's leadership table has led to several overarching lessons:

• Leadership has a responsibility to ask the right questions. It is true that, "We make our world by the questions we ask."

• Champions of this new paradigm require patience, tenacity, empathy, flexibility, abiding hopefulness, and a seat at the leadership table.

• Engagement in a hands-on process like decision making personalizes a construct as vague as sustainability and increases the likelihood of its adoption as a working ethos.

• Campus culture directs the working definition: for Warren Wilson, sustainability best infuses the community as a habit of mind rather than an outcome.

• Sustainability practiced as a decision-making framework strengthens community engagement by legitimizing a more diverse stakeholder pool.

• Leadership engagement in the sustainability discourse influences campus engagement.

• Positive results lead to further use of the model.

• Over time, decisions will result in either positive or negative consequences which will help to ground truth the nebulous destination called "sustainable."

Discourse and Action Advance the Mission

Warren Wilson's history is steeped in innovation that addresses the pressing issues of the day with a practical engagement in solutions. We believe that this approach resonates with the broader task of higher education. Our hope is that the discourse and the actions that advance Warren Wilson's mission to define responsible citizenship for the twenty-first century will contribute to discussions everywhere.

Acknowledgments

For their contributions to the shaping of this chapter the author especially wishes to thank Paul Bartels, PhD, Division Chair of the Sciences and former Faculty Sustainability Facilitator; Ben Anderson, Director of Media Relations; Richard Blomgren, Vice President for Admission and Advancement; Sandy Pfeiffer, PhD, former Warren Wilson president; and the members of the President's Advisory Council.

Notes

1. Read full resolution at www.aaup.org/AAUP/pubsres/academe/2003/JA/AW/AM.html.

2. Learn about pattern language at Christopher Alexander's website: www.patternlanguage.com.

3. Explore the college's formal commitments at www.warren-wilson.edu/environmental/sustainability/main.php.

4. Visit www.warren-wilson.edu/~ELC/sustainability/sustainable_decision_making.php to learn about this model.

References

Berry, Wendell. 1994. Conserving Communities. Address for Seed Savers Exchange Annual Conference and Campout, Decorah, Iowa, 1994.

Wheeler, John A. 1974. The Universe as Home for Man. *American Scientist* 62 (November/December): 683–691.

16

Sustainability as Turnaround: The Case of Unity College

Mitchell Thomashow

Unity College, founded in 1965, is a small, environmental liberal arts college in Maine. Its curricular emphasis is science, service, and sustainability, with a strong field-based, experiential approach to learning. Its small student body (570), relatively compact size (90 acres), and rural location provide outstanding opportunities for sustainability initiatives, especially those involving alternative energy and organic agriculture.

When I arrived at Unity College in July 2006 as the new president, I was green in two ways. I was "green" as in naive—an inexperienced, "newbie" college president. I had never worked in an undergraduate setting, or with a board of trustees, and I had never been the chief executive of an organization. I was also "green" as in being a long time advocate for environmental sustainability. I made it clear to the search team that my most prominent aspiration was to enable Unity College to become a truly exemplary sustainable campus.

Unity, I was told, by both the search team and the search firm, was a "diamond in the rough." The college possessed heart and grit, interesting students, a hands-on faculty, an experiential approach to learning, and unlimited potential. Yet it was not very well known nor was it particularly distinguished. It was not selective in its admissions process, its curriculum was rather traditional for an environmental liberal arts college, and it had no signature programs or facilities. Unity College derived its revenue almost exclusively from tuition and was, to put it mildly, resource strapped. It had just been through a difficult stretch that resulted in mistrust regarding the administration. The college desperately needed active and engaged leadership. It was poised for significant change and a much-needed turnaround. I was naive, as well, in that I didn't have a sense of the scope of the challenge I signed on for.

Fortunately, there was a small core group of intrepid students, staff, and faculty who had initiated a variety of sustainability initiatives, including comprehensive energy assessments, modest gardens, and a few courses. Yet these were spotty approaches never fully endorsed by the college administration, and surely not perceived as deeply rooted in either the mission or the master plan for the college. Consequently, the sustainability advocates were a bit jaded and isolated when I arrived, feeling that they never had the depth of institutional support they required. They were skeptical as to whether I would really be able to make a difference, worried particularly about the resource limitations, the lack of sustainability awareness of the board of trustees, and the relative campus indifference to these challenges, particularly at a so-called environmental college. They wondered, too, whether their new president had the administrative experience, the "technical" sustainability expertise, and the fundraising capability to make it all work. They were correct to have such doubts. My challenge was not only to build sustainability initiatives into the DNA of the college, but also to help the college gain confidence in its own ability to move forward on these issues.

Thanks to the collaborative work of an extraordinary group of staff, students, and faculty, the undaunted support of the board of trustees, the growing national sustainability movement, and the receptiveness of both the campus and the community, we were able to transform Unity College into an exemplary sustainable campus. We did this on a shoe-string budget, what we referred to as "real-time frugal sustainability." It was clear to me as a first-time college president that many aspects of Unity College's turnaround could be framed within the sustainability agenda. We integrated all of the crucial indicators for improving a college's academic and financial standing (selectivity, retention, recruitment, reputation, academic excellence, community service, fiscal stability, fundraising, governance, student life, and campus morale) around our collective emphasis on sustainability initiatives.

This five-year effort embodied many aspects of leading a "turnaround" effort. Although Unity is a very small college (570 students) on a rural campus in an out of way place, I am convinced that the basic principles of our approach are relevant to any college or university. A great characteristic of American higher education is the extraordinary variety of types of institutions. Surely every institution will forge its own idiosyncratic path. Yet there are patterns of change intrinsic to a sustainability turnaround. This essay aspires to encapsulate some of the key features of the Unity College experience, by elaborating on a dozen rules of thumb.

(1) Sustainability Is the Turnaround

A stunning convergence links the volatile global economy with planetary ecological challenges. On the one hand, individuals, communities, and nations alike are facing extraordinary economic uncertainty. Pressed by unprecedented debt, at a variety of institutional and personal scales, there is a budget-balancing mood afoot. The premise is that by overspending, we have robbed future generations of their wealth. The solution is to cut budgets, live within our means, stash cash, and invest prudently. Yet the economy will only be recharged when there is enough spending and investment to catalyze growth and productivity. The ecological challenge is similar. By "overspending" our resource base, we have "overtaxed" the biosphere, straining the future of human and ecological systems so we can live affluently in the present.

Sustainability is essentially a response to this planetary economic and ecological challenge. Its premise is that there is a correspondence between the economy and the biosphere. We have to simultaneously balance our economic and ecological budgets, conserving (saving) our resources, and investing them prudently and wisely. Hence the idea of sustainability asks us to think more carefully about how we live, suggesting that ecological criteria serve as the foundation of economic decisions. The economy should still thrive, produce, and grow, but it must do so in a more ecologically balanced way.

Higher education is at a similar crossroads. It is under enormous pressure to reduce costs, provide the public with value for its investment, and develop measures of accessibility and accountability that balance learning and value. Like governments, many campuses are thinking deeply about their priorities, and giving careful thought to educational and financial resilience. In that way, colleges and universities all require "turnaround" agendas. From curriculum to infrastructure, across constituencies, the role of presidential leadership is to guide campuses through these difficult times.

Sustainability is the turnaround. Whether we are describing energy innovations and efficiency measures, campus food-growing systems, green construction and materials, or the curricular changes that ensure a vital and prepared twenty-first-century workforce, colleges and universities can save money, invest in the future, work with the community, become crucibles of innovation, and lead the way to a sustainable future. These initiatives matter for the campus itself, the surrounding community, the regional and national economy, and global ecosystem services.

When college presidents articulate this convergence, when they embed these ideas deeply in the DNA of their campus, when they challenge faculty to translate this reality into the basic curriculum for undergraduates and professional schools, when they challenge the senior leadership to use their political authority to implement sustainability initiatives, then their institutions embody the very turnaround that is required of the whole community.

(2)   Demonstrate the Linkages between Sustainability, Mission, and Finances

At Unity College, I was convinced that building sustainability initiatives into the core of the college's DNA would provide its constituents with a coherent mission, establish Unity as a leader in the field, and provide a framework for all aspects of my presidency. Further, a sustainability mission was consistent with institutional values and could be applied specifically to the Unity College turnaround challenge, from infrastructure development to curriculum. I understood that all of the key planning documents, financial orientations, and political constituencies required alignment, agreement, and consensus.

I started with the board of trustees. As a new college president, my priority was to visit board members at their homes to better understand their values and visions for the college. I conceived these visits as a mini-research project. I designed a suite of questions to provide consistency and data for a full report. One question addressed the perceived meaning of sustainability. Unity was unique in that the board of trustees represented an interesting variety of environmental and political perspectives. There was a notable "rod and bullet" crowd of avid fishers and hunters. They were conservative politically, disdainful of taxes, and frugal in their outlook. There was also a more politically progressive constituency of environmental activists and NGO types. I found that everyone was intrigued with the idea of sustainability. The progressives liked its consistency with their ecological world view. The conservatives embraced the inherent cost-savings and efficiency. To further enhance this consensus, the interim provost and I conceived the term "real-time, frugal sustainability" to distinguish the Unity College approach. By this we meant that Unity's would apply a hands-on approach, geared to specifically low-cost campus improvements.

Next was the budget process. This involved several stages over a five-year period. Initially my priority was to open the process to the entire community. We built trust and emphasized good communication about budget expenditures. Second, I insisted that the sustainability coordinator (see below) work closely with the Vice President of Finance to ensure that all decisions around buildings and procurement were closely scrutinized for both fiscal and ecological criteria. Third, when I initiated a search for a new chief financial officer, I wrote the job description so as to highlight the college's emphasis on sustainability. We supported this orientation by sending her to a variety of sustainability-related finance workshops. Eventually a sustainability outlook permeated all budget decisions on campus.

Simultaneously I initiated a new master-planning process (Unity 2020). Although the college had been through this process before, and was somewhat skeptical about having to do so again, we emphasized campus-wide participation, with much student input, and a clear sustainability focus. By engaging in this consensual decision-making process we further broadened the campus commitment to sustainability. We rewrote the campus mission statement, updated the strategic plan, and discussed our "real-time, frugal sustainability" approach in all campus publications. The public relations people wrote numerous stories about our efforts; we initiated several sustainability-related blogs and "branded" the campus philosophy and working methods accordingly.

(3) Build Sustainability Initiatives into Job Descriptions

At one of my first senior staff meetings during the earliest days of my presidency, I suggested that we build sustainability initiatives into job descriptions and annual evaluations. While discussing their annual performance goals, employees would generate sustainability-related tasks that would improve all aspects of their operations. I weathered a skeptical response, listening to the customary litany of excuses, at which point I good-naturedly stood up and started to leave the room. I said that I thought I was hired to become the president of "America's Environmental College," Unity's bold motto, but surely this was the wrong place. It was clear that the group got the message. I sat down and we had a serious discussion about how to implement this idea.

In subsequent discussions senior staff discussed their sustainability goals with their teams. Within a year this approach had an enormous impact on campus. The Dean of Student Life, in conjunction with the Director of Residential Life, and ultimately the residence hall advisers, developed a suite of behavior change ideas, events, and competitions. The Vice President for Enrollment Management worked with the Dean

of Admissions and the admissions counselors to develop sustainability-
relevant recruitment and marketing strategies. The Director of College
Advancement geared our fundraising efforts around Unity as an exemplary sustainability campus. The events coordinator planned a "green"
commencement. By my third year on campus, these efforts were so intrinsic to the life of the institution that I would learn second-hand of exciting
initiatives. It was no longer just my agenda. Sustainability was becoming
incorporated into most aspects of campus life.

(4)   Hire and Empower a Sustainability Coordinator

I am inspired and delighted with the number of colleges and universities
that now employ sustainability coordinators. These positions take on a
variety of forms and titles depending on the size, orientation, and disposition of the institution. If you visit the annual Association for the Advancement of Sustainability in Higher Education (AASHE) conference, there
are hundreds of these professionals, coming from all kinds of substantive
backgrounds, with a diverse set of skills and experiences. They represent
a new vanguard of institutional change.

Yet these positions are all relatively new (mainly developed since 2005),
contain highly ambitious portfolios, and ask the individuals involved to
do the work of a dozen people. This is due less to the insensitivity of their
supervisors than the daunting tasks at hand. Further, most of these folks
have some kind of technical expertise, or they are sustainability general-
ists, but they are unlikely to have management or leadership training.
Their professional originality is unsurpassed, marked by the fact that in
many cases they created unique occupational niches, which have now become intrinsic to the field—the new sustainability professional. Given the
complexity of their challenges, it is easy for their work to seem stuck in a
morass of institutional bureaucracy, and often that is how they perceive
their impact.

One of the best ways to deal with this situation, regardless of institutional scale, is to have the sustainability officer report directly to the
president or vice chancellor of the institution. At a very large university,
the sustainability officer should take on the status of vice president. At
a smaller college, there is every reason for the coordinator (or whatever
the title) to report directly to the president. In my experience this ac-
complishes a great deal. Most importantly the coordinator now has the
required stature to get things done, especially if she or he is perceived as
one of your closest advisers. Secondly, you have weekly updates as to

the various sustainability operations on campus. Third, you can give the coordinator specific guidelines about the most important things to accomplish. In the case of Unity College, I emphasized four priorities: (1) galvanize the students and employ them as your work force; (2) make sure that the Climate Action Plan (as required by the American College and University Presidents' Climate Commitment) is moving forward; (3) work with students and faculty on the STARS (Sustainability Tracking, Rating & Assessment System) process; (4) network well with your peers in the region to insure collaborative problem solving and mutual support.

(5) Use the Bully Pulpit

I used my college presidency as an opportunity to reiterate the importance, meaning, virtue, and challenge of sustainability. For starters, I considered the number of hours I spent in a given week attending meetings and/or events. My responsibilities included weekly meetings with a senior team, various committee assignments, individual appointments, board of trustees meetings, gatherings of professional associations, keynote addresses, and an assortment of cyclical events, including commencement, convocation, parents welcome, and other introductions.

My calendar was typically bookended with such commitments. The wonderful challenge of this schedule is to find a way to say something meaningful, without repeating yourself too often, and to do so in such a way that different constituencies look forward to hearing what you have to say. My view is that college presidents have much more influence than they think, and much less than they would like to have. These public appearances, regardless of size or importance, represent a terrific opportunity. One college president once said to me that such speaking engagements are the best chance she ever had to demonstrate educational leadership.

A leader must often encourage people to remember why they, in their shared mission or goal, do what they do, why their work is important, how they can maximize their impact, and how they are contributing to a greater good. I thought (and hoped) that people looked forward to our meetings because they had a purpose, and they were constantly framed within the broader sustainability initiatives of our college. Internally, students, staff, and faculty seem to enjoy being reminded of our collective vision, and they shared with me their appreciation for different perspectives and takes on it. Externally, our constituencies were excited to hear about what we were doing and were intrigued to follow our progress.

If the leader handles this challenge well, other members of the organization will take similar roles. It is good practice to send students, staff, faculty, and senior leadership to a variety of conferences and gatherings. When they carry a sustainability vision and express it intelligently and discretely, they take greater pride in their institution, and have a better understanding of how their work contributes to a collective effort.

The whole college becomes an educational leader, or bully pulpit if you will, to call attention to its efforts, explain its significance, and frame its mission within the larger generational context of sustainability leadership and planetary well-being. The president's role is to articulate the new sustainability-related mission, and then the institution, in turn, articulates it.

(6)   Practice What You Teach

On a college campus, a dynamic community where people explore values, ideals, and aspirations, it is necessary that we practice what we teach. And we learned to start where we live! The various constituencies (students especially) are always ready to point out hypocrisy, inconsistency, deflection, ambiguity, or ambivalence. Indeed, an important leadership quality is the willingness to listen to such criticism, while simultaneously acting respectfully and exercising legitimate authority.

I found that on a small college campus (but this is certainly true at all institutions), the community observes its leader and itself very carefully. How you live and the choices an institution makes will be the ultimate arbiter of its values and commitments. Symbolic gestures and practical life habits are closely scrutinized.

When I arrived at Unity College, there wasn't any presidential housing. I suggested to the board of trustees and the whole campus community, that we construct a Leadership in Energy and Environmental Design (LEED) Platinum–certified, zero carbon, presidential residence that could serve as the focal point of our future sustainability efforts. It was essential that we do this in a way to bring attention to our efforts and yet do so without ostentation. Our commitment to sustainability had to match the resource-strapped ethos of our campus. Hence the residence had to be small, reasonably priced, and reflect a blend of private and public objectives. Thanks to the inspiration and vision of Tedd Benson (Bensonwood Homes), we built the Unity House, a brilliant solar home that became a landmark and a source of pride for the entire campus. We financed it by using the president's housing allowance as the monthly payment, and taking a modest chunk of capital from our precious plant fund.

There is much to say about the various challenges involved while initiating and completing this project, including the legitimate skepticism from some campus constituencies who questioned the priority of such an expense. In my view the Unity House was a testimony to the college's commitment to sustainability, allowing us to bring distinguished visitors to campus, and providing a locus for fundraising efforts (including a green residence for students). The Unity House brought outstanding publicity to the college, helped recruit my successor, and made a wonderful public statement about living what we teach. It became a great source of pride for the college.

This project was merely the keystone for dozens of "practice what you teach" campus efforts, including growing more food, serving more local food in the cafeteria, serving local food at catered events, experimenting with a variety of alternative energy sources (wood pellets, wind), planting wildflower gardens, exploring composting and recycling options, initiating rural carpooling, and an entire gamut of operational and facilities improvements.

Every institution has an array of similar choices. When the college president aspires to live as a role model for sustainability it is more likely that the whole college will join the effort. The entire community will be better prepared to exercise sustainability leadership.

A caveat. Despite our best efforts, we inevitably made mistakes, and there were countless ways that we could have done more or improved our policies. Further, the idiosyncrasies and inconsistencies of our efforts were inevitable. Its far better to use such mistakes or dilemmas as teaching opportunities, than it is to be defensive about them, or to fall into a precious political correctness that will only encourage detractors.

(7) Reward Innovation

Whenever I met a new faculty member, I would suggest several priorities. "Your job," I said, "is to train a new generation of sustainability leaders who can enter the workforce and make a real difference in their communities. Take them into the field, provide them with rigorous hands-on experiences, try bold and engaging teaching techniques, and deepen their enthusiasm for learning. If you come up with interesting new ideas and approaches, we'll find ways to support, encourage, and reward you." I asked the faculty to overhaul the curriculum, and develop a sequence of programs that reflected our strengths, emphasizing science, sustainability, and service. I told them that I wouldn't interfere in their discussions, but I was always available to help.

We created a senior staff spirit that emphasized service to the campus. Our administration aspired to make things easier, provide opportunities, reduce bureaucracy, and open channels of communication. We kept our doors open and performed a great deal of "management by walking around." We encouraged staff professional development, especially around sustainability, change management, and organizational process.

Like many resource-strapped colleges, we were always vigilant regarding our budgets. Our challenge was finding ways to reward innovation without adversely impacting the bottom line. We developed two modest revenue streams for supporting sustainability initiatives. First, I kept a discretionary fund in the president's office. It was designated to support student, faculty, and staff development for innovative sustainability ideas. We sent mixed teams to conferences, offered small seed grants to interesting campus projects, and worked with all campus constituencies to figure out inexpensive ways to try out interesting ideas. Second, we made sure that the College Advancement Office was geared toward finding support for sustainability initiatives. We received numerous small grants to enhance vegetable growing infrastructure, install a wood pellet heating system, perform a comprehensive energy analysis, promote community wind energy assessment, build a small barn, and support faculty research.

A primary function of senior leadership is to provide a learning and working environment that enhances collaboration, facilitates creative thinking, encourages risk taking, and celebrates success. The quickest way to catalyze campus buy-in is to reward the innovators and to let them know they have your support.

(8)   Utilize the Arts

Art provides a cognitive advantage. At the core of understanding sustainability, biodiversity, and climate change is a perceptual challenge. These issues require a broad understanding of spatial and temporal variation, the foundation of assessing environmental change. Sustainability, above all, requires an understanding of scale. Art projects use imagination to convey scale. They are a bridge to scientific understanding. Further, art projects catalyze some of the emotional responses surrounding these issues, from despair and grief to wonder, celebration and gratitude.

At Unity College, we emphasized the arts and humanities using three convergent approaches—publications, gatherings, and public art. I organized a meeting with several of the humanities faculty and asked them if they were interested in developing an annual publication to explore creative sustainability, a journal that would include prose and artwork. We quickly agreed that this would enable us to establish Unity College as a national sustainability voice, especially if we organized a statured editorial board, and sought refreshing new ideas and contributions. The journal was funded out of the president's office. With a very modest budget, and the outstanding work of students, staff, and faculty, we created *Hawk and Handsaw: The Journal of Creative Sustainability*.

Second, we received funding support to organize an "Art of Stewardship" conference. We brought fifty artists, scientists, and sustainability professionals to campus. We asked them to envision the college as a campus canvas for environmental art. They presented us with several dozen ideas, including mandala sand paintings, murals on the sides of buildings, recycled-materials art sculptures, soundscape designs, native plant sculptures, and landscape artwork capturing the movements of flora and fauna.

Third, several members of the arts faculty were inspired to implement the conference ideas by using their classes accordingly. They used the art curriculum to engage their students by developing a suite of public art projects on campus. Within months, the entire campus took on a new look. Art projects would spontaneously appear in all kinds of campus venues. The faculty also worked closely with local artists to utilize the entire campus as a community gallery.

These projects were constructed at minimal expense and provided students, faculty, and community artists with a wonderful venue for displaying their work. The campus became much more interesting, more attractive to visitors, and a source of great pride for the artists.

Sustainability should entail aesthetics every step along the way. The people who live in a place should have opportunities to make it their own through ephemeral and permanent artistic installations. This has the great advantage of making a campus a more vital and dynamic place. Even better, every art project contributes to the sense that the campus is a place in space and time, a living and working environment that creates an aesthetic mark on the landscape. Ultimately, this kind of a collaborative process allows the campus to experience reciprocity between the built environment and the ecological landscape.

(9)   Participate in Regional and National Networks

Ideally, each college and university is a node in a wider sustainability network. In the spirit of experimentation and collaboration, institutions develop uniquely interesting approaches to climate action planning, food growing, materials use, governance, and curriculum. Allocating time and resources to a broader collaborative approach contributes to an emerging collective voice. In the United States, many sustainability organizations have sprouted since 2005, including AASHE, the American College and University Presidents Climate Commitment (ACUPCC), and the United States Green Building Council (USGBC). The remarkable emergence of these organizations, parallel to the development of regional and local groups, provides an extraordinary network of expertise, consultation, and innovation.

In formulating and implementing Unity College's sustainability voice, we emphasized the importance of a committed participating membership in these organizations. This allowed us to share our expertise, learn from our colleagues, participate in multiple conversations, see our own work from a broader perspective, identify ourselves as an aspiring contributor, further craft our "sustainability" brand, help the college gain visibility, and ultimately provide funding support. Equally important, we rewarded our innovators by sending them to a variety of conferences, webinars, and colloquia, encouraging them to offer presentations, join committees, and apply for awards. Our innovators included students, staff, and faculty, many of whom would engage in projects together, and join with their cohorts at other institutions. In my role as college president, I would attend many of these meetings, bring assorted teams with me, and provide support (as possible) for the necessary memberships and collaborations.

(10)   Integrate Sustainability and Community Service

Community service was central to Unity's sustainability initiatives. This served numerous objectives—constructive partnerships with a range of community non-profits, assistance to neighbors, and meaningful, hands-on student work. These projects contributed to the college's visibility, spawning funding partnerships, improving student retention, providing superb public relations and press coverage, ultimately resulting in enhanced college pride.

Community service was the foundation for interesting curricular applications. Faculty, staff, and students developed a magnificent portfolio of service projects, including community wind assessment programs, local energy retrofits in low income communities, food growing partnerships to enhance local food capacity and relieve regional hunger, and water quality testing programs, among many others. Students would report on their work at semester-end campus conferences, join their peers at other institutions, and continue these commitments during their breaks.

During the spring break, students self-organized regional service projects. The Student Government Association, with the support of the administration, developed a ten-day program at various sites in Maine, visiting communities that required assistance with a variety of sustainability initiatives. This kind of student leadership was one of the most inspiring aspects of campus life and became central to the ethos and identity of the college.

(11) Balance Urgency and Patience, Boldness and Compassion, Innovation and Tradition

Our sustainability initiatives were inextricably linked to substantial governance changes, the essence of Unity College's turnaround. In highlighting our achievements, I do not want my enthusiasm for our collective efforts to diminish the difficult challenges that accompany change. In most organizations, as in everyday life, people are typically resistant to change. There are many reasons for this, deeply embedded in the nature of organizational life and personal psychology. A full explanation of these dynamics is beyond the scope of this paper. I wish to reiterate the necessity of reflective change management, the importance of social intelligence, and the inevitable controversies that emerge in turnaround processes. In my experience I discovered that I was perennially balancing three interlocking tensions—urgency and patience, boldness and compassion, innovation and tradition.

As a new college president, I was driven by the converging necessities of institutional change and the sustainability imperative. Whenever possible, I reminded the campus that we had to adapt to the rapidly changing higher education environment, and we had a responsibility to make a strong commitment to sustainability. Yet, we could not move faster than the capabilities of the college would allow. On the one hand, there were some campus constituencies demanding that I take quicker action, and others that were very worried at what they considered the rapid pace of institutional change. We were moving too quickly for some and too slowly for others. The challenge for leadership is to find the right pace of change. This requires a good understanding of an institution's capacity for change. The leader has to patiently promote all the reasons why change is essential.

I understood that it would be easiest to work with staff and faculty who were most ready to change, and difficult to work with those who were change averse. I also had to recognize the importance of emotional regulation, for myself and for the campus. If I moved too quickly, only a few constituents would follow. If I moved too slowly, the college wouldn't change as quickly as required. If I pushed too hard, I would overtax myself and the campus. If I was lax, I would be perceived as ineffective, and I would be personally unhappy.

The sustainability agenda was ideal for conveying the urgency of change. Its values were conducive to campus identity. Its implementation allowed us to become a distinctive regional and national voice. The "assessment" requirements, such as the ACUPCC climate action planning process and the STARS program, allowed for a convergence between campus and planetary urgency. Still, our resources were limited and it took discretion and deliberation to build a consensual approach to this challenge.

I considered the balance between urgency and patience on a daily basis. I explored this issue both personally and publicly. As a leadership team and as a campus, we considered the pace of change. How quickly should we proceed? What is the campus carrying capacity for change? There is no formula for making this assessment beyond common sense, broad consultation, and social intelligence. We promoted a change agenda to the limit of people's capacity to internalize the process, erring on the side of urgency, but never forgetting the need for patience. I am convinced that raising this issue publicly helped convey its importance and brought a deeper understanding of how we could collaboratively achieve the required balance.

Some decisions, including personnel, budget, governance, and curriculum required bold measures. Others require compassion. Whenever I made a bold decision I had to reassure some constituencies that I understood the consequences of the decision, that I appreciated their concerns, and that I was considering the best interests of the whole organization. I never expected everyone to agree with me, but I hoped that if I acknowledged everyone's concerns, and then carefully explained my rationale, we could reach a common understanding. Typically we could find this balance. It was absolutely crucial that all members of the senior staff could act accordingly, recognizing that we were all learning how to manage change together.

Essentially we were changing the culture of the college. We were becoming a learning organization, capable of adapting to dynamic external circumstances, learning how to improvise, willing to make a mistake or two along the way, capable of embracing diverse points of view, while coordinating a unified approach to the future oriented around our sustainability agenda. As the leader, I had to help the college find its collective voice, enhancing its strengths, paying homage to its history and traditions, while enabling new directions and opportunities. Too much tradition holds you back. Too much innovation is upsetting.

Earlier in my tenure, a student asked me why sustainability was so important. She was an avid hunter. I asked her what she did with a deer after she killed it. She went into a lengthy explanation as to how she used all parts of the animal and that by doing so, she paid respect to the hunting tradition and the spirit of the animal. I explained to her that such a mentality was the very basis of sustainability and that Unity College was aspiring to take a similar approach to its future.

(12)   Celebrate Your Accomplishments

Given the daunting tasks of organizational change, the planetary sustainability challenge, and the volatile economy, it is easy to wonder whether one's own actions make any kind of difference. Every change agent asks such questions, and often despairs in the enormity of the burden. Yet the process of change yields its own rewards, and one can take great pleasure in the simple satisfactions of a job well done, achieving a common goal, and the sequence of seemingly minor accomplishments that add up to something much greater.

The task of leadership is to celebrate these accomplishments at every opportunity. There are dozens of ways to do this, from rewarding individuals, to calling attention to innovative ideas, to recognizing collective achievements. Everyone responds differently to accolades and congratulations. It is crucial to establish an atmosphere of community accomplishment.

What we find over time is that we accomplish much more than we ever thought we could, especially when we link individual efforts to the collective good. As I consider the five years I spent at Unity College, I am amazed at the number of sustainability initiatives that are now permanent aspects of college life. In a given moment, it never seemed like we were moving as fast as we needed to, and I was always aware that our progress was tentative, precarious, and based on sheer perseverance and collective will. As a leader, I would remind people of all the good work they were doing, but how much improvement they still needed to make. I do not think this feeling ever goes away, especially in regard to higher education, our planetary predicament, and the necessity of sustainable solutions. Indeed, we will not rest until we commonly acknowledge that sustainability is the turnaround, and it must become the basis of how we learn to live, and hence the very foundation of higher education.

17

Transformational Leadership at Furman University: Tradeoffs and Transitions

Angela C. Halfacre

Furman University, founded in 1826, is one of the United States' leading private liberal arts colleges. Furman's campus in Greenville, South Carolina, is nationally acclaimed for its beauty and the university's commitment to sustainability and community partnerships. The residential student body of 2,700 comes from all over the nation and around the world.

Transformational Leadership

When David E. Shi was inaugurated as Furman University's tenth president in 1994, he brought with him from Davidson College a career-long commitment to environmental stewardship. A cultural historian by training, he had written an influential book in 1985 titled *The Simple Life: Plain Living and High Thinking in American Culture*. For him, sustainability was both a personal passion as well as a civic and professional responsibility. For Shi, as a Furman professor explained, "sustainability wasn't an initiative, it was an imperative."[1]

It is one thing to promote sustainability at a college where a significant number of students are engaged in the effort, but it is much more challenging on a campus where few students are so inclined—and some are openly hostile to the premises and practices of sustainability. In this chapter, I explore how transformational, "top-down" presidential leadership made sustainability a strategic priority and cultural norm at Furman University over the past twenty years. That Furman is situated in upcountry South Carolina, one of the most ideologically conservative regions in the nation, makes this case study even more illuminating.[2]

What David Shi was able to achieve over sixteen years illustrates that transformative leadership involves much more than mere managerial skills; it involves the strategic repositioning of an institution to align its ideals with its actions (Gordon and Berry 2006; Manolis et al. 2009).

Transformational leaders are skilled communicators and ongoing learners who are adept at inspiring and empowering others to be change agents (Burns 1978; Bass 1985; Bennis and Nanus 1985; Northouse 2007). Transformational leaders create a compelling vision and possess the conviction and charisma to see it implemented—even in the face of considerable early resistance.[3]

The American South and the Furman University Context

Sustainability advocacy in the American South—a region distinctive for its suburban sprawl, car culture, reliance on coal-powered electricity, and widespread skepticism about environmental activism—poses particular challenges. At Furman in the 1990s, student, faculty, and staff critics lampooned sustainability as a misguided liberal crusade and a misappropriation of precious resources, a presidential priority lacking any immediate relevance to longstanding university priorities. The percentage of Furman freshmen during the decade of the 1990s who believed it "essential" or "very important" to become involved in programs to sustain the quality of the environment dropped from 41 percent to 19 percent (Annual Furman First Year Survey). Yet over time the persistence of transformational leadership in the face of such inertia generated profound cultural and sociopolitical changes on campus and in the larger community.

A university president determined to make sustainability and institutional priority must identify ways for key elements of the campus community to "buy in" to the new paradigm in the process of initiating new programs and encouraging new behaviors. The stunning beauty of Furman's 750-acre campus provided an initial rallying point to preserve the integrity of the landscape while making it more sustainable. Soon after his arrival at Furman, President Shi discovered a small but earnest group of professors and students (the Environmental Action Group) dedicated to promoting a multidisciplinary program in environmental studies (created in 1999) as well as fostering greater campus engagement with urgent environmental issues.

First Steps

With each passing year, Shi focused on sustainability-related initiatives that collectively would change the trajectory of Furman's ambitions from being a top regional college to being a college of national distinction in the field of environmental stewardship. To do so, he first recruited senior administrators eager to adopt aggressive approaches to energy management, "green" construction principles, curricular innovation, and behavioral change. He also worked closely with faculty to promote environmental studies. "As president," a faculty member recalled, "he gave the green light to move ahead, which stimulated our creative thinking." In 1995, for example, the departments of Earth and Environmental Sciences, Biology, and Chemistry launched the River Basins Research Initiative, a massive student/faculty research project analyzing how the rapid rate of development in the upcountry region of South Carolina was affecting water quality. The initiative evolved into the largest single research project in Furman's history. Funded by numerous outside grants, the ongoing multidisciplinary effort eventually came to involve over a dozen professors from seven departments as well as hundreds of students.[4]

Building Trustee Trust

By 1996, the combined efforts of engaged faculty, staff, and students across the campus had enabled the president to convince the trustees to designate environmental responsibility as an explicit priority of the university's new strategic plan, titled Furman 2001. This was no mean feat, for the trustees, like those at most institutions, included many who were initially skeptical of the significance and relevance of such initiatives. Some of them went along with Shi's recommendation not so much because they agreed with its premises but because they trusted his strategic judgment. Because of Furman's conservative cultural context, Shi emphasized the practical, bottom-line benefits of increased energy efficiency and renewable energy systems as well as the potential leadership role that the university could play on a national level. In discussing the strategic significance of sustainability with the trustees, he repeatedly referred to energy conservation projects as constituting a new form of "endowment" for the university in that they provided perennial budgetary savings for the college. He also championed the many other institutional benefits afforded by a broad-based emphasis on environmental stewardship: curricular innovation, new fundraising opportunities, and unique community-based research projects and municipal collaborations. Explicit trustee support was a crucial step in implementing Shi's vision, for it provided the university's commitment to sustainability with immediate legitimacy and credibility as well as access to resources. Not everyone embraced the new emphasis. Several students, especially self-identified conservatives, as well as faculty and staff members, expressed skepticism about such a comprehensive initiative, but the criticism was blunted by the board's action as well as Shi's ability to garner outside grants for most of the innovations.[5]

With the official endorsement of the board of trustees, Shi systematically set about integrating sustainable practices and projects across the university. For example, in 1998 he encouraged the board of trustees to require that all new campus buildings and all significant building renovations qualify for the U.S. Green Building Council's Leadership in Energy and Environmental Design (LEED) certification program. In 2003 Furman became the first organization in South Carolina to construct a LEED-certified building. By 2012 the university boasted eight LEED-qualified buildings.

In 2004 the board of trustees led the way among institutions of higher education in formally adopting environmental stewardship and sustainability as one of the five "pillars" of the Furman educational experience. Before doing so, the trustees engaged in a robust debate about the strategic viability of sustainability. Some questioned whether sustainability was simply a fad. How did it relate to the university's mission? In the end, however, they endorsed the idea, in large part because Shi persuaded them that "a sustainable campus will help endow the institution's future—in perpetuity." The trustees also trusted Shi; he had forged long-standing relationships with them in the process of addressing other needs (higher academic standards and faculty salaries, new facilities, greater diversity), and his efforts had paid off. While no trustee emerged as a champion of the strategic significance of sustainability, the board as a whole supported Shi's willingness to be a crusader in this arena. The trustees also liked Shi's emphasis on the academic dimensions of sustainability and the many opportunities for experiential learning it afforded, both on and off campus. As a former board chair recalled, the trustees were convinced that Furman graduates would benefit from the opportunity to understand sustainability "within a context of real world issues." The university's updated strategic plan in 2004, titled Engaging the Future, called for the university to "strengthen its commitment to the environment by promoting sustainability through educational programs, campus operations/construction practices, and public awareness initiatives." Shi's encompassing vision of sustainability, remembered a trustee, was breathtaking in its scope and distinctive for its emphasis on curricular and co-curricular opportunities. According to a professor, the president promoted a "holistic understanding of sustainability beyond simply 'greening the campus.'"

Next Steps: Assessment

In 2001 Shi appointed a Strategic Planning Working Group on Environ-mental Initiatives composed of trustees, faculty, staff, and students. Their task was to create an omnibus plan for integrating the principles and practices needed for Furman to become a truly sustainable campus. Over an eighteen-month period, the group crafted specific sustainability goals and initiatives with concrete numerical targets, projected budgets, and designated staff and faculty supervisors. The group's report, released in December 2003, provided an in-depth analysis of the university's sustain-ability commitment and achievements, as well as many recommendations to integrate sustainability more broadly across the campus and within the Greenville community.

During 2005 Shi was asked to co-chair the greater Greenville com-munity's own long-range strategic visioning process, called Vision 2025. Not surprisingly, sustainability quickly emerged as one of its hallmarks. That same year, Shi authorized the first comprehensive energy-use au-dit in Furman's history. It came on the heels of an ecological resource and footprint analysis of the university conducted by two student vol-unteers under faculty guidance. In 2005, Shi also contracted with Ida Phillips Lynch, an environmental journalist based in North Carolina, to develop an inventory of the university's sustainability efforts, strengths, and weaknesses. He had come to realize that there were so many sustain-ability-related initiatives occurring across the campus that no one knew everything that was happening, not even himself. Lynch interviewed many faculty, staff, students, and trustees. Her resulting "white paper" confirmed how much had been accomplished while highlighting the need to engage more students in the efforts. As she concluded, "Although the University's sustainability efforts have been effective from the top-down, they have yet to permeate student culture." A professor who joined the faculty in the fall of 2005 characterized the mainstream student senti-ment at the time:

It seemed that environmentalism, and for that matter sustainability, still carried a stigma [among most students]. It was perceived as an agenda being pushed by a small group of radical patchouli-wearing, dread-locked, tree-hugging student environmentalists whose job it was to get in the way of economic progress and somehow crimp the American lifestyle. The funny thing was that . . . the Environ-mental Action Group at that time was [actually] a small group of forward think-ing, environmentally-minded students, and their appearance no different than the typical Furman student. They were well dressed, well-kept, and extremely civil.

While there was burgeoning interest in sustainability across the campus, misperceptions were rampant, especially about the use of university funds for sustainability activities. To better engage—and inform—the students, Shi in 2005 asked Scott Derrick, the Director of Student Activities, to take on the additional duty of generating more student involvement with the university's sustainability efforts. Derrick, in turn, formed an Environmental Sustainability Committee composed of faculty, staff, and students. Within two years, it had become evident that such efforts needed a full-time director as well as a dedicated Center for Sustainability to provide more effective coordination of the university's rapidly expanding activities.

The academic year 2006–2007 was climactic for Furman's sustainability efforts. That year, David Shi was one of the first signatories of the American College and University Presidents' Climate Commitment (ACUPCC). He was also appointed to the ACUPCC national steering committee. That same year, the university launched the Year of the Environment, a year-long series of programs, speakers, and events promoting greater environmental awareness on campus. Also in 2007 the Andrew Mellon Foundation awarded an $850,000 grant to provide startup funding for the annual operations of Furman's new sustainability center, an idea first suggested by faculty members. But the center first had to be built and financed. To that end, Shi formed a unique partnership, years in the making, with *Southern Living Magazine*, Duke Energy Corporation, and an array of other vendors and contractors to construct a state-of-the-art LEED Gold-certified building to showcase environmentally sensitive construction practices and renewable energy systems. The "showcase home" served as a cover story in *Southern Living* magazine as well as the home for the new Center for Sustainability. Shi and Furman's provost, Dr. Thomas Kazee, endorsed the idea suggested by professors that the new center be administratively housed in the Division of Academic Affairs. They also agreed that the center's first director needed to be someone with experience as a classroom teacher, as a scholar, and as an academic administrator. I was pleased to be offered the position in 2008.[6]

Centering Sustainability

As the first director of Furman's Center for Sustainability (named for David E. Shi upon his retirement in 2010), I have been in a unique position to evaluate the strengths and weaknesses of transformational leadership designed to excite interest in sustainability on campus and in the greater community. I also have benefited from the multiyear groundwork of the administrators and staff members, trustees, professors, and students who helped make the university's commitment to sustainability holistic as well as self-sustaining. In July 2008, when I arrived at Furman to begin my work both at the Center for Sustainability and as a professor of political science and earth and environmental sciences, I was eager to help the institution advance its sustainability goals by adopting a more explicit systems-wide approach. I also worked with others to form a broader campus-wide coalition engaged with the sustainability effort so as to nurture mutually beneficial relationships and build even more trust in the enterprise.

After initial meetings with various students, professors, staff members, and administrators, including President Shi and Provost Thomas Kazee, I learned that the university's prolonged emphasis on sustainability had generated criticism as well as praise. Not everyone agreed with the university's commitment or applauded Shi's "crusading" leadership. Furman's "top-down" strategy had won national awards and attracted much attention, but it had also generated grumbling about other campus programs being shortchanged. Shi and Kazee acknowledged that any such designated strategic emphasis would generate charges of favoritism, and that was especially true with the sustainability campaign because it was readily linked by critics to a "liberal" agenda. A staff member reflected that "having sustainability as such an integral part of seemingly every discussion may have actually turned some people off to the concept." The political dynamics on campus made it important for me to curb my own enthusiasm for sustainability so as to reach out to all campus stakeholders and defuse misperceptions. On several occasions, I made mistakes typical of newcomers—often vacillating between the need to be decisive and energetic (and likely overstepping my bounds) while also being patient and deliberate enough to learn the values and nuances of a new campus culture before launching new initiatives. Throughout my career, I had stressed that sustainability necessarily involves a delicate balancing act involving frequent tradeoffs (economic, environmental, social equity); my new role required me to develop a better understanding of the particular tradeoffs needed at Furman while focusing on ways to involve all the various campus constituencies in the activities of the sustainability enter, especially faculty and students.

In 2008, sustainability was definitely "in the air" at Furman, but it suffered from continuing misperceptions across the campus about what sustainability meant, and what its role at Furman should be. Did it entail energy conservation and recycling, green buildings and new courses? Or all of those things and more? Many students remained indifferent and some were quite hostile. Several charged that their tuition dollars were funding the administration's "pet project," although, in fact, the funding was largely provided by corporations, foundations, donors, and government agencies. A 2009 editorial in the student newspaper expressed a common concern among conservative students: "Many of the ideas being tossed around for Furman's climate plan seem to be more of the same ill-advised policies, including restricting driving [and] covering acres of campus with unsightly and inefficient solar panels" (Mills 2009). At the same time, some staff members embraced the emphasis on sustainability as an opportunity to encourage controversial policy changes on campus they had long wanted. For example, a staff member sought my support in moving the university to a four-day work week; other staff members wanted me to endorse imposing additional restraints on faculty and staff travel to conferences.

I focused my initial campus conversations on asking questions and listening. I discovered that some professors had benefited from various sustainability initiatives related to campus operations and energy management to develop new curricular experiences and innovative teaching/ research opportunities. As many professors said, the president and provost created an environment where faculty members could dream big and think creatively about how best to incorporate sustainability into the academic arena. As one key faculty member put it, "David Shi led by providing space for ideas." By 2008, the Furman faculty had overwhelmingly approved a landmark general education requirement: every student must take at least one course examining human interaction with the environment. In addition, the university had raised millions of dollars in external funding to support various sustainability operations, programming, and facilities, including a new science building with dazzling sustainability components.[7]

What was not yet finalized was the scope of my position as director of the Center for Sustainability. There were few models to draw from, and the expectations across the campus were many and varied—and even contradictory at times. While it was exciting to have the opportunity to shape the precise elements of my job description in the first year, there were also widespread misperceptions about my role and that of the new center. I had arrived at Furman as an administrator with faculty status. I was eager to continue my research agenda, finish a book project that had been a decade in the making, and teach courses related to environmental policy and sustainability. The Sustainability Planning Group (later re-named Sustainability Planning Council) was ready to move forward with the crafting of the university's Climate Action Plan; I was asked to chair these efforts. Others wanted me to promote the Furman Farm and other sustainability projects on campus, help with the consideration of additional renewable energy platforms, serve as a host for visitors (including prospective donors) and more. A growing number of students were interested in working on sustainability-related research and taking classes with a new social scientist interested in environmental/community policy, perceptions, and problem-solving projects (i.e., I taught the first Environmental Policy course at Furman in 2009). As a new director, I also was appointed to numerous campus committees including: the President's Council, Administrative Council, and Department Chairs/Program Directors' Council.

The number of hats I was wearing was bewildering, and the scope of inquiries and expectations was dizzying. During one day in my third month on campus, I learned that the $850,000 check from the Mellon Foundation to establish our Center for Sustainability had arrived; that same day, I was called by a campus staff member who asked what type of toilet paper should be used in the Welcome Center. For understandable reasons, my position had become a catch-all resource for anything related to sustainability on campus—and often in the Greenville community as well. So throughout my first year I worked with the provost, to whom my office reported, to refine my priorities and educate the community about the actual scope of the center.[8]

During my first months on the job, I confirmed that the university's emphasis on sustainability provided an ideal bridge to the community and a framework for organizing innovative curricular and co-curricular research projects. At the same time, some members of the administration, I gradually realized, were providing only lip service in support of the president's focus on sustainability while privately denigrating it and expressing frustration with Shi's "obsession" and Kazee's preoccupation. None of this was surprising, of course. A decade before, people had made the same criticism of Shi's emphasis on engaged learning as the center-piece of the university's pedagogical approach. Campus communities are like all organizations: no major initiative (except salary increases) garners complete support. As I came to better understand the dynamics of Furman's campus politics, I focused on those areas that seemed to have the most strategic importance, especially as the onset of the Great Recession pinched the university's resources.[9]

Leveraging Leadership: Bringing More People under the Umbrella

Since 2008, we have stressed the importance of sustainability as a holistic educational experience that includes broad campus participation in strategic planning, faculty development, curricular innovation, and meaningful community partnerships. The institutional commitment by the board of trustees, the participation in the University Presidents' Climate Commitment, and the creation of the Center for Sustainability all set the stage for cascading institutional commitments and benefits, often in highly visible ways.

As a team, the administrators, faculty, students, and staff committed to Furman's focus on sustainability went to work after 2008 at a faster and even more committed pace. We expanded the Sustainability Planning Group to create a 124-member Sustainability Planning Council (yes, 124 members). Our strategy in expanding the number and diversity of participants in our planning efforts was to get more people across the campus inside the sustainability "umbrella," to help shift the emphasis from it being the administration's "pet project" to being one of the university's signature programs. As the Council explained to the campus community, sustainability "is integral to our institutional identity. It is what we are as an institution and not simply a program or set of programs." We also strove to encourage better communication and more engagement across the campus, and to draft a Sustainability Master Plan for the university. So we intentionally created a huge council to create a critical mass for spirited discussions and wider dissemination of information. We followed Provost Kazee's advice to "bring some of those who were skeptical of these initiatives into the conversation, to hear their arguments, and to ensure no one could say that we'd stacked the deck in favor of particular outcomes."

Since its inception, the Shi Center for Sustainability has deepened the engagement of the *academic* community in the university's sustainability efforts. The Shi Center is much less about campus operations than it is about educating students. Since its opening in 2008, the center has supported faculty members from all departments as they integrate elements of sustainability into their courses and research. Faculty development opportunities have included workshops for faculty funded by the Mellon Foundation (one-fifth of all faculty have participated to date), the center's affiliate faculty program (whereby professors capitalize on their existing research and teaching interests to create interdisciplinary collaborations), faculty sustainability research fellowships awarded to a handful of professors each year, and supporting interdisciplinary research around particular systems (e.g., food) and sense of place (e.g., environmental history / geography of Greenville). Making faculty collaboration across disciplines and departments a focal point of the center's mission has helped to "mainstream" the center into the academic program and community.

Students now have the opportunity to study sustainability through courses across the curriculum, and they may also take advantage of Furman's multidisciplinary sustainability-oriented "concentrations." In 2010, the faculty unanimously approved the nation's first undergraduate major in sustainability science offered by a private liberal arts institution. Gaining such robust approval was not easy, however. When the new major was first proposed in 2009, it was tabled because some faculty claimed that the administration was pressuring the faculty to design such a major. These claims had no basis in fact; the professors who created the major had conceived the idea over a decade before. Other faculty questioned whether sustainability science is a legitimate field of study. Such concerns led to an informal effort by several professors, especially the major's primary architect Brannon Andersen, to better explain the premises of the new major. Such efforts had dramatic results. When the proposal came up for a vote a second time, it passed without objection. By the fall 2012, there were forty-four students majoring in sustainability science. This expansion of the curriculum provided another tangible example of the relevance of sustainability to the university's academic program.

Still another major benefit of the university's emphasis on sustainability has been the opportunity to forge an array of new connections between Furman and the Greenville community. When I first met President Shi in 2008, he and I agreed that sustainability was especially suited for experiential learning activities. That has proven to be the case. Various faculty/student research projects, internships, and participation on community boards and task forces have enabled students, faculty, and staff to be more engaged than ever in the Greenville community. For example, when the City of Greenville unveiled its Greener Greenville sustainability and climate action plan at a public meeting in 2012, half of the ninety participants in the open forum were Furman students, faculty, or staff. Such collaborations between campus and community are exactly the type of rich learning experiences I had hoped we would have organized by year four of the center's work. Another major development in our efforts was the decision by the trustees to launch a fundraising effort in conjunction with President Shi's retirement. That project generated almost $2 million in endowment to subsidize the operations of the Center for Sustainability.[10]

Top Down to Transformational Leadership

Furman's top-down approach to incorporating sustainability may not be the ideal model, but it can be an inclusive, effective, and even necessary approach on campuses where student interest is initially tepid or even antagonistic. As Elizabeth MacNabb, the director of environmental programs for the Associated Colleges of the South, emphasized in 2010, "while it's important for sustainability to bubble up from the bottom . . . it MUST also come down from the top in order for serious change to occur." The presidential emphasis on sustainability for over a decade helped Furman generate substantial momentum and national attention as well as garner outside funding ($13 million in five years).

But is top-down sustainability sustainable? In 2009, during my first year as the center's director, Shi announced his plan to retire in June 2010. At the end of my second year, Provost Kazee accepted the presidency at the University of Evansville in Indiana. So within a matter of months, the two people who had initiated and led Furman's award-winning sustainability programs were gone. However, Shi's transformational leadership and Kazee's astute ability as an implementer left a deep imprint. When the board of trustees announced the search process for Furman's new president in 2009, the editorial board of the student newspaper declared that it would be crucial for the selection committee to choose a president who shares "the values of sustainability, diversity, and global awareness" (Editorial Board 2009). More comprehensive evidence of shifting student attitudes came in the form of a university-wide perception survey conducted by the center for sustainability in 2008 and 2011. In 2008, only 12 percent of Furman students believed that sustainability should be a high priority at the university. Just three years later, in 2011, 70 percent believed it should be a high priority of campus life. What had begun in 1994 as one president's inspiration and a handful of faculty members' innovation had become a prominent aspect of the campus culture. At the end of 2011, Furman's senior associate academic dean observed that sustainability "had become ingrained in Furman's culture; it is part of the fabric of our community. We no longer need to bring it to the forefront of everyone's attention because it is now a part of our mindset." Yes, there remains an ongoing challenge to reinforce the purpose and nature of sustainability as a new administration establishes different priorities, but sustainability retains its much of its significance and visibility.

In sum, the story of how sustainability has become a compelling new ethic at Furman and across higher education is as complicated and varied as it is inspiring. It shows how sustainability operates at the very nexus of liberal education and provides a concrete example of how colleges and universities can view sustainability-related initiatives as constituting a new form of endowment. As a Furman student observed in responding to another student's criticism of the sustainability efforts, "If examining ways to preserve life on earth isn't worth spending time on throughout our educational journey, I'm not sure what is" (Morris 2009). However contested the sustainability story has been at Furman, it has provided the university—and the Greenville community—with enduring benefits. As a professor noted in 2012, "David Shi was certainly a visionary who was absolutely instrumental in establishing Furman as a campus sustainability leader, and it will inevitably define his legacy."

On the eve of his retirement in 2010, Shi told a national audience that sustainability at Furman had become "a core principle and a transformational force." He highlighted the emergence of a "cadre of student leaders" who had become committed to promoting sustainability across the campus and in the community. "The fabric of campus life has indeed been altered." But he stressed in concluding that "the good work of nurturing our environment, whether a campus or a community, is never over. Nor should it be."

Acknowledgments

My sincere appreciation to editors Peggy Barlett and Geoff Chase as well as other critical and helpful contributing respondents and readers of earlier versions of this manuscript; these individuals helped to sharpen the focus of the chapter, improve substantially the tone and texture of the text, and correct factual errors.

Notes

1. For this chapter, I followed an ethnographic approach, and used my own participant observation data collected since 2008. Importantly, I conducted semi-structured interviews via phone and electronic communication in January and February 2012 to gather other perspectives that had more historical connection to the sustainability effort. I also analyzed the thematic content of several documents (including the student newspaper and other materials such as internal reports) to help illuminate the dynamics of the Furman case over the past twenty years. Interview data from seven board of trustees, five professors, and five administrators (including President Emeritus Shi and former provost Kazee) are critical in my analysis to inform my first person account. I am very appreciative of the time and energy these respondents put into helping me shape this story.

2. A 2009 Gallup poll ranked South Carolina the sixth most ideologically conservative state in the United States.

3. For a brief overview of the transformational (and transactional) leadership models, see Northouse (2007,175–179).

4. The participating departments are Biology, Chemistry, Environmental Science, Sociology, Political Science, Economics, and Philosophy.

5. See Furman's two websites that host information about the history of sustainability at the university: (1) Sustainability at Furman www.furman.edu/sustain and (2) David E. Shi Center for Sustainability www.furman.edu/shicenter. These two websites were designed to share information about the Furman's efforts, but also to distinguish the overall university commitments from the academic Shi Center's programs.

6. From my ethnographic data collection (including interviews and participant observation), faculty most associated with the early and significant efforts to promote sustainability include: Brannon Andersen (EES), Frank Powell (Health Sciences), William (Bill) Ranson (EES), and Wade Worthen (Biology).

7. For example, since 2008 approximately $8 million in external funding has been secured.

8. I got so many calls or emails in the first months that did not relate to my specific expertise that we experimented with the creation of a "student sustainability help desk" to address the questions that flowed in about recycling, light bulbs, electronics, and toilet paper. These questions were most often related to campus operations and individual behavior choices.

9. For example, when asked to coordinate several efforts to help the university network with other sister schools (especially through The Duke Endowment Task Force on Environmental Sustainability and Community Engagement; collaborations with the Associated Colleges of the South; and connections with Rocky Mountain Institute schools). I focused on building bridges to other colleges. I reached out to other faculty to prioritize further the curricular opportunity for innovation and carefully began focusing my own efforts around how the curriculum could further connect to the community. I took the "long view" about the center's vision and my role in it, and was very patient—especially in those first couple years—with explaining to the campus community that sustainability was much more than recycling. My primary goal was to win over the people who remained honestly ambivalent about the sustainability campaign while addressing continuing misperceptions and dogmatic opposition. That is an ongoing process, but the results have been positive.

10. The student Fellows, funded through grants from the Andrew Mellon Foundation, Bank of America, and the Arthur Vining Davis Foundations, have been engaged in innovative research and service activities in the community. One of the greatest challenges the Shi Center still faces is explaining its coordinating role without seeming to take responsibility for *all* aspects of sustainability on campus and in the community. We have organized our current staff (Associate Director Yancey Fouche, Program Coordinator Katherine Kransteuber, Administrative Coordinator Cassie Klatka) to meet our center mission, and their individual and col-

lective contributions are critical to its success. It took three years for us to clarify the individual and overlapping responsibilities for each staff position.

References

Bass, Bernard M. 1985. *Leadership and Performance Beyond Expectations*. New York: Free Press.

Bennis, Warren, and Burt Nanus. 1985. *Leaders: The Strategies for Taking Charge*. New York: Harper and Row.

Burns, James MacGregor. 1978. *Leadership*. New York: Harper and Row.

Editorial Board. 2009. Replacing Shi. *The Paladin*. October 16.

Gordon, John C., and Joyce K. Berry. 2006. *Environmental Leadership Equals Essential Leadership: Redefining Who Leads and How*. New Haven, CT: Yale University Press.

Manolis, Jim C., Kai M. Chan, Myra E. Finkelstein, Scott Stephens, Cara R. Nelson, Jacqueline B. Grant, and Michael P. Dombeck. 2009. Leadership: A New Frontier in Conservation Science. *Conservation Biology* 23 (4):879–886.

Mills, Christopher. 2009. Don't Follow the Fad. *The Paladin*. February 6.

Morris, Susannah. 2009. The Good of Being Green. *The Paladin*. May 23.

Northouse, Peter Guy. 2007. *Leadership: Theory and Practice*. 4th ed. California: Sage.

Shi, David E. 1985. *The Simple Life: Plain Living and High Thinking*. New York: Oxford University Press.

V

Accountability

18

Sustainability Strategic Planning: Establishing Accountability in a World of Distractions

Julie Newman

Yale University, founded in 1701, is the third-oldest institution of higher education in the United States. The campus is located in New Haven, Connecticut, just minutes from Long Island Sound and comprises approximately 400 buildings across 330 acres on the Central Campus. Yale currently supports a community of 11,600 undergraduate and graduate students.

I believe that the field of sustainability in higher education is still at a fragile stage in that we live in a world of competing priorities, paradoxes, distractions, and short attention spans, combined with the fear of the science of climate change. It is our responsibility, as sustainability professionals, to ensure that the sustainability commitments made by our institutions will continue to surface and remain rooted in the midst of all of this. A commitment to sustainability must outlast the daily emergencies while paving the way toward a new future. Such a commitment cannot rely on the whim of the leader in the moment. The course of action from vision to implementation calls for walking a fine line between enabling a creative process of continuous improvement over the long term while setting and achieving incremental, measureable, and impactful goals along the way. As a field, we must ensure that these commitments continue to encourage transformation and do not force us to settle for a non-transformative evolution in the long run.

Our realities today present us with a pressing need to raise the bar on accountability. This chapter raises a series of questions as to what the role of accountability is in building a sustainable campus and how accountability plays into a process of transformation. I have come to these thoughts through the process of the development of the Sustainability Strategic Plan for Yale University and watching the transformations in the institution and my own role in reshaping and strengthening one campus's commitment to becoming sustainable. My reflections upon the process of goal setting, communication, implementation, and accountability have led to a series of new questions—which may not be answerable today, but raise a number of interesting conundrums that warrant deeper analysis and understanding.

The Evolution of a Sustainability Office

I came to Yale in 2004 and founded the Office of Sustainability a year later in 2005. Upon arrival at Yale I was charged "to position Yale as a national and international model and leader in institutional sustainability—through education, outreach, research, and partnership." A sustainability committee of students, staff, and faculty, known as the Advisory Committee for Environmental Management, had built a strong foundation for sustainability at Yale over a period of four years prior to my arrival. My position originally reported to both an associate vice president of facilities and a deputy provost enabling me to bridge the academic and operational divide in the early stages. Since 2005 the Office of Sustainability has grown from an original staff of one (me) with a few graduate students to a staff of ten full-time equivalents, five of which reside in my office and the other five are involved in facilities planning, energy conservation and waste management as well as transportation options, and dining on campus. Our work continues to be supported by roughly fifty-five research assistants, both graduate and undergraduate students.

In 2007, only two years after founding the Office of Sustainability, Yale's president, Richard Levin, chose the office as one of the focus units for a regular but thorough review. Led by an external committee of Yale alumni, the reviewers were charged to assess and recommend how best to strengthen and broaden Yale's sustainability efforts. The development of a campus-wide Sustainability Strategic Plan was one of two recommendations that emerged from the eighteen-month review process. The other primary recommendation was to shift the reporting structure of the office from the previous dual report, to a singular reporting structure to the vice president of the university. This change alone lifted the importance of Yale's commitment and sent a strong signal across the university indicating that Yale was serious about sustainability.

In May of 2009, President Levin began the strategic planning process by tasking the Office of Sustainability with facilitating its development with campus-wide input. The university's vice president chaired a Sustainability Task Force of fourteen people representing administration, staff, and faculty and was asked to develop sustainability goals for all operational divisions. The intent was to develop a strategic plan that would publicly state and demonstrate Yale's commitment to sustainability beyond a single greenhouse gas reduction target that we had already adopted. The development of our Sustainability Strategic Plan has been a pivotal moment for the university's desire to be and remain a leader in campus sustainability, nationally and internationally.

The committee spent six months reviewing current trends and analyzing goals from other schools as well as leading industry. At that point there were only a few comprehensive plans to reference as compared to today. Each of the task force members worked with a subcommittee within their division to come up with a set of recommendations and potential targets that were intended to be visionary, yet achievable. Before going public, the plan had to be endorsed by the president and his cabinet as well as the Corporation (Board of Trustees). Today, Yale's Sustainability Strategic Plan is framed by a three-year timeline (2010–2013) and encompasses forty-five distinct goals divided between twelve different units.[1] Our office is responsible for ensuring that our goals are met and that the outcomes are both measured and communicated. (See table 18.1)

Influence without Authority

With the excitement and relief of the sustainability strategic plan came also the realization that our office faces the challenge of accountability from inception to implementation. The common challenge that the majority of sustainability officers face, myself included, is that not one of the operational areas reports to the Office of Sustainability, yet we are held accountable for the actions of these units in relation to meeting our sustainability objectives. In the end, a failure to achieve the stated goals

Table 18.1
Yale University Sustainability Strategic Plan: Sample Quantitative Goals

Area	Goal by 2013 (2009 Baseline)	Unit Responsible
Waste Management	Reduce municipal solid waste by 25%.	Facilities
Recycling	Increase rate of recycling to 25%.	Facilities
Food and Dining	Increase sustainable food purchases to 40%.	Dining
Paper Use	Reduce copy-paper use by 25%.	All
Energy Use	Reduce energy use by 15%.	Facilities and All
Transportation	Reduce single-occupancy vehicles on campus by 1–3%.	Transportation and All

reflects on the performance of our office. As a sustainability officer, my success relies upon my ability to demonstrate *influence without authority*. We must learn to strategically align ourselves with the units throughout campus to leverage a whole system response.

Campuses committed to sustainability recognize the need to embrace practices and policies that are considered to go beyond basic, legal compliance and therefore rely on voluntary measures. To date, there are no fines or penalties for being unsustainable. One attribute of a sustainable campus is that it deliberately leverages the public domain to hold the institution accountable to its end goals by establishing internal mechanisms of measurement and verification. There is an emerging trend and opportunity to report progress through voluntary mechanisms such as the Sustainability Tracking, Assessment & Rating System (STARS), and many universities have established reporting mechanisms unique to their situations. Since STARS has only been recently developed, it is currently unclear whether an outside voluntary reporting system has the capacity to hold an institution accountable to its goals to the same extent that is possible with an internal system. The external system is particularly tested when a new leader, who was not the signatory, is put in place.

Making Sustainability a Priority at Yale

We built the foundation for the strategic plan over a five-year period prior to the commencement of the planning process. This involved the combination of working relationships between the Office of Sustainability and a multitude of operational units, supported by a series of successful pilot projects. For example, in the early stages of the Sustainable Food Project, new menu choices and more sustainable procurement from local farms were piloted in one dining hall, which made expansion to the whole campus easier. With our transportation goal, we recognized that while encouraging carpooling reduces fossil fuel use and has the long-term economic benefit of reducing the need to build future parking garages, the short-term consequence is loss of parking fee revenues. In our pilot project, we targeted just a few crowded parking lots and will continue to encourage carpooling in an incremental way, to soften the impact on the Transportation Department's budget. Once Yale passed an aggressive greenhouse gas reduction goal in 2005, the Facilities Department demonstrated the ability to reshape the way in which energy was produced and purchased. A new emphasis was placed on reducing greenhouse gas emissions, and the cost per kilowatt hour is now calculated together with the metric tons of carbon dioxide equivalent eliminated, thereby guiding decisions toward both cost savings and greenhouse gas reductions. Such pilot projects enabled us to reduce the risks of innovation (or the perceived risks) for our administrative colleagues, and allowed the strategic plan goals to strengthen informal ties across the campus. I have learned that good intentions alone will not revolutionize a campus, though they certainly provide the foundation for a successful transformation. Today, most of these relationships have evolved from good intentions driven by the 2013 goals to ensure solution development, innovation, measurement, and accountability.

To set the three-year goals, our committee built on those past experiences, using the combination of current measureable trends (waste, energy, transportation) and gaps in resource-management planning (water, stormwater, land). A prior commitment that all new construction be designed to Leadership in Energy and Environmental Design (LEED) Silver specifications subsequently enabled a seamless transition to a commitment to a LEED Gold standard. Yale dining had already pioneered sustainable food choices and developed metrics that showed students were served 30 percent sustainable food in 2010; we moved that commitment to 40 percent. A greenhouse gas reduction target was in place to seek 43 percent reductions from 2005 levels by 2020; we set an energy reduction goal of 15 percent by 2013 to illustrate the rate of reduction that was essential to achieve our long-term goal.

Incremental Sustainability

One of the primary challenges that we must grapple with as sustainability officers is "what counts as sustainable?" Moreover, with limited time, financial resources, and personnel, where ought our efforts to go? Some campus directors build visibility by banning water bottles, installing water bottle fillers, and passing out free coffee mugs. These are certainly strategic and doable initiatives, but do such projects portray the right message? In addition to the type of project, the other questions we must grapple with include how much water and energy ought we use? How far should our food travel? How much waste should we really be producing? In some cases, like greenhouse gas emissions, we have some guidance as to what our universities ought to be emitting. However, in the case of water use or land management, that specificity is currently more difficult to prescribe. Inspirational goals such as zero waste and zero carbon have emerged in recent years, but such a bold, lofty commitment needs to be both well defined and boiled down to incremental steps in an effort to move an entire system in that direction. In short, the goal-setting process calls for a sense of vision and direction as to how the operational systems ought to function, both independently and systemically. This is a much more complex endeavor than we tend to acknowledge.

Is it sustainability if the action is driven only by frugality or financial gain? I find this to be one of the most dangerous aspects of our work, particularly in a time of financial crisis. I worry that it may undermine the full triple-bottom-line thinking to allow financial gain to trump other concerns. At the same time, cost-cutting benefits of many parts of the plan are attractive to the units and widen the circle of people who are seen as contributing to sustainability efforts. Such a broader base of partnerships is good and greater efficiency is essential moving forward.

Another hard part of fostering sustainability involves counting dollars saved; in the context of fiscal crisis, some units do not want to admit that they could find any cost-savings, because that money will just be taken away from them. Even for schools not in financial crisis mode, one can imagine downsides to honesty in cooperating with a strategic plan accountability process.

Setting a series of quantifiable and measureable goals requires reliable data and therefore reliable systems by which to collect the data in the same manner, year after year. For a plan to be successful, the combination of a reliable data collection system and clear direction is essential. The process by which the data are collected and analyzed by the staff must be institutionalized and systematized concurrently in order to outlive personnel changes over time. The quantitative goals are essential for measuring and demonstrating progress over time.

Not everything we are committed to doing or would like to do can be understood and measured quantitatively, however. At Yale, we are in the process of developing a series of more qualitative principles that expand the framework for decision making in areas such as ecosystem management, stormwater, and landscaping. As we manage the campus's open spaces, we are seeking to craft principles that will help include ecological as well as aesthetic and recreational aspects of land use. Currently, Yale has no stormwater management plan, but runoff from our compact, urban campus affects two river watersheds and the nearby Long Island Sound. Taking into account the interactions with nearby watersheds (and local biodiversity) may affect decisions about new buildings and expanded hard surfaces to reduce stormwater runoff and improve groundwater recharge. Principles that embody all the dimensions of sustainability can frame a new relationship between Yale's built and natural environment. The quantitative and the conceptual goals play two distinct roles in ensuring success and calling for accountability.

We also debated the frequency and scale of reporting for our plan. We agreed it has to work easily within existing data collection mechanisms within the institution. At Yale, we currently report progress on an annual basis; however, we are working on putting future systems and mechanisms in place that will allow for quarterly reporting for appropriate units, such as the medical school campus or the procurement office. The mechanics of collecting and reporting may be cumbersome but are doable. Reporting requires a level of diligence, consistency and precision to ensure reliable results.

The Evolution of the Sustainability Officer

In my experience at Yale, I put plenty of emphasis and up-front planning into the reporting-out mechanism, but had not anticipated the new role that I was about to take on. With real power comes a shift in my role in the system *from advocate to enforcer*. This shift may not suit every sustainability officer's talents or preferences. As soon as the plan was endorsed and implementation began, my role had to evolve to hold my peers and those at higher levels accountable for the promises made in the report. Moreover, I was going to be held responsible from the highest level of administration as to how my peers were performing in relation to the promised outcomes. These are fragile working relationships and ones that must be carefully and deliberately maintained. At the same time, these relationships can be the most rewarding and fulfilling part of the job.

What is clear is that institutional tweaking of operational systems such as waste, energy, and water will enable us to be successful with our 2013 goals. These incremental achievements do not represent all that is gained, however, they reduce risk for future goal setting, build confidence with the stakeholders, evoke short-term incentives, and publicly demonstrate Yale's ability and willingness to move toward a sustainable future. What happens when the burden of success and accountability falls on the behavior of community members is not so clear. For example, why is it so difficult still for people to use correctly a single-stream recycling bin or to alter the daily patterns of how they get to and from work?

One of the greatest leadership challenges we face as sustainability professionals in higher education is the need to keep an institution's commitment to sustainability on the priority list—and if possible, at the top of the priority list—in the midst of many other competing priorities, financial setbacks, emergencies, and personnel changes. We need to be encouraged and rewarded to take risks and also to think creatively to ensure that a transformation can take place without crumbling the foundation or alienating the troops. Until sustainability in all of its forms (standards, guidelines, curriculum, innovations) is institutionalized and second nature, it will be considered a competing priority or not a priority at all. Ultimately, a highly developed and yet flexible system of accountability combined with an incentive revolution may be the foundational linchpin of successfully becoming a sustainable campus.

Notes

1. Campus planning, building design, and construction; waste management; transportation; food and dining; environmental health and safety; energy and greenhouse gas emissions; water use; land management; finance and business operations; procurement; cleaning and maintenance; educating and engaging the community.

19

Transforming the Silos: Arizona State University's School of Sustainability

Charles L. Redman

From its roots as a Territorial Normal School established in 1885 to train teachers, Arizona State University in Tempe developed into a comprehensive metropolitan research university for the twenty-first century. More than 72,000 students from all 50 states and some 120 countries enroll at ASU each year.

Creating a New Institutional Structure

In January 2007, Arizona State University (ASU) initiated its School of Sustainability (SOS) by offering Master's and PhD degrees, and one year later it began its undergraduate program that would lead to BA and BS degrees in Sustainability. Looking back, this was a very special moment in the development of ASU and perhaps for academia in general. The initial impetus for this innovation came from the top. ASU's president, Michael Crow, who took office in 2002, felt strongly that sustainability captured what he believed was needed to meet the challenges of the twenty-first century and, for the broader society to address them, academic institutions needed to lead the way and would have to re-invent themselves. Crow had training in science-policy analysis and could speak authoritatively about transforming the way universities address academic challenges. Believing that a sustainability approach was fundamental to meeting the social and environmental challenges facing society, he challenged ASU to infuse sustainability throughout the university and build a totally new academic program. However, the university was not ready—a foundation had to be laid.

ASU has a long history of doing interdisciplinary environmental research, and in many ways that was foundational for launching our sustainability initiative. The evolution of those projects over the past fifteen years made them a "training ground" for sustainability by encouraging social scientists to work with natural scientists, especially in our Central

Arizona–Phoenix Long Term Ecological Research project that engaged close to two hundred faculty and students in interdisciplinary research focused on the city (Grimm and Redman 2004). At the same time, I served as co-director of this and other projects that brought research even closer to graduate education through two National Science Foundation (NSF) Integrative Graduate Education and Training grants in Urban Ecology that led students and faculty to contemplate new models for graduate education. The final piece of the foundation was put in place by a new NSF grant, Decision Making Under Uncertainty, which focused on solving real-world problems in partnership with the community while conducting basic research on developing decision support tools to improve water-management decisions in the face of climate change.

With these and other projects providing many faculty members with an optimistic view of what could be achieved, Crow was ready to take the next step. The crystallization of his efforts came in the spring of 2004. Together with William Clark of the JFK School at Harvard and John Schellenhuber, he assembled a distinguished group of ten international sustainability scholars at a secluded resort in the Yucatan to discuss how to bring sustainability into the international university system. While everyone present was committed to sustainability education, only Michael Crow had the leadership position within a university to effect changes on the ground.

The creation of ASU's School of Sustainability identified the Center for Environmental Studies as the starting point. The first step was to transform the existing center into the Global Institute of Sustainability (GIOS), and my title was changed to be director of the institute. The mission of GIOS was to find a way to promote and integrate sustainability activities across the campus by building on the former center's research achievements and expanding the work to include more disciplines, more applied work, more geographic diversity, and most importantly, to incubate a full-fledged and independent school granting degrees specifically in sustainability (i.e., the SOS). Although the university administration was ready to invest resources in this initiative, GIOS received a financial and recognition boost from a gift of $15 million from philanthropist Julie Wrigley. To receive a gift of this size even before the program began helped speed the process and also lent weight to establishing the new program. In this way, the new unit would not be tied to the traditions and disciplinary limits of an existing program and in fact could be designed to break down former barriers and facilitate the integration of these programs.

Faculty Engage in the Planning

Although the initial impetus for the SOS and continuing support for its activities came top down from the university president, he then stepped back and the balance of actual planning and implementation came from faculty and eventually from students themselves. The process focused on a series of meetings of faculty who had expressed interest in sustainability or been recommended by their chairs to represent their department's views. These meetings had representation from virtually the entire spectrum of disciplines at the university. Many gifted members of the faculty were attracted to these planning efforts: first because of my success in being co-director of the three large research projects mentioned above, second because of the buzz around the Wrigley gift, and finally because they thought sustainability was exciting. More than one hundred faculty participated in these meetings and of these about forty became the official faculty of the School of Sustainability when it enrolled its first students in 2007. None of the faculty had formal training in sustainability, but all of them believed that the challenges of the times required a more interdisciplinary and aggressive approach than currently existed. Thus, two and a half years of active planning led to the opening of the School of Sustainability, with evaluation and major refinements of its program continuing up to the present (Miller, Munoz-Erickson and Redman 2011).

It is not clear whether the key factor in ASU's establishment of the School of Sustainability structure was the interdisciplinary success of the antecedent organization (Center for Environmental Studies), my own belief in the great potential of interdisciplinarity, or the composition of the faculty planning groups. Looking back, it was a natural progression from where each of us began in terms of our own training, current research, and objectives. We had not yet conceived a specific roadmap to lead us to attain sustainability, and we even deferred the debate on defining the term or setting limits on what disciplines could be included. The end result was a consensus that created a school reflecting the belief that strong interdisciplinarity was the primary pathway to understanding, teaching, and contributing to sustainability.

We debated what to call the school and which degrees we would offer. The initial proposal was to use the term "sustainability science," following Robert W. Kates and his colleagues (Kates et al. 2001). Interestingly this proposal received stiff resistance from engineers, architects, humanists, and some social scientists who were part of the planning meetings because it misrepresented their perspectives. Similarly "sustainability studies" was rejected as not reflecting the strong science component. We were all sympathetic to the notion that a plurality of perspectives would be useful to achieving sustainability and that this school should be open to diverse viewpoints and not be housed in a particular college or limit its coverage to a single domain such as energy or environment. This initial framework for the School of Sustainability represented what I would now call an eclectic approach to sustainability. That is, if one brought together the appropriate disciplines and partners, one could effectively address sustainability challenges. This left open the question whether a distinctly new approach or methodology needed to be created. It also, at least in my mind, meant that all disciplines and professional schools were welcome into the discourse, and by extension, into planning the SOS.

The curriculum that was designed for the first year included two introductory courses that all students would take as an entering cohort. The first initially comprised sections reflecting what we saw as the major perspectives on sustainability; the second was to be a composite of the range of methods that might be needed. After that, we offered a series of "perspective" courses, each encompassing the views of a suite of traditional disciplines such as the human dimension, ecosystems, economics, technology and the built environment, and policy. These were complemented by a series of "challenge" courses such as urban dynamics, water management, energy systems, and in subsequent years ethics and food systems. The other feature of the curriculum was a series of hands-on "solution" workshops where students and faculty from various disciplines would work together on addressing a real world problem. In this way our curriculum reflected two key components of sustainability as we first saw it: the centrality of interdisciplinary collaboration and the emphasis on solving real world problems while pursuing academically defined research.

Students Seek Changes

From the moment we began to offer this curriculum, the courses evolved in response to student input and the experience of faculty working under a new set of expectations. Students have been particularly important in questioning and redirecting our efforts as they are not just experiencing the curriculum, but have also risked their futures by committing themselves to a field and academic degree with no track record of careers and professional success. Whether or not this initial curriculum is the best approach to sustainability education is something we continue to debate, but clearly it was successful in terms of student interest and in meeting the expectations of faculty. We limited the entering graduate class (Masters and PhD combined) to 25 students (a reasonable cohort for the introductory class), with 87 applicants the first year, 150 the second year, and 250 in the third and fourth years. In 2008 we introduced an undergraduate major in sustainability (based on roughly the same principles as the graduate degree), and by the second year there were 600 majors! Rather than allow the number of majors to continue to grow to what would have been unmanageable numbers given budgetary constraints on hiring new faculty, it was decided to limit the number of majors by raising requirements to among the highest in the university. In order to meet the student demand for sustainability, we established a three-pronged approach: a major for those most committed, a minor (established in 2010) for those who want a substantial exposure, and disciplinary-based sustainability courses for those who want to know about it in the context of their primary studies. Each of these "levels of intensity" has substantial audiences and satisfies an important need in our educational framework.

The success of any curriculum is most directly reflected in the impact on students and their future achievements. Clearly, we need sustainability graduates to be leaders, to be change agents, and not simply among those who want to fit into already well-established career tracks. Given that in many ways students are ahead of faculty in their early commitment to sustainability, students should often assume the role of teachers, and professors should be willing to learn from students. Toward that end, students at the School of Sustainability are key to organizing solutions workshops, running their own reading groups on topics of their choice, and holding a monthly town hall where they raise questions and suggest solutions to faculty, staff, and administrators. As an additional outlet for their creativity and to solicit input from those outside the school, they have formed their own journal. *The Sustainability Review* is open source and available globally (www.thesustainabilityreview.org).

Our hope is that each graduate in thesis or dissertation work (and later in a career) will demonstrate an understanding of five basic elements of sustainability and the ability to apply those elements. Students should first possess an *awareness* of the challenges facing society and the interconnectedness of the world, including a solid understanding of earth and social system dynamics. Second, they need to nurture the *creativity* needed to develop and deliver innovative solutions; we will not be able to build a sustainable world without it. Third, they should be *stewards* of natural, cultural, and human resources that we are endowed with, protecting them and fostering new growth. Fourth, as a community, we must promote *institutions* that continuously learn, adapt, and anticipate so that they not only are responsive to the issues of today but are ready to address issues as they emerge in the future. And finally, students and the rest of us should hold *values* that enhance inclusiveness, equity, and justice in all that they do.

Six Cornerstones of Our Approach

As of June 2010, the faculty and students of the SOS have immersed themselves in a continuing, all-encompassing, inquiry on whether to continue in the established direction or to once again fundamentally reorganize themselves and what they are doing. Although the school has been established as an independent administrative unit with a mandate to create a novel approach, the reality is that the inertia of traditional approaches is difficult to overcome. A major stimulus for change has come from the addition of new, junior faculty. These are the first faculty who were hired directly into the School of Sustainability and hence are more inclined to consider it as fundamentally new and distinct from existing disciplines rather than a transitional unit whose value derives from effectively joining approaches developed in the antecedent disciplines. Whether the school ultimately develops into a more closely integrated set of previously established perspectives or a wholly novel and distinctive perspective of its own is yet to be determined.

We identified a set of six cornerstones that define the school and its aspirations. First, we focus on identifying and addressing a series of sustainability challenges/opportunities that we refer to as "wicked problems" (Kates and Parris 2003). By that we mean they are important, urgent, and complex and do not yield to simple solutions or optimal tradeoffs. Eliminating poverty, protecting biodiversity, and mitigating human-caused climate change are all examples of sustainability challenges recognized for decades by many, but still without adequate solutions. Unfortunately, the tools of traditional science have proven ineffective in solving these challenges (Grunwald 2007; Ramo 2009). Given their high level of uncertainty and the need to incorporate conflicting value systems, coupled with the complexity of solving global problems one locality at a time, a new paradigm is required, and the educational system must be transformed to accommodate that paradigm.

Second, there are multiple ways of knowing and in fact there may be more than one "truth" for each situation. A study that incorporates the methods of one discipline alone is almost certain to result in an incomplete picture of the phenomenon despite most practitioners' belief that their disciplinary methodology produces complete knowledge. If multiple perspectives are employed in an inquiry, a fuller picture emerges, though sometimes aspects of the results may be in conflict. The goal is for sustainability scientists to employ epistemological pluralism to develop methodologies that encourage the maximum input while creating the means to integrate these findings (Miller et al. 2008). The goal is not simply to develop a common language and agree to compromise on accepting elements of each approach, but rather to find additional value by learning from other disciplinary paradigms. This approach to interdisciplinarity requires mutual respect among practitioners as well as a working knowledge of the collaborating perspectives.

The third cornerstone is that research and problem solving should not be seen as separate activities and that scientists, practitioners, and stakeholders should work together in the co-production of knowledge leading to solutions (Cash et al. 2003; Kates et al. 2001). We use the term *transacademic* to indicate the kind of work that goes well beyond the bounds of academia to enlist the help of people who have worked on a problem and who often have a direct interest in its solution. To be most effective, this type of partnership should start early in the process, when the problems are being defined and the investigative methods developed. In some cases the solution to pressing challenges may also result in new theoretical insights, as suggested by what Donald E. Stokes (1997) has termed "Pasteur's Quadrant," a class of research methods that both solve scientific problems and generate societal benefits.

The distinction between basic and applied research that has emerged in traditional disciplines becomes much fuzzier (or nonexistent) when viewed from a sustainability perspective. This has enormous implications for a reorganization of the faculty reward structure (especially promotion and tenure expectations), and how graduate students are encouraged to design their careers. We not only are considering some of what had been considered gray literature on a par with peer-reviewed publications, but are developing approaches to identifying excellence in engaged research where traditional metrics are inappropriate. It also means that conducting research and problem solving becomes more contextual and often place-based, since the times, places, and people involved in each situation are unique. In addition, research and problem solving are reflexive activities in which the investigators may have both explicit and implicit impacts on the course of investigations and the ultimate results (Grunwald 2004). Despite the unrealistic expectation of complete objectivity and detachment often attributed to the "scientific method," sustainability scholars must accept the additional challenge of explicitly and intelligently dealing with the importance of context and the implications of reflexivity.

If the solution of real-world problems is at the core of sustainability, then it is apparent that real-world learning experiences should be an essential element of the educational process at every level (Brundiers, Wiek, and Redman 2010). This is the fourth cornerstone. Effectively working with problems and people in the real world necessitates a series of skills and experiences that are not often emphasized or even available in the normal academic career. Real-world learning experiences promote working with students from different disciplinary backgrounds, working effectively in teams, communicating and working with those outside academia, and the ability to lead and find ways to bring together the differing values and opinions of those you work with or serve. At an advanced graduate level, this may take the form of the "solution workshops" described in the SOS curriculum where real-world problems are identified, specific clients are often secured, and teams of faculty and students with diverse backgrounds collaborate on finding sustainability solutions. Real-world learning experiences should also be available in other forms such as internships, and we also believe that most classes should have some aspect of this in their syllabus, even if it is as simple as a visiting lecturer from the community or taking the class to visit a local agency or company. At an even earlier stage in the curriculum, one might have class projects that involve such experiences on or off campus, role-playing activities, and team-building exercises.

The fifth cornerstone is an explicit concern with possible future states, with the objective of moving the system toward sustainability. Part of this is an emphasis on change as a normal condition and a willingness to consider even more dramatic transformations as essential to moving the system toward a more sustainable state. Another element of this approach is being able to work with possible, expected, as well as desired futures generated from a variety of methodological approaches such as simulation modeling, scenario analysis, and uncertainty analysis (Swart, Raskin, and Robinson 2004). Implicit in an emphasis on futures is recognizing the necessity of working with input from stakeholders and an ability to incorporate diverse values attributed to alternate outcomes by different participants. The planning and managing for particular conditions in the future implies the ability to deal with numerous tradeoffs in which there will be winners and losers. Beyond that, there is a high degree of uncertainty in what will happen even with the best planning, so the nature of the tradeoffs will continue to shift over time.

The final cornerstone of an SOS education is that beyond the basics graduates have a series of additional competencies, such as critical inquiry, quantitative and qualitative analyses, and written communication (de Haan 2006; Wiek, Withycombe, and Redman 2011). In fact, for many disciplines, specific competencies are not explicitly identified, but rather "good pieces of research" are cited as defining the field and student aspirations. Beyond specific methods of data collection and analysis, the student is not directed at the real personal competencies that may have made that research effective. This traditional approach to directing graduate education has the unintended consequence of promoting business as usual and equating quality research with an appeal to authority. Sustainability education cannot rely on implicit objectives or assume that students learn "by experience"; nor can the field aim to replicate what has been achieved in the past. If transformational research and problem solving is the objective, then we must be ready to break with past practices.

Based on our discussions of these cornerstones, from a review of the literature on key competencies in sustainability education, and drawing from our own experience, we proposed five competencies essential to successful sustainability research and problem solving (Wiek, Withycombe, and Redman 2011).

• *Systems thinking* is key to understanding the challenges, how they are situated in the larger world, and the cascading sets of implications of various actions.

• *Anticipatory competence* allows one to envision and construct possible, likely, and desirable futures for the system under study.

• In thinking about alternative futures and decision making in general, it is necessary to weigh the values of various outcomes as they are held by the different stakeholders. This *normative competence* is rarely emphasized in scientific pursuits, but if we are to be effective in guiding the future we must be able to incorporate values, perceptions, and attitudes.

• In order to achieve the desired futures and values, one must have the *strategic competence* of being able to formulate the strategies to implement sustainability ideas in actual real world settings.

• Finally, *interpersonal competence* involves teamwork skills, communication abilities, and leadership qualities. These skills are widely acknowledged as essential, but are rarely an explicit part of graduate education.

Whither Sustainability Education?

The question that all of this has brought to the fore is whether sustainability education should be a gradual transition from current interdisciplinary programs adhering to and intensifying many of the approaches already current at research universities, or does it require a sharp break with the traditional way of conducting research and problem solving? There is little question in my mind that the first choice is more comfortable. This is a logical progression for many researchers who already embrace interdisciplinarity and want to enhance those efforts. It also is easier to operationalize within current institutional settings because it retains the value of individual disciplines and their administrative units. However, for many this alternative is a positive step over the status quo but is insufficient to address the challenges of today. For those who want to follow the second choice, serious institutional change must accompany an effective approach to sustainability. The question then becomes: Can we radically improve interdisciplinarity through epistemological pluralism, becoming disciplinary translators, infusing real world learning experiences at all educational levels, valuing applied alongside basic research, and restructuring our educational pedagogy around the five new core competencies of sustainability education?

These are difficult questions to answer without years of experience at attempting each alternative and tracking the success of graduates of both. It is likely that both positions can be effective in training sustainability practitioners and should be pursued. One would expect that the first alternative of intensifying the interdisciplinary collaboration of current disciplines will be followed by the majority of programs. In fact there is a chance that the second alternative is unrealistic and may fail or may itself result is a situation not unlike the first. However, there is a chance that it may succeed and form the basis of much-needed institutional and societal change. Hence, it is my belief that it is the obligation of the School of Sustainability and other willing institutions to follow the second, more radical, program of a experimenting with the development of a transformational approach to meeting the grand challenges of sustainability.

References

Brundiers, Katja, Arnim Wiek, and Charles L. Redman. 2010. Real-world learning Opportunities in Sustainability: From Classroom into the Real-world. *International Journal of Sustainability in Higher Education* 11 (4):308–324.

Cash, David W., William C. Clark, Frank Alcock, Nancy M. Dickson, Noelle Eckley, David H. Guston, Jill Jäger, and Ronald B. Mitchell. 2003. Knowledge Systems for Sustainable Development. *Proceedings of the National Academy of Sciences of the United States of America.* 100 (14, July 8):8086–8091.

de Haan, Gerhard. 2006. The BLK "21" Programme in Germany: A "Gestaltungskompetenz"-based Model for Education for Sustainable Development. *Environmental Education Research* 1:19–32.

Grimm, Nancy B., and Charles L. Redman. 2004. Approaches to the Study of Urban Ecosystems: The Case of Central Arizona-Phoenix. *Urban Ecosystems* 7:199–213.

Grunwald, Armin. 2004. Strategic Knowledge for Sustainable Development: The Need for Reflexivity and Learning at the Interface between Science and Society. *International Journal of Foresight and Innovation Policy* 1 (1–2):150–167.

Grunwald, Armin. 2007. Working towards Sustainable Development in the Face of Uncertainty and Incomplete Knowledge. *Journal of Environmental Policy and Planning* 9 (3):245–262.

Kates, Robert W., William C. Clark, Robert Corell, J. Michael Hall, Carlo C. Jaeger, Ian Lowe, James J. McCarthy, et al. 2001. Sustainability Science. *Science* 292 (5517):641–642.

Kates, Robert W., and Thomas M. Parris. 2003. Science and Technology for Sustainable Development Special Feature: Long-term Trends and a Sustainability Transition. *Proceedings of the National Academy of Sciences of the United States of America* 100 (14):8062.

Miller, Thaddeus R., Timothy D. Baird, Caitlin M. Littlefield, Gary Kofinas, F. Stuart Chapin III and Charles L. Redman. 2008. Epistemological Pluralism: Reorganizing Interdisciplinary Research. *Ecology and Society* 13 (2):46.

Miller, Thaddeus R., Tischa Munoz-Erickson, and Charles L. Redman. 2011. Transforming Knowledge for Sustainability: Towards Adaptive Academic Institutions. *International Journal of Sustainability in Higher Education* 12 (2):177–192.

Ramo, Joshua Cooper. 2009. The Nature of the Age. In *The Age of the Unthinkable,* 3–19. New York, NY: Little, Brown & Co.

Stokes, Donald E. 1997. *Pasteur's Quadrant: Basic Science and Technological Innovation.* Washington, DC: Brookings Institution Press.

Swart, Rob, Paul Raskin, and John Robinson. 2004. The Problem of the Future: Sustainability Science and Scenario Analysis. *Global Environmental Change* 14 (2):137–146.

Wiek, Arnim, Lauren Withycombe, and Charles L. Redman. 2011. Key Competencies in Sustainability—A Reference Framework for Academic Program Development. *Sustainability Science* 6 (2):203–218.

20

Fair Trade, Social Justice, and Campus Sustainability at the University of Wisconsin Oshkosh

James W. Feldman and David Barnhill

The University of Wisconsin Oshkosh has been educating the residents of northeastern Wisconsin since 1871. Approximately 13,500 students currently attend the university, which lies on a 174-acre urban campus located along the shore of the Fox River.

In spring 2011, ten students from the University of Wisconsin Oshkosh (UW Oshkosh) traveled to Guatemala on an alternative spring break trip where they learned first-hand how their morning coffee is grown and marketed. The students spoke with growers who had withdrawn from the Fair Trade movement—an alternative market that pledges a living wage to producers of commodities such as coffee, tea, and chocolate—because they had not received the benefits promised. The students returned to campus with serious questions about the movement and their university's commitment to it. This raised an important concern because in fall 2008, UW Oshkosh had become the first campus in the United States to declare itself a "Fair Trade University." The campus Fair Trade Committee responded to the students by calling an open forum, where the students joined interested faculty and staff in exploring the complexities and contradictions of this dynamic and complex social movement.

The alternative spring break experience, and the discussion it generated, demonstrates how Fair Trade has advanced the university's larger sustainability goals. By declaring itself a Fair Trade University, the university committed to raising awareness and making certified Fair Trade products available on campus. In the four years since this declaration, Fair Trade has become an integral part of our campus sustainability initiative, one that cuts across operations, outreach, and curriculum. While the commitment has required some operational changes in purchasing and in dining services, the goal has always been to move beyond operational concerns. The Fair Trade declaration has allowed the university to serve as a community forum for this important issue, as a vehicle for sustainability as a lens of critical inquiry, and as a mechanism for enacting the university's commitment to social justice.

The international Fair Trade movement has traditionally been focused on the buying and selling of products and the attempt to provide producers of selected food commodities (such as coffee, tea, bananas, and chocolate) and cultural goods in the developing world with a fair, living wage and access to good markets. It recognizes the inequities built into the global economic system and tries to reduce them by ensuring that trade works in the interests of both producers and consumers to enable more sustainable forms of exchange while also ensuring production practices that protect the environment. The university movement grew from the Fair Trade Town movement, both of which started in England in the early 2000s. In the United States, the town of Media, Pennsylvania, picked up the banner in 2006 and became the first Fair Trade Town in the nation, and the university movement is gaining momentum, as well.

Securing the Fair Trade Declaration

At the University of Wisconsin Oshkosh, efforts to educate the community about Fair Trade and promote the sale of Fair Trade products began in the spring of 2005. In the fall of 2007, David Barnhill, the director of the Environmental Studies Program, started a campaign to become a Fair Trade University and received a positive reception from faculty and students. All agreed that a public institutional commitment—including approval by our four governance groups (faculty, academic staff, students, and support staff)—would maximize our educational and promotional efforts. Another motivation was to help jump-start a Fair Trade University movement in the United States. We felt that if we made such a commitment, others would seek that status and a national organization might develop. And, yes, another motivation was institutional visibility and public relations: being the first Fair Trade University in the country would be a distinction we could trumpet.

The timing of the campaign was motivated partially by operational requirements. In summer 2008, the university planned to publish a request for new dining services proposals—the contract that would govern on-campus food service for seven years. If Fair Trade was to have a significant role in our food service, it needed to be in that contract. Through negotiation and persistence, we were able to have included in the request a statement about the four principles of sustainability in food: Fair Trade, organic, locally grown, and humanely raised. While we realized that much of our food would not embody those principles, our efforts did result in a commitment to Fair Trade on the part of Sodexo, the company that successfully maintained its status as our food service provider and pledged to serve Fair Trade coffee and tea on campus, as well as other products as they became available.

With this success behind us, we decided to push for a stronger institutional commitment. Declaration as a Fair Trade University aligned with several previous steps that that the university had taken. In 2002, UW Oshkosh had joined a handful of other campuses in officially endorsing the Earth Charter, an international declaration of social and ecological interdependence that grew out of the 1992 Rio Earth Summit. The Earth Charter lists as its key principles: respect and care for the community of life; ecological integrity; social and economic justice; and democracy, nonviolence, and peace. Becoming a Fair Trade University was a way of putting that earlier declaration into practice. In 2006, the university adopted a comprehensive Campus Sustainability Plan that committed us to making the university more sustainable in our operations, research, outreach, and teaching. The Fair Trade declaration would advance these goals, as well.

Institutional change—particularly in places with a strong tradition of shared governance—never comes easily, and securing the Fair Trade declaration required constant negotiation at both the campus and system levels. In the fall of 2007, we reviewed the criteria in the United Kingdom and consulted with the head of the Fair Trade Town campaign concerning the wording of a declaration. David Barnhill adapted this resolution to fit the UW Oshkosh context and presented it to the provost's office as well as to those in charge of university dining. During the remainder of that academic year, we took the proposal to the four governance groups, and by May 2008, all four had endorsed the proposal. Some members of the administration were concerned, however, about potential legal implications of the declaration, leading to a consultation with the attorney representing the University of Wisconsin System. The attorney altered some of the wording, which required another round of endorsements from the campus governance groups. Those endorsements were secured just before the fall 2008 semester began, and Chancellor Richard Wells proclaimed UW Oshkosh to be a Fair Trade University on opening day of the semester. The declaration committed UW Oshkosh to serving certified Fair Trade coffee and tea on campus, to selling certified food items and handcrafts at university stores, and to raising awareness about the campaign. Our group celebrated, and then we realized that this was not so much an achievement but rather the beginning of the real work that needed to be done.

From the outset, the goal of the Fair Trade declaration has been to move beyond operational concerns and to make Fair Trade a part of the university's sustainability initiative. One of the motivations for the campaign, and one of the stated reasons the Chancellor supported this declaration, was that Fair Trade combines the ideals of social and economic justice with the goal of protecting the environment. While the jobs versus environment dichotomy is routinely cited by those seeking to exploit both workers and our natural resources, Fair Trade aims to improve the lives of farmers, workers, and artisans in the developing world while mandating that environmentally friendly methods (often but not always organic) are used. For all of the progress that universities across the country have made toward sustainability, commitments to social justice are often the hardest to secure and to assess; social justice is often the weakest of the "three pillars" of sustainability (ecology, ethics, and economics). The Fair Trade declaration serves as a tangible commitment to social justice principles. "Sustainability goes well beyond being 'green,'" Chancellor Wells explained. "It includes social justice as well. By becoming a Fair Trade University, UW Oshkosh is making a commitment to do our part toward helping workers around the world get a livable wage and humane working conditions. As a large institution, UW Oshkosh can play an important part in shaping the future and in supporting green practices on all levels."

The institutionalization of Fair Trade at the university helps to spread the word about the values and benefits of Fair Trade while promoting the purchase and sale of Fair Trade products. Instead of occasional events initiated by a small group of faculty and students and scattered sales of Fair Trade coffee and chocolate, Fair Trade is now part of the university identity. Almost all coffee and tea sold on campus is Fair Trade, and we are exploring other possibilities as well. Leaders in university dining, the university bookstore, and the student union convenience store understand and applaud this, and they are aiming to expand the sale of Fair Trade products.

Fair Trade has also become an avenue for student engagement. Our paid intern is effective in supporting the issues on campus while she develops her leadership skills, having presented at two national Fair Trade conferences. We have started a "Fair Trade Ambassador" program, in which students learn about the movement and then educate student groups. One of our alternative spring break options in 2011 and 2012 had students doing service learning work in Guatemala with a Fair Trade grower.

Raising awareness about and understanding of Fair Trade has become one of the primary focuses of the campus-wide campaign. Campus events on Fair Trade have become a regular feature of our Earth Charter Week in October and Earth Week in April, in addition to special Fair Trade events. Halloween and Valentine's Day are times to sell certified chocolate and to educate people about the "dark side" of conventional chocolate production through poster sessions, invited speakers, film screenings, and "reverse trick-or-treating." Over 40 percent of the world's chocolate comes from the Ivory Coast, where plantations often subject children to unsafe, abusive working conditions (Mistrati and Romano 2010). Promoting and distributing fairly traded chocolate helps to educate consumers and bolster chocolate producers who ban child labor, pay a living wage, and practice environmental conservation. In early December, student environmental groups and the university book store cooperate to put on a Fair Trade Festival—a special holiday sale of Fair Trade products and a way to inform people of how the lives of artisans in India or Latin America are improved by buying their products.

Of course there have been challenges. The selection of Fair Trade goods available at a price that our students can afford remains narrow. The Fair Trade coffee that is served by catering is not always marked as such—missing an educational and promotional opportunity. And many of the students and staff who work in dining facilities remain unaware of what Fair Trade means—and sometimes unaware of the fact that they are selling Fair Trade coffee themselves. New students are always arriving, and especially since a high percentage of our students are transfers and do not reside on campus, it is difficult to spread the word about Fair Trade. Inertia exists in our operations, and it is easy to slip back to old habits. While it was relatively easy to stock the convenience store with chocolate and to get dining services to sell coffee, expanding the sale of Fair Trade products quickly becomes constrained by lack of availability or contract restrictions.

Fair Trade and the Critical Analysis of Campus Sustainability

Fair Trade has made its way into the classrooms at UW Oshkosh, as well, and has helped to further the university's commitment to infusing sustainability into the curriculum. An innovative business course, for example, pairs a field experience visiting coffee producers in Peru with a project requiring students to prepare a business plan for a Fair Trade coffee house in the United States. An introductory course in Environmental Studies discusses Fair Trade both as a part of the emerging alternative food system and as a component of the UW Oshkosh Sustainability Initiative. A team-taught honors course for first-year students focuses on the social, ethical, and economic dimensions of the issue. A writing-intensive course in the English Department designed for first-year students concentrates on the Earth Charter and discusses Fair Trade as a practical application of the charter's principles. Two upper-level anthropology courses—Economy, Nature, and Culture; and Globalization—make Fair Trade a central component of the syllabus. A professor in the College of Education and Human Services also teaches a course on globalization that considers Fair Trade. At least two study-abroad courses (one in business and one in English) have dealt with the topic through site visits to producers. Fair Trade has also become a regular component of our Winnebago Sustainability Project, a two-day workshop for faculty interested in infusing sustainability into their courses.

Benign and altruistic as it might seem on the surface, Fair Trade is a complicated and contested issue ripe for classroom analysis. Indeed, it functions exceedingly well as a mechanism for moving sustainability beyond prescription and turning it into a lens of inquiry—a way of analyzing and understanding complicated social and environmental issues (Sherman 2008). "At the heart of fair trade lies a fundamental paradox," explains sociologist Daniel Jaffee. "In its efforts to achieve social justice and alter the unjust terms of trade that small farmers face worldwide, fair trade utilizes the mechanisms of the very markets that have generated those injustices" (Jaffee 2007, 1). This raises all sorts of interesting questions about the motivation and practice of Fair Trade. Should the goal of the movement, for example, be to increase the amount of coffee or other products sold "fairly"? Advocates of this approach suggest that this will spread the benefits of Fair Trade widely and have aggressively courted large market players such as Starbucks, Proctor and Gamble, and Nestlé. Critics contend that allowing these corporations to use the Fair Trade label might lower standards in areas such as wages and environmental quality and might turn Fair Trade's promises of a living wage into a marketing ploy. Other critics question the role of third-party certifiers, seeing certification as an extra step imposed from the global north onto the global south, and one that increases the cost of the products and threatens to lower the income that actually reaches producers in the developing world.

The "direct trade" of coffee has emerged as a response to these concerns—but this alternative has its own issues. Direct-trade advocates claim that they are building a more truly alternative market—one based on transparency and a closer relationship between producers and consumers. But by moving their businesses away from the domestic and international Fair Trade organizations, direct-trade advocates forego the opportunity to secure independent third-party certification of the prices and wages that they pay and the production practices they depend upon. These and other questions have led to a recent splintering of the Fair Trade movement that has created a complicated maze of organizations, labels, and competing strategies for success.

Scholars from a wide variety of fields have begun to investigate the questions and challenges raised by Fair Trade. Anthropologist Sarah Lyon (2010) has explored the meaning of Fair Trade, both for coffee producers in Guatemala and also for consumers, and has determined that participation in Fair Trade has benefits and costs for each group. Daniel Jaffee (2007) concludes that fair trade growers in the Mexican highlands can sometimes earn more than conventional producers, but that Fair Trade does not always deliver on its promises. Other scholars have investigated the preservation of cultural practices, women's empowerment, economic structures and prospects, and the implications of globalization, demonstrating the richness of the questions raised by the movement.

A recent senior seminar in Environmental Studies, taught by Jim Feldman, serves as an example of the way that Fair Trade's contested meanings can provide the backdrop for critical inquiry into the purpose and impact of sustainability practices. The course started with a series of common readings on sustainability and Fair Trade focused on the above issues. Students then wrote individual research papers on topics such as the labeling of cultural goods, the local distribution of Fair Trade products, the risks of "cooptation" of movement ideals by corporate sales campaigns, and the prospect of using a Fair Trade–like system to guard against abusive child labor practices. In addition, students completed team projects in which they revamped the university's Fair Trade website and created videos about Fair Trade and the university's commitment to it. In doing so, they wrestled with questions about how and why the university was conducting its Fair Trade campaign. Some suggested that the university's motivation had more to do with public relations than with helping producers in the developing world; others believed that the ultimate goal of raising awareness about Fair Trade—both its promises and its controversies—served as justification enough on its own. In other words, students took the complicated real-world issue of Fair Trade and dissected the social, economic, and ecological implications of its global and local manifestations—exactly the kind of critical responses to sustainability that many universities are trying to build into their curriculum and course offerings. Such enquiry asks all of us in higher education to interrogate the practices we pursue on behalf of a sustainable future.

The Fair Trade University movement has spread beyond UW Oshkosh. As of Janurary 2013, twelve other campuses have achieved Fair Trade University status. A national steering committee has formed to promote and coordinate the university movement, as well as to approve new Fair Trade universities and to conduct an annual review of all campuses. The first national Fair Trade Town and University Conference was held in September 2011.

Many challenges certainly remain. General awareness is still relatively low. Numbers of faculty involved are still small, and those with interest may remain unsure how to incorporate Fair Trade into their classes. Programming events about Fair Trade that are engaging and innovative require constant attention and imagination.

But four years after UW Oshkosh became the first Fair Trade University in the country, the results are encouraging. Fair Trade has become an important component of the university's sustainability initiative, one that cuts across operations, teaching, research, and outreach. It has provided an avenue for the application of sustainability as a lens of critical inquiry, both inside and outside of the classroom. And most importantly, it has provided a way for the campus community to engage directly with the social, economic, and environmental aspects of sustainability, demonstrating how improving lives and protecting the environment can be achieved simultaneously. We need more such opportunities—at the University of Wisconsin Oshkosh and throughout higher education.

References

Jaffee, Daniel. 2007. *Brewing Justice: Fair Trade Coffee, Sustainability, and Survival*. Berkeley: University of California Press.

Lyon, Sarah. 2010. *Coffee and Community: Maya Farmers and Fair Trade Markets*. Boulder: University of Colorado Press.

Mistrati, Miki, and U. Roberto Romano. 2010. *The Dark Side of Chocolate*. Bastard Film.

Sherman, Daniel. 2008. What's the Big Idea? A Strategy for Higher Education Curriculum. *Sustainability: The Journal of Record* 1 (June): 188–195.

UWO First in U.S. to Become a Fair Trade University. 2010. University of Wisconsin Oshkosh. http://www.uwosh.edu/today/1188/uwo-1st-in-us-to-become-a-fair-trade-university.

21

Creating and Sustaining a Student Movement at San Diego State University

Grant A. Mack

San Diego State University is an urban, hilltop university of 283 acres that enrolls roughly 30,000 undergraduate and 5,000 graduate students. The university is one of three research-focused Hispanic-serving institutions in the United States and has no ethnic majority population.

As a freshman entering San Diego State University (SDSU) in fall 2007, I never realized how involved I would become in university activities, let alone the influence I would have on the entire campus community. This is the story of how I, along with many other students and the Associated Students at SDSU, came to embrace sustainability concepts through various initiatives and goals in a short five-year period. The Associated Students at SDSU is a non-profit public benefit corporate auxiliary of the university, a type of organization unique to the twenty-three California State Universities. Auxiliaries manage and operate specified university services, such as food and dining operations, university giving, and research funding. At SDSU, the Associated Students is entirely student directed, with an elected student board of directors called the Associated Students Council, and five elected student executive officers. The auxiliary oversees an annual operating budget of roughly $22 million for various programs and eight facilities. The culmination of SDSU's student sustainability efforts was the approval of the Associated Students Corporate Sustainability goals, which guarantee a level of institutional continuity for our sustainability efforts into the future. These goals are guiding not only the Associated Students, but also San Diego State University and the entire California State University system, into a sustainable future.

Founding the Enviro-Business Society (e3)

Some student groups at San Diego State University had been strategizing and actively campaigning for various sustainability-oriented policies and initiatives for years, before they were ever formally embraced by the Associated Students. In spring of 2005, three fraternity members founded the Enviro-Business Society (e3) to promote modern business practices based on the three pillars of a sustainable system: ecology, ethics, and economics. Using alternative economic theory, e3 sought to demonstrate how maximizing profit can lead to a sustainable future.

The Enviro-Business Society began by recruiting a strong network of hard-working, passionate, and motivated students in the spring and fall semester of 2005. Benjamin Crawford, the founder and president, decided that each year the organization would focus on a particular environmental theme for their events and educational marketing campaigns to raise environmental awareness throughout the campus community. Heather Honea, an energetic, young marketing professor, was recruited as the organization's faculty adviser. Heather guided the students' numerous flash marketing campaigns and educational events that were launched throughout the 2005–2006 academic year, culminating in a resurrected Earth Day celebration. A highlight of the day was an eco-fashion show in which clothing designers from New York, Los Angeles, San Diego, San Francisco, and Montreal collaborated with hair and makeup artists to debunk the myth that organically grown fabrics and recycled clothing cannot seduce the high-fashion runways of the world.

When the e3 founding members graduated, Ian Beven was elected president, and he believed that students were the change enablers for the rest of the world and that this generation of students would be the "green" change that society needed. The Enviro-Business Society employed grassroots strategies and hosted various educational events, guest speaker forums, and teach-ins. SDSU even created an upper-division business-marketing course for the e3 executive officers, granting them academic credit for their marketing and public relations work on campus.

The next step for the organization was to strengthen ties with other campus partners, especially the campus-wide Associated Students auxiliary, the Aztec Shops auxiliary (which manages the university bookstore, dining services, and other retail operations), the Division of Undergraduate Studies, and the Physical Plant department. By spring 2007, e3 leaders worked with the Associated Students to craft an environmental policy platform for the Associated Students Council candidates. In collaboration with key administrative personnel, the e3 also organized a monthly Green Lunch Bag meeting to discuss sustainability practices on campus and, most importantly, break down the barriers that existed among the siloed university departments. The lively meetings of faculty, staff, and students at the Green Lunch Bag meetings eventually evolved into several sustainability-related efforts and organizations. Earth Day 2006 evolved into Earth Week 2007, which consisted of a Green Film Festival, organic food tasting, a Global Warming Action Summit, a Green Lifestyles Fair, a concert, and a weekend beach cleanup. A final success was that the incoming Associated Students president appointed the outgoing e3 leader to serve as the first Associated Students Green Commissioner under the direction of the Associated Students president himself.

First Steps to Recycling and Alternative Transportation

With the Associated Students auxiliary now actively supporting the Enviro-Business Society goals, real progress could be made in the 2007–2008 academic year. The first effort was to expand the campus recycling program. Students carried out an extensive analysis of the current practices and recommended that the administration change the ratio of trash bins to recycling bins from 15:1 to 1:1. The university president, Dr. Stephen L. Weber, supported the students' efforts, and by the end of spring 2008, almost half of the trash bins on campus had been converted to recycling containers. Thousands of dollars in tipping costs were saved, and the campaign also reduced the amount of waste sent to landfills.

Meanwhile, e3 recognized that transportation to and from SDSU's urban campus contributed greatly to the university's overall environmental impact. A major impediment for students living near campus was the existing campus-wide ban on bikes and skateboards; large fines were issued for riding on campus. This policy encouraged students living a mile or more from the university to drive to campus, which contributed to an increase in traffic, noise, and greenhouse gas emissions. In November of 2007, e3 hosted a bike crusade, a peaceful demonstration for the removal of the bike/skateboard ban and for an alternative transportation policy.

Like most students in the Associated Students auxiliary, I began as a board member on the University Affairs Board, one of the sixteen boards and committees within the organization responsible for any and all issues that affected student life. I began my position on the board with a good friend of mine from high school, who was also interested in student government. We both joined the Associated Students in the middle of the fall 2007 semester and quickly became friends with the organization's five executive officers.

My first major task as a member of the board was to collaborate with the Enviro-Business Society leadership to draft a bike lane resolution to remove the ban on bikes and skateboards and support the development of designated bike lanes on campus. I was initially averse to this task because I did not see the value or the purpose of alternative transportation options. However, as time went on, I began to see the possible benefits of bike lanes and became inspired by the Enviro-Business Society's dedication and passion. When all was said and done, the resolution was presented to the Associated Students Council, and it received unanimous approval in the spring of 2008. Alternative transportation policies then moved to discussions between the Associated Students and university administration. Meanwhile, Earth Day 2008 became a fun, educational, and consciousness-raising celebration including the first-ever local sustainable businesses fair with over 200 participants and an evening concert joined by 4,000 students.

Financing Major Projects through the "Enhance, Evolve, Innovate" Fee

Moving forward with sustainability efforts on campus, the next step was the development of a major student programming initiative called the Enhance, Evolve, Innovate campaign. Led by the Associated Students Green Commissioner, executive officers, and student representatives, it proposed to increase student fees by $20 per semester to fund six new programs.

In March 2008, the Associated Students launched the campaign to gain support for the fee. Students made presentations throughout the campus and engaged in grassroots marketing to inform students about the initiative, which passed by 64.6 percent. The Associated Students was now authorized to create and implement those six transformative programs: Aztec culture project, study abroad scholarships, new legal and financial services for students, increased student organization funding, a week-long sustainability-focused spring festival, and Associated Students sustainability facility upgrades.

Facility Upgrades: The Green Love Initiative

With the newly created Green Love Sustainability Advisory Board, the Associated Students president appointed Erica Johnson as the new Associated Students Green Commissioner and chair of the board. Green Love (for short) was responsible for administering the fund for Associated Students sustainability facility upgrades. The first task was to form the board with over thirty students interested in sustainability. Glen Brandenburg, director of the Mission Bay Aquatic Center (a public water-sports facility run by the Associated Students) was recruited as the board's adviser. I became the first student recruited and was asked to be the board's vice chair. I knew very little about environmental issues or policy, but this moment changed my entire college experience.

By the time the fall 2008 semester began, we had developed a road map for the year and finalized criteria for the $250,000 allocation. The board, entirely made up of students, decided to allocate funding in phases to the "low hanging fruit" projects such as lighting and water efficiency retrofits for each of the eight facilities operated by the Associated Students. The board also approved the installation of over 150 kilowatts of solar photovoltaic capacity located at two Associated Students operated facilities.

With the Green Love board projects determined for the school year, the board decided to expand its authority. Seeing facility retrofits as too narrow a focus, Green Love approached the Associated Students executive officers for additional funding for a Sustainability Educational Awareness campaign. The request was hotly debated but was then approved by the Associated Students executive committee. I was tasked with this campaign, which focused on environmentally responsible giveaways, such as reusable bags and reusable water bottles and the distribution of sustainable lifestyle information. Halfway into the year, it was common to see students throughout the campus carrying their Green Love reusable water bottles and reusable bags.

Continuing the educational programming into the spring semester, the Green Love board also expanded the Green Lunch Bag meetings into a public speaker series. The program hosted local San Diego officials, progressive business leaders, and SDSU faculty to talk about their policies, programs, and research on environmental topics to an audience of students, faculty, staff, and administrators. An organic lunch was provided by the Green Love board for those who attended. The event attracted an enthusiastic crowd of students and continued to build bridges across the campus.

Work on the bike lane proposal also continued. A local landscape architecture firm was hired to develop a comprehensive study and recommendations for the construction of bike lanes on campus to address the university administration's concerns. Once the study was completed in April 2009, the collaborators in the Associated Students and Enviro-Business Society were hopeful that permanent lanes would be constructed.

Earth Day 2009 evolved into the inaugural GreenFest Spring Festival, funded by the Enhance, Evolve, Innovate initiative. The three-day event was a trial run for the Associated Students and became a signature for the university auxiliary. In addition, the celebration included the first-ever campus Farmers Market organized by the Enviro-Business Society. The Farmers Market was a huge success as thousands of students lined the campus walkways for local organic fresh food.

ModernSpace: A LEED Platinum Student Union

At the end of the 2008–2009 academic year, a critical effort emerged to rethink plans for the renovation of the existing student union facility. Constructed in 1968, it was the first student union in the entire California State University system. After thirty years, the facility was not meeting the needs of the student population, which had grown from 15,000 to over 30,000 students. The Associated Students had been working with the University Campus Design, Construction and Facilities Planning office for over ten years to assess the condition of the facility and design major repairs and renovations. Several initiatives to increase student fees to build a new facility were launched under the campaign name of ModernSpace—in 2002 (which failed) and in 2006 (which succeeded). Despite work by outside consultants and the university project managers, the project stalled in 2008 due to the economic downturn and other cost escalations. The slow and arduous progress the Associated Students had made over the previous eight years had led to an expensive and unattainable project, and the ModernSpace subcommittee comprising students and administrators made a decision to move forward with a smaller renovation.

With many others on the ModernSpace subcommittee, I was concerned that the project had been completely gutted. There was only one alternative. In April 2009, we proposed that the Associated Students scrap the current project and construct a new student union building that would not only include all the design and programming elements of the original initiative but would achieve Leadership in Energy and Environmental Design (LEED) Platinum certification (the highest green building rating that could be achieved through the US Green Building Council). We needed to convince not only members of the ModernSpace subcommittee, but the Associated Students Council as well. The Green Love board drafted a resolution in support of the new vision, and almost immediately the proposal was criticized by various university administrators and students for being too ambitious in a difficult fiscal time. Despite the initial outcry against the project, the Associated Student Council representatives were persuaded through extensive and informative dialogue. When the final vote was tallied at the Associated Students Council meeting, both the new construction proposal and the LEED Platinum resolution passed, with only two representatives out of fifty-two opposed. A new course was set for the ModernSpace project, and another fee initiative in the spring of 2010 would be required in order to finance it.

Sustainability at the Forefront

A new and exciting year began in August 2009. I was appointed the Associated Students Sustainability Commissioner (a name change from Green Commissioner) and was elected to serve on the Associated Students Council another year. Over the summer, e3 engaged the Aztec Shops auxiliary to discuss the feasibility of hosting a weekly Farmers Market on campus. Negotiations were extended and challenging, but when the fall semester began, the San Diego State University Farmers Market opened, and by the end of fall, the e3-managed market had twenty-two vendors and was a popular attraction for the entire campus community.

The Associated Students Green Love board launched both Zimride, an online ride-sharing program, and Zipcar, a car-sharing program for the university. Along with the continuation of the Sustainability Educational Awareness Campaign and the Green Lunch Bag Series, these programs were quickly adopted by the campus community. Both e3 and the Associated Students continued to produce GreenFest, a week-long sustainability-focused Earth Day festival, including a business fair, farmers market, eco-action center, student organization tables, and a music festival. The event was building a campus tradition and helped students look forward to activities in the coming year.

With eight months of planning, spring 2010 also saw the launch of the marketing campaign to win a new $94 per semester fee increase for the ModernSpace initiative. The Green Love board and Enviro-Business Society led the LEED- and "green" features component of the campaign. After all of the presentations and open forums, the final vote was taken, and the ModernSpace initiative passed with a 54.4 percent approval! Despite the economic downturn, students looked beyond the now and instead believed in the future. The Associated Students had done it and construction of the first LEED Platinum building in the entire California State University system was nearly underway.

The Green Love board then turned its attention back to the construction of bike lanes on campus. After many meetings and heavy negotiations, the Associated Students executive officers and I proposed that the University Senate policy banning the use of bikes and skateboards be substantially amended. We received support from both the University Environmental Health and Safety Senate Committee and the University Senate Sustainability Committee to designate lanes located in the campus interior. The University Senate approved the policy modifications, though some concerns about mobility issues remained.

Institutionalizing a Movement

In March 2010, I was elected to serve the student body as president of the Associated Students auxiliary. I realized early on that I only had a year before graduation, so I focused on institutionalizing the progress made over the previous five years and on recruiting and mentoring future sustainability advocates at SDSU and within the Associated Students.

The fall semester was a trial period for one designated bike lane, which supporters were determined to see succeed. The Associated Students then developed a bike safety and educational campaign to inform students of the policy changes and the proper use of the campus bike lane. It took the entire campus community all of fall semester to become familiar with the designated lane. But, by the end of the semester, the trial lane felt like a natural part of the campus culture. A massive increase in bikes and skateboards on campus was a testament to the interest in alternative transportation efforts. And particularly important was the documentation to show no increase in bicycle and skateboard accidents.

After developing and approving a bike and skateboard resolution, conducting a comprehensive study, negotiating with the Faculty Senate and university administration, and constructing a temporary designated lane, the time had finally come to approve the construction of permanent bike lanes throughout the campus. The Associated Students Council allocated funding for the campus lanes in April 2011. The permanent bike lanes were completed in August 2011 and have become a tremendous asset and feature at San Diego State University.

The Associated Students also completed the construction of a 23-kilowatt solar photovoltaic array at the Children's Center daycare facility, offsetting roughly 33 percent of the total energy used on site. Though small in comparison to other solar projects completed by the Associated Students, it nevertheless represented a significant investment for the facility.

Another project was determining the proper level of on-site renewable energy needed to reach LEED Platinum certification for the new student union. We found that a 173-kilowatt solar array would be the minimum needed. However, thanks to the Associated Students management team and a creative financing strategy, it was possible for us to double the size of the solar array to 373 kilowatts and thereby offset an estimated 50 percent of the facility's total electricity use.

After almost a year of analysis, a LEED consulting firm hired by the Associated Students finished developing a comprehensive plan for each student-managed facility to achieve LEED Operations and Maintenance certification. This plan, along with the progress Green Love had made, would form the backbone of the much-anticipated Associated Students Corporate Sustainability goals. These goals were designed to guide the organization's sustainability decisions and actions for the next nine years. The goals stipulated that:

• All Associated Students-managed facilities will achieve LEED for Existing Buildings: Operations & Maintenance Silver certification or better by 2020.

• All Associated Students–managed facilities will achieve zero net-energy (consuming only the electricity it generates on or near the facility from renewable energy resources) by 2020.

• The Associated Students will encourage its full-time and part-time employees to embrace sustainable lifestyles by implementing programs and incentives to engage in socially and environmentally responsible behavior.

On March 16, 2011, the Associated Students Corporate Sustainability goals were presented to the Associated Students Council and unanimously approved. This momentous policy commitment ensured the Green Love board's role within the Associated Students and gave me the assurance that our progress would continue even after my graduation.

Creating a Sustainable Future

When I graduated in May 2011, I looked back over what had occurred at San Diego State University in the past four years and reflected that I had never expected to be part of such tremendous change. My story is not so different from other students at universities across the country. It is a story filled with innovative ideas, perseverance, insurmountable obstacles, and above all else, change. Students like me at SDSU did not realize the impact we would have, but we knew that we could be the drivers of a new way of thinking. We established tangible goals with real outcomes and committed ourselves to seeing those goals accomplished. The story I have told is far from over, and there is still much progress that must be made. There is now a new cadre of students who have become advocates of environmentally sustainable initiatives, students who were mentored and guided just like me. These students have and will continue what we started, that much I am certain.

VI

Professional and Personal Transformation

22

Living the Questions: Contemplative and Reflective Practices in Sustainability Education

Marie Eaton, Kate Davies, Michael Gillespie, Karen Harding, Sharon Daloz Parks

Introduction: What Motivates Us?

As college and university teachers across a broad array of disciplines, we have come to believe that the scale of the global environmental crisis poses unprecedented challenges to the future well-being of the planet and all humankind. We also believe that this crisis challenges underlying values and beliefs that have shaped the dominant Western culture for the past two-and-a-half thousand years, calling us to rethink how we might best respond. We believe that, as educators, we have a vital role to play in facilitating the transition toward a more sustainable society and, further, that contemplative and reflective practices are important for this transition. Behind our common sense of purpose lie multiple intellectual and educational experiences, as illustrated by these brief descriptions from the authors of this chapter.

Marie: Recently one of my students said to me, "We're studying all these problems, and they seem so big, like an open wound, a cut that gets bigger and bigger and there's nothing to heal it." Although I have multiple reasons for incorporating contemplative and reflective practices into my teaching, this student spoke directly to the feelings of despair and loss of hope that often overwhelm those of us who study and teach about sustainability. Many of the courses I teach at Fairhaven College of Interdisciplinary Studies at Western Washington University address intersections between society's structural inequalities and the political and economic systems that keep these structures in place. For example, in my course called Food for Thought, we explore the ideas of food pathways and how significant changes to our climate, coupled with patterns of unsustainable consumption, create food insecurity and lack of access to safe, healthy food for all. I often feel like Cassandra of Troy when my students do not want to believe the often-gloomy scientific predictions, or slide into despair or feel overwhelmed, so I engage in this work not as a simple intellectual exercise, but rather because like others, I am called to respond to these emotions—emotions that I also experience. I have come to understand that contemplative practice enlarges our capacity to navigate the suffering, grief, despair, fear, or hopelessness that arises when environmental issues are studied deeply.

Mike: As a long-time philosophy teacher who has also taught courses in environmental ethics, I am especially interested in ways that many of our common assumptions—about the relationships between humans and nature, our value orientations and cultural presuppositions, and what meaningful responses to these issues might look like—are challenged by our global ecological crises and their regional expressions. When the assumptions that lie behind our usual modes of problem solving are themselves at issue, we must explore Sharon Daloz Parks's interpretation of what Ron Heifetz calls *adaptive challenges*. These are conditions that cannot be addressed with expertise already in hand and thus require new learning and innovation—even the transformation of our worldview and the exploration of new patterns of response (Parks 2005). One component of such exploration will be the enhancement of our own and our students' capacities for reflection and contemplation, two components of intelligence that are not currently as attentively cared for in higher education as they might be. Yet careful, emotionally rich, personal, and dialogical thinking about the connections between knowledge and experience, along with the cultivation of sustained nonjudgmental present-moment awareness, require time. Can we imagine a culture and educational institutions with time for that kind of thinking? Can we recover contemplation in the intellectual life?

I believe that within this query itself is an invitation for each of us to become more attentive to our place in the world, to experience and think deeply about our own localities, our bioregions. What shifts might be required to genuinely see things locally, but not automatically in terms of city, county, state, and national boundaries? What might it take to move through a life seen, and cared for, in terms of an affinity for the Northwest Coast and the Salish Sea? Can development of receptive modes of consciousness, reflection, and contemplation enhance such an awareness and affinity? This does seem to be a particularly rich possibility for certain sorts of classroom activities and fieldwork. In my teaching at the University of Washington Bothell I have been designing a series of reflective activities I call "quiet noticing," which utilizes walking, sitting, careful observation of places, and other means to encourage students to experience connection to the places they live in already and to bring these experiences to reflective recognition. These reflections can then be used to relate to both the conceptual themes of courses and to rethinking what it means to live in this bioregion.

Kate: The contemplative practices that lie at the heart of Quakerism and Buddhism, silent worship and meditation, have sustained and nourished me for many years. I have been drawn to explore how to use these and other similar practices in my professional life as an educator, so that students can experience the benefits I have enjoyed. Teaching at Antioch University Seattle's Center for Creative Change has given me many opportunities. At Antioch, I prepare graduate students to become leaders of social change in sustainability, organizational development, management, and other areas, and I teach courses in sustainability, critical thinking, global pluralism, communication, and environmental policy. In my professional work on contemplative practices, the questions I have been drawn to consider include: What is the role of contemplative practices in an educational system whose purpose is seen as preparing students for jobs and careers? How can I introduce contemplative practices into the classroom, when so few of my students have any concept of contemplation and most are frantically busy in their everyday lives? And in an educational system increasingly driven by learning outcomes, how can I measure the benefits of contemplative practice in my students?

Sharon: The seeds from which this project has grown were planted in May 2008, when Jean MacGregor from the Curriculum for the Bioregion project (see chapter 5) and I (in my role as senior fellow and principal of Leadership for the New Commons, an initiative of the Whidbey Institute), convened a small planning group in the Farmhouse at the institute. The eight members of this initial group began by sharing their long-term personal commitments to reflective and contemplative thought along with their concerns about the current status of sustainability education on campuses. We all were keenly aware that very complex problems are often presented superficially without the deep analysis and sustained thought that might move students toward more viable and meaningful responses. Together we identified about thirty colleagues who valued sustainability education from diverse disciplines in the colleges and universities (and a non-profit or two) of our bioregion, and who might be good companions in a larger faculty learning community.[1]

Further, we chose to invite only people from within our own bioregion in order to enhance our ability to gather face-to-face and to encourage participants to share rides or use public transportation when traveling to our meetings. This partnership between the Curriculum for the Bioregion and the Whidbey Institute is highly compatible because the central commitments of the institute embrace: (1) a commitment to the environmental challenge as the critical issue of our time, because it so profoundly affects every sector of society and calls upon every discipline of the academy; and (2) the recognition that at the heart of the environmental challenge is a call for a deepened contemplative consciousness. Thus the Whidbey Institute—a retreat center on seventy acres of forest and meadowland— has served as a fitting home place where this faculty learning community could find its voice, courageously grapple with complex questions, and cultivate new pedagogical practices.

Karen: During my three decades teaching chemistry and environmental science at the community college level (Pierce College), I have been troubled by the apparent disconnect between how chemistry is typically taught and the ecological challenges that we face. My personal contemplative practices as well as my experiences as a Courage and Renewal facilitator[2] have helped me understand how turning away from the busyness of our lives and taking time to slow down can have an impact on how we think, what we think about, and how we act. When I attended the initial meeting of the steering committee for the Curriculum for the Bioregion project in 2004, a small group of us engaged in a conversation about the need for a contemplative/reflective strand within our work around sustainability education. I realized then that I had found colleagues who shared my concern about disconnections between learning and living and the impact they can have on teaching and learning for a sustainable future.[3]

As the Curriculum for the Bioregion project grew and developed, the desire to explore the impact of contemplative and reflective practices within sustainability education arose repeatedly, in multiple settings and from many different individuals. So, I was delighted when we made a decision to form a faculty learning community to explore how these practices might be integrated into our teaching and how they might impact our ability to respond in new ways to the environmental challenges facing us.

Our Faculty Learning Community

As a result of our shared awareness of the environmental crisis and by our strong desire to prepare our students to respond to it creatively, in 2008 we decided to form a faculty learning community within the Curriculum for the Bioregion project. We hoped to build a professional community of practice, through which we could develop and articulate a pedagogy that incorporates reflective and contemplative practices into sustainability education and to develop models for ourselves and for others who feel called to integrate sustainability into college and university courses across the curriculum.

The goal of our faculty learning community was to explore how contemplative and reflective practices might become components of larger efforts to counterbalance current societal behavior patterns that privilege consumption, busy-ness, and unsustainable patterns of living. Our work together was characterized by reflective practice, originally defined by Donald Schön as "the capacity to reflect on action so as to engage in a process of continuous learning" (Schön 1987). Schön also made a distinction between reflection-*in*-action (reflection during action) and reflection-*on*-action (reflection after action).

Our work together used both approaches. We have reflected-*in*-action during our meetings by thinking on our feet. Our conversations were spontaneous, free-flowing, and only lightly structured. We resisted the temptation to resort to conventional answers and instead held the questions open, expressing our ideas as provisional, tentative, and even half-baked. We made the road by walking it—and it was a road with many turns. We also reflected-*on*-action by exploring how our individual experiences teaching reflective practice and our shared experiences in the faculty learning community have impacted our teaching and our individual and collective learning. Indeed, this chapter is a manifestation of reflection-*on*-action as we seek to share some of the gleanings from shared experiences.

Because we came from disparate institutions and disciplines, we wanted to create a shared background from which we could explore the role of contemplative and reflective practices in higher education. To support this goal, we distributed a set of readings prior to each retreat. Participants were asked to note the quandaries and predicaments stirred up by the readings and to pay particular attention to the ideas that most arrested their attention. For example, during our first weekend retreat we discussed Stephanie Kaza's "Being with the Suffering," which addresses despair and hope in the face of today's planetary challenges. This led us to wonder if teaching students how to *sit* might just amplify their despair. So, together we explored how *being with the suffering* is different from *wallowing in the suffering*, noting Kaza's observation that only by opening ourselves to suffering can we transform it (Kaza 2008). We also recognized that that the stirring of minds and hearts happens frequently in many subject matters (especially when university-level education is successful) and contemplative practice does not necessarily amplify these responses more than other pedagogical strategies. Moreover, shared contemplative time may also have the benefit of helping individual students understand that they are not alone as they face disturbing details about our ecological challenges.

Two ideas have been central to our work together: a committed, consistent group and a willingness to explore uncharted waters. Through repeated gatherings of the same individuals, we have been able to "cook" our ideas and deepen our learning in ways that are difficult in highly porous groups where people come and go. Because inquiry has been a central feature of our group process, much of the following narrative is framed around questions we have explored together. We have learned to sit patiently with difficult, potentially unresolvable questions as well as with our own feelings of frustration, fear, and hope. By suspending our desires to advocate for our own individual ideas and to critique the ideas offered by others, we gave each other permission to "try to live the questions" (Rilke 2001, 8) without the need to articulate answers prematurely or unilaterally. We have no doubt that our experiments in learning to share practices of reflection and contemplation transformed the way we have been able to work together.

Living with the Questions

Over the four years we have worked together, the questions that have emerged and been held by the group followed two major themes: questions about contemplative and reflective practices as pedagogical strategies, and questions about how to respond creatively to the global ecological crisis. These generative questions have helped us learn new ways to think and behave in the face of adaptive challenges.

What Is the Relationship between Reflective and Contemplative Practices?
At our early retreats we explored the relationship between reflective and contemplative practices. Are they separate and distinct? Are they perhaps complementary? Or is it even appropriate to try to differentiate them? Some of us were tempted to propose definitions for these terms, but we soon realized that given the number of perspectives in the room, it would be more fruitful to explore their actual use in the classroom. Our discussions ranged over many options, sometimes exploring reflection and contemplation together as capacities relatively distinct from analysis and

argument, sometimes contrasting reflection and contemplation with one another. Some of us wanted to see reflective and contemplative capacities on a continuum, while others of our number strongly disagreed, believing the step to non-judgmental present awareness should have a distinct integrity.[4]

As we held the question about the relationship between contemplation and reflection and continued to explore our genuine and often heartfelt differences in our views, our faculty learning community grew into a shared understanding about these terms. For us, reflection generally connotes active cognition. It often draws on memory, reinforces associations, and may assist us as we move from initial thoughts into more enduring meaning and understanding. Consistent with Schön's definition, the objective of *reflective* practice is to ensure a more accurate and relevant understanding of a situation, which will facilitate more desired and effective outcomes. Reflective practice provides the pause to explore beliefs, values, and interpretations of reality, and requires a particular kind of focused attention. Reflective practice is widely accepted in the academy, codified in practice in many professional disciplines and pedagogical approaches (education, engineering, leadership studies, service learning) and in the assessment and evaluation systems in many alternative colleges.[5]

Contemplative practice, on the other hand, is characterized by relaxed yet concentrated presence of mind. Less common in the modern academy, it is often experienced as opening a space for other forms of understanding even as one is grounded within the space occupied by one's body. The contemplative mind is not about active thinking, but rather holding a space in silence, maintaining an openness that may allow for understanding and knowledge, or for spontaneous or intuitive insight, that does not arise through discursive thought. Contemplation is characterized by a mind attuned to an awareness of itself as it attends to the world.

Can We Teach What We Practice?

Although the participants in this learning community share a commitment to the value of contemplative and reflective practices in our personal lives, we found ourselves wrestling with questions about the appropriate role of such practices in our professional lives. Although some of us expressed concern about finding the time within our courses to include reflective practices such as journal writing, there was general agreement that these activities were very useful for deepening student learning. But, when the focus of our conversation moved toward less mainstream pedagogies, such as meditation and guided visualization, the anxiety level increased for many of us. It was not unusual to hear comments like, "Well, maybe that works well in your course, but I'm not sure it really fits in my situation."

The lack of comfort with certain types of contemplative practice mirrored differences in disciplinary focus as well as variations in institutional climate. Not surprisingly, our colleague, Karen Gaul, who teaches in a program on yoga and sustainability at The Evergreen State College, felt much more comfortable integrating meditation practices into her course than Karen Harding, who teaches a required chemistry course at a community college. The fit of deeply contemplative practices also varied from one institution to another. In some institutions there was widespread support among faculty and students for including practices such as meditation within courses. For example, Elizabeth Sikes teaches environmental philosophy and ethics at Seattle University, a Jesuit institution whose mission is "to educate the whole person," and she sees meditation as a natural fit with course content. On the other hand, Rosalie Romano, who teaches in Secondary Education at Western Washington University, a secular, publicly funded institution, finds more uneven collegial understanding and support for contemplative pedagogical strategies. Part of the issue, of course, is that practices like meditation are closer to activities found in spiritual traditions than to those typically seen in most educational institutions.

Is It Appropriate to Draw on Spiritual Traditions in Classroom Settings?
These discussions about the inclusion of contemplative practices in classroom settings led to another recurring question about the appropriateness of drawing on practices that often are based in spiritual traditions. At an early meeting, Marie Eaton raised the concern that integrating contemplative work into the classroom may appropriate practices that are often deeply connected to cultural or historical contexts. Patricia Killen, a historian of Christian traditions at Gonzaga University, helped us puzzle over what happens when contemplative practices are disconnected from the wisdom traditions that ground them and how to honor their origins, especially as higher education is now largely secular and relatively few students engage in contemplative practices of their own. Our early exchanges on this topic were heated, with varied perspectives expressed. Some felt that the value of the practices was so significant that we should not worry too much about the sources; others wondered if there are ways to honor the contemplative dimensions of all of the

world's faith traditions. Still others simply felt confused and anxious about the challenge these questions posed about their own classroom practices.

In addition to questions related to the spiritual-secular divide, we explored obvious and inevitable questions such as what might constitute appropriate assessment of student participation in contemplative activities. For example, how, if at all, should we as educators assess a student's progress with respect to contemplative and reflective work? If such assessment is desirable, are there appropriate ways to determine the quality or efficacy of student participation? Rather than assessing individual students, should our assessments be based on how these practices affect the tenor of classroom discussion? These questions remain alive in our ongoing work.

Can We Practice What We Teach?

As we have engaged reflective and contemplative practices as components of education for sustainability and justice in our region, we have increasingly recognized the importance of these same practices of attention for our own gatherings. A key shift occurred when, after our first major retreat, we realized we had not fully embodied our own convictions about the power of contemplation as we designed the agenda for our time together. Though we planned for reflective space in the meeting, including silence to process ideas before discussions and some significant written reflective prompts, we struggled with time constraints as we made decisions about how to include contemplative time. However, while debriefing the first meeting, the planning team realized that in our effort to spend time wisely and make progress toward our goals, we had lost our own confidence in using contemplation in the midst of an academic seminar. We had scheduled contemplative time only in optional, early-morning sessions.

We found that we continually had to resist and reexamine our inclination to stay in the intellectual territory that we, as faculty, are typically comfortable navigating, and thus reevaluate our own assumptions about what cognition means. As we negotiated our own challenges of moving between discursive thinking and the contemplative mind, we noticed all the triggers in academic settings that move us into analytical space and became aware of our collective failure to tap into other means of understanding and learning in our professional lives. We needed to remind ourselves that many of the metaphors that appear in stories, illustrations, songs, poetry, and even maps relate to the concepts we were exploring, and that the use of metaphors can bypass the limitations of expressing ideas solely through exposition. Symbolic image—in word, gesture, paint/pencil/pixel, or musical theme—may open a path toward understanding by engaging the senses as well as the mind. Sharon Daloz Parks noted the parallels between our work and the period of seed to harvest in the natural world, which reminded us to be conscious of these metaphors as we developed the next retreat agendas. The fact that this issue arose among a group of people who value the potential of including contemplative and reflective practices illuminates how difficult it can be for faculty to integrate these practices into a classroom setting when colleagues and students alike may be actively skeptical of their worth.

When we realized the implications of our own omission of these practices in our meeting times, the planning team decided to use the faculty learning community as a testing ground for how reflective and contemplative practices might be more fully integrated into a learning environment. The team modified the format for subsequent meetings to include more shared silence, reflection, and solitude. We actively integrated typical academic modes and cognitive activities of reading, discussion, and writing with other ways of knowing, and sought to create occasions for people to share what they are already doing to incorporate contemplative practices on behalf of a sustainable future. For example, during one session, Marie Eaton, a professional singer as well as a former dean, guided us through an activity in which we each voiced a sustained sound (but not necessarily holding one pitch) while moving freely through a large open space. Over several minutes, toning loudly enough to be heard but softly enough to hear others, and being mindful of our breath, we gradually moved toward the center of the space, each holding a tone but allowing it to be influenced by the others, each listening attentively. Then silence. We each kept our own voice, so to speak, yet came into an interdependent resonance with the others, held in an envelope of silence.

Similarly, another important effort to integrate contemplation into our process involved rethinking how we, as individuals and as a group, engaged with selected readings. At the first faculty learning community meeting, we launched into the discussion of the readings with little preamble, as we often do in our classes. In subsequent meetings, as we sought to create an environment more conducive to thoughtful interactions and deeper discussions, we decided to sit together in silence for twenty-five to thirty minutes prior to discussing the readings. We asked participants to just sit quietly during this time, rather than use the time to pore over the readings. For example, in preparation for a recent retreat, participants were asked to read "To a Future Without Hope" by Michael P. Nelson (Nelson 2010) and "How to Be Hopeful" by Barbara Kingsolver (Kingsolver 2010). During our conversation, we found ourselves wondering whether approaching the world with a sense of gratitude was more appropriate than maintaining a sense of hopefulness about the future. As Suzanne Fest, who teaches eco-psychology and research design at Antioch University Midwest, said, "When we get up in the morning with hope, it's a set up for disappointment. If one gets up with a sense of gratitude, there's a sense of invitation and expansive mind. Hope is not the goal, but a side-effect." David Levy, who teaches in the Information School at the University of Washington, felt that part of our human predicament was that we lack clear language for talking about how to be simultaneously grounded in the reality of our present situation while maintaining a positive vision of the future. Holly Hughes, an English Department faculty member at Edmonds Community College, reminded us of Emily Dickinson's sense that "'Hope' is the thing with feathers" (Dickinson 1999, 12). The image that came to Holly in response to our conversation was that the earth is a natural system; she will heal herself if we are willing to be aligned with her.

Although it is difficult to convey the depth and richness of our conversations in these short examples, we found that sharing quiet time together allowed questions and ideas to arise that would have been unlikely without our preparatory silence. In addition, the group silence seemed to change the tenor of our time together. These experiences (as well as our experiences with our students) confirmed our belief that although contemplative practices such as sharing silence are different from conventional classroom work, integrating these practices into courses is likely to have the same effect on students that it has had on us: deepening our dialog, helping us shape more apt and provocative questions, and encouraging a sense of community.

How Can We Respond Creatively?

As we wrestled with the question "how can we respond creatively to the global ecological crisis ourselves and how can we help our students to make their own creative responses?" our starting place was to consider current responses. Three are easily discernible; we see them in ourselves, in our students, and in society at large. The first is grief and despair. The second is denial—whether it is denial due to a lack of awareness of the scale of the crisis or disbelief that it is really that bad. And the third is to get out there and just fix it—to do something, now. But none of these responses are likely to help improve the situation.

The reasons why denial and despair are problematic are obvious, but the "fix it" strategy is also tricky. We live in a highly technological and instrumental culture; it fosters the false assumption that any problem can be fixed. Many attempts at "fixing" environmental problems fail because of the inherent unpredictability of human and natural systems. One need only think of the unforeseen consequences of the widespread use of the insecticide DDT on wildlife and human health, or of BP's numerous attempts to stop the flow of oil from the Deepwater Horizon rig in 2010. As David Orr said more than twenty years ago, one of the myths of education is that *"with enough knowledge and technology we can manage planet Earth. . . .* But the complexity of Earth and its life systems can never be safely managed" (Orr 1991, 52). Moreover, "fix it" strategies are characteristically piecemeal and disconnected, responding to one problem at a time, failing to take into account the radical interdependence of all life. Thus, they are inadequate and incommensurate with the scale of the global ecological crisis.

So how can we respond creatively and appropriately to support our students as they make their own creative and appropriate responses? Our discussions used two sets of ideas—namely the distinction between technical problems and adaptive challenges and the distinction between receptivity and instrumentality. Sharon Daloz Parks, drawing on the work of Ronald Heifetz and Marty Linsky (2002),[6] defined the distinction between technical problems and adaptive challenges, noting that technical problems (even though they may be complex) can be solved with knowledge and procedures already in hand. In contrast, adaptive challenges require new learning, innovation, and new patterns of behavior (Parks 2005). This perspective was helpful in our thinking, and we agreed that although technical fixes may play a part in addressing the challenges of sustainability, the scale and magnitude of the global ecological crisis requires adaptive responses that are necessarily creative.

We also found it helpful to consider David Levy's (2007) work on receptivity and instrumentality, asking ourselves whether contemplative practices can cultivate a deep receptivity to, and acknowledgment of, our situation, while recognizing that we do not know what to do in the instrumental or technological sense. Yet we are all active in the world, so our ongoing question is now: If reflecting deeply about sustainability moves us away from fix-it and instrumental responses, then what might receptive engagement look like?

Karen Litfin, who teaches in the Political Science Department at the University of Washington, triggered a third strand in our thinking, about "making a creative response." At one of our early retreats, she challenged us to reflect on the question: "What exactly do we want to sustain in the face of our own impermanence, mortality, and the survival of the planet?" Her question moved us to acknowledge that deciding what we want to sustain involves choices about what we *should* do, rather than what we *can* do, based on our deepest ethical values. Second, it led us again to an appreciation that receptivity and openness to adaptive challenges requires more than rational knowing; it also involves affective and somatic ways of knowing. Complementing reason and rationality, contemplation and reflection can help us to navigate feelings of despair and grief.

Applying What We Learned

Over the years that we have been meeting, we have developed a variety of contemplative and reflective classroom processes oriented toward deepening learning, inspiring civic action and reform, contributing to hope, and encouraging a symbiotic relationship between hope and action as we seek to enhance bioregional sustainability. Although each of us had experimented with strategies in our own classrooms, we wanted to create a broader professional platform to cultivate shared understandings of best practice and to create greater visibility for the effectiveness of reflective and contemplative pedagogies. We also generated many other forms of written work including theoretical essays, expositions of teaching-and-learning activities, and informal responses that helped shape agendas for subsequent meetings, which are available at the Curriculum for the Bioregion website.[7] A few examples follow.

Marie: When I teach Food for Thought, a course exploring the environmental and human impacts of the industrialized food system, I find that students often come with unsophisticated ideas about the economic, political, and social pressures that have created these systems and simplistic ideas about possible solutions. For example, when studying genetically modified seeds, their first response is typically outrage. To help complicate their thinking we examined not only corporate greed but also the impetus of people of good intention to develop genetically modified seeds as a response to world hunger, I draw on strategic questioning models as the basis for assignments that ask students to think about problems related to industrialized food production differently. Students learn to ask, what information do I *not* have or what parameters influence this situation that I am *not* considering? What judgments and assumptions may block my ability to see this situation, and are there other people who could help me examine the problem from a different perspective? Through this questioning they are better able to interrogate the complex intersections of poverty, hunger, and profit seeking that led to the Green Revolution and to explore more nuanced alternatives.

Kate: At Antioch University Seattle's Center for Creative Change, our entire pedagogy is based on reflective practice. We emphasize this approach to learning in two sequences of required courses (Comstock and Yamamoto 2007). In the Methods for Sustainable Change sequence, taken in the first year of graduate studies, we ask each student to write a weekly reflective journal responding to a series of questions designed to deepen their understanding of how assumptions, expectations, and beliefs influence what they feel, think, and do. As the first year progresses, we expect them to engage in collaborative reflective practice with their peers about events they have experienced together in their classwork by sharing and discussing their individual journals. In their second year, we require students to take a course sequence called Applications of Sustainable Change, in which they engage in collective reflective practice on a nine-month social change project conducted in an organization or a community of their choice. In this work, they participate as change agents in a co-created project, learning from their collective experiences.

Others in our learning community have devised classroom activities that attempt to link personal reflection, somatically based attentiveness and major global environmental issues. At the end of a two-week section on global climate change, Karen Litfin asks students to focus on a spectacular visual image from NASA that shows the narrow blue band of the earth's atmosphere. She then invites them to relax deeply and to observe their emotions and bodily sensations as she reminds them of some of the political and ethical quandaries related to global climate change that they have been studying. Though students who wish to opt out of this ten-minute exercise are given permission to leave, very few do. As students focus on their breath, Karen guides them through a meditation, reminding them that humanity has embarked upon a planetary experiment and that we all will be living in the results of that experiment. She then asks them to consider who they are in relation to this changing world and to simply take note of all that arises within them. The first time Karen offered this exercise, she was curious about its effectiveness, and so she conducted an anonymous online poll. All of the respondents, minus one, felt that they benefited and expressed gratitude for the respite from their harried lives.

Over seventy percent of the students reported gaining "significant insights into my sense of self in a changing climate" (Litfin 2012).

Gleanings and Other Questions

During the four years we have worked together, we have shared lively meetings, deepened our learning and engaged in meaningful work, reminding ourselves of our own needs to seek balance in this increasingly fast-paced world. We all agree that our meetings themselves became nourishing, that our shared silences created a container for conversations that were rich because they encouraged the use of multiple lenses and protected differing perspectives. Another important feature of our interactions has been the equality of participation among all members regardless of rank or institutional affiliation. Leaving behind the institutional hierarchies we tend to carry in our minds has fostered the development of an openness and sense of trust that allows us to explore our enduring questions and a willingness to freely disclose our uncertainty and vulnerability in new terrain. The sense of shared purpose and the opportunity to integrate our personal practices with our professional work has strengthened our commitment to collective and collegial work and continues to inspire us to develop new questions about where we might go from here.

We also continue to explore the possible connections between reflective and contemplative practices in education and the development of a deeper understanding of our own bioregion. It is a profound challenge: the patterns of our daily lives are so highly conditioned that coming to see (to perceive and move among) the ecosystems in which we live, and to consider their fragile future, are daunting challenges. They would be such in any case, but in a world of electronic immersion amid busy-ness, quietly paying attention to the quality of one's local natural environment, requires a conscious effort.

We hope this chapter shines a light on the power of meaningful purpose, commitment to long-term work, depth of inquiry, and the value of experiments in reflection and contemplation in the life of teaching and learning. We also hope that it serves to promote commitment to collaborative work, as now we must all learn how to face daunting challenges together, rather than as individuals. Further, perhaps this account of our small microcosm of deep connectedness and shared commitment can inform not only the work of other college and university faculty but all who seek ways of responding creatively to what Thomas Berry described as the "Great Work" of our time.

Acknowledgment

The authors would like to acknowledge the significant contributions that the work of the entire faculty learning community made to the development of the ideas and themes of this chapter.

Notes

1. See www.evergreen.edu/washcenter/bioregion for roster of participants.

2. www.couragerenewal.org.

3. See Chapter 5 for a fuller description of this a regional effort to support faculty in a variety of disciplines as they develop learning activities that integrate sustainability into their courses.

4. These varied dimensions of reflective and contemplative capacities are explored more thoroughly at http://www.contemplativemind.org.

5. Many of the schools in The Consortium of Innovative Environments for Learning (CIELearn.org) share narrative reflection as an assessment and evaluation tool.

6. See Ronald A. Heifetz and Marty Linsky, *Leadership on the Line: Staying Alive Through the Dangers of Leading*, 2002, p. 14.

7. See http://bioregion.evergreen.edu for a complete list of retreat readings.

References

Comstock, Don, and, Britt Yamamoto 2007. Social reflection for social change. Preparing adult learners to be change leaders. *Proceedings of the American Association of Higher Education conference*. Available at http://ahea.org/files/pro 2007comstock.pdf.

Dickinson, Emily. 1999. "Hope" Is the Thing with Feathers. In *The Poems of Emily Dickinson*, ed. R. W. Franklin, 12. Cambridge, MA: Harvard University Press.

Heifetz, Ronald A., and Marty Linsky. 2002. *Leadership on the Line: Staying Alive through the Dangers of Leading*. Cambridge, MA: Harvard Business School Press.

Kaza, Stephanie. 2008. Being with the Suffering. In *Mindfully Green: A Personal and Spiritual Guide to Whole Earth Thinking*, 15–32. Shambhala Books.

Kingsolver, Barbara. 2010. How to Be Hopeful. In *Moral Ground: Ethical Action for a Planet in Peril*, ed. Kathleen Dean Moore and Michael P. Nelson, 452–457. San Antonio: Trinity University Press.

Levy, David. M. 2007. No Time to Think: Reflections on Information Technology and Contemplative Scholarship. *Ethics and Information Technology* 9 (4):237–249.

Litfin, Karen. 2012. Personal communication.

Nelson, Michael P. 2010. To a Future Without Hope. In *Moral Ground: Ethical Action for a Planet in Peril*, ed. Kathleen Dean Moore and Michael P. Nelson, 458–462. San Antonio, Texas: Trinity University Press.

Orr, David. 1991. What Is Education For? Six Myths about the Foundation of Modern Education and Six New Principles to Replace Them. *In Context* 27:52.

Parks, Sharon Daloz. 2005. Leadership for a Changing World: A Call to Adaptive Work. In *Leadership Can Be Taught*, 1–18. Harvard Business School Press.

Rilke, R.-M. 2001. Letter IV (16 July 1903). In *Letters to a Young Poet*, 8. Modern Library.

Schön, Donald A. 1987. *Educating the Reflective Practitioner: Toward a New Design for Teaching and Learning in the Professions*. San Francisco, California: Jossey-Bass.

23

Cultivating Pedagogies of Resilience: Practicing Place, Expanding Perspectives, Sustaining Life

Bobbi Patterson

A private, medium-sized research university, Emory University enrolls 6,000 grad-uate and professional students and 7,000 undergraduates in the liberal arts and business. Half of the main Atlanta campus is preserved forest, though located twenty minutes from downtown Atlanta in a mixed neighborhood of historic homes, suburban shopping malls, and dense urban corridors.

Some consider me an outdoor junkie. Time in wilderness, whether hiking, kayaking or camping, not only wakens me to the power of places but also nourishes my commitment to sustainability. None of my Religion Department colleagues flinched when I asked to take our long untaught course, Religion and Ecology, out of mothballs and give it a go.

We Start Where We Are

Our fledgling campus sustainability efforts had incorporated some lessons about place, citing campus history, flora and fauna, and cultural contexts. So, I supplemented the course title, Religion and Ecology, with Emory as Place. Our classroom experience would be open to intellectual, tactile, emotional, and spiritual learning and teaching. My design, goals, and objectives drew on transformative pedagogies and contemplative practices, which spanned from the personal to the collective (Kolb 1984; Mezirow 1991 and 2010; Patterson 2010). Readings, films, and videos addressed American environmental histories and challenges through the lenses of religious cultures and thought. We confirmed and contrasted those writers' and practitioners' assumptions, facts, and conclusions using our local and bioregional settings as comparative data. Experiential learning framed everything we did in our campus walks, outdoor assignments, fieldtrips, and campouts. Students wrote weekly, using a range of reflective and analytic formats to create a semester-long portfolio.

As we tested and interpreted arguments and encounters in real time and space, we discovered our own approaches to complex questions of human-creatures-plants-place interactions and interdependencies. Drawing particularly from Buddhist and Christian perspectives on American environmental issues, we dug deeper into ethical questions about ecological responsibility and social justice. We also learned about meditation practices, many of which built from "natural" relationships.[1] Sensory-based assignments drawing on simple phenomenological approaches to learning emphasized observation involving smell, touch, and sound. Students chose a natural site on campus (using their own definition) and returned weekly to watch and compare. These exercises kept us literally grounded as our analytic and critical thinking matured. Within a few weeks, we found ourselves focusing on these key questions: What does the environmental crisis have to do with the places that sustain us? What counts when using the word *place*? How and when do we feel connected to places—or not? What do these connections tell us about our social, political, religious, and cultural lives? How do we move from understanding these connections to acting for positive, sustainable change—now and lifelong?

Class readings expanded to include analytic and testimonial texts by Stephanie Kaza, Sally McFague, Howard Thurman, and others. Poems and essays by Gary Snyder, David Wagoner, and Mary Oliver extended our understandings. We ambled in our campus forest, identified plants, tracked animal pathways, and enriched our emergent environmental knowledge by taking into account our relations with those creatures and natural processes. Simultaneously, we read reports of Atlanta's sprawl, consequences of over-building, water shortages, and the asthma epidemic among children. The links grew complex and intersecting as our "book learning" also became whole body realizations. We sometimes smelled the trash-filled and semi-polluted South Fork of Peachtree Creek, which runs beside our campus woodlands. Learning that this water contaminated the southwest Atlanta playgrounds of the Boys and Girls Club children, who trick-or-treat each fall on our campus, tightened the intellectual connections and also our throats. A field trip to the neighborhoods of these children confronted us with literal signs of our inescapable interdependence: "Park Closed! Danger: Health Hazards."

Pulling back these layers of interdependence broadened and intensified the implications of our lifestyle choices on campus and beyond. Threats to sustainable biodiversity of the Piedmont forest and to our basic health now extended to human relations, ethical responsibility, and public policy. As sustainability questions thickened, we read more about local ecosystem, economic, and equity matters, while also contemplating—sitting with—the suffering and beauty of place. We analyzed data and sustainability models for increased thriving as we tried to put them to work in our written reflections and active engagement on hikes, neighborhood field trips, and campouts. Active and exploratory scholarship like this not only challenged our worldviews about nature, race, and class, but also our resources for hope and resilience. Creating a classroom of trust and safety, we brought back our questions, shock, and fears while striving to form positive responses (Patterson 2005). Our unfolding classroom covenant of respect, critical inquiry, and personal transformation kept us moving forward.

During the last few weeks of class, I explicitly invited students to see themselves and their lives as part of the ongoing, unfolding hope for global sustainability: "What will your chapter be?" Students majoring in biology, political science, sociology, and religion began claiming their own nascent but growing expertise as the foundation for taking next steps. Along with texts, some students drew on revised or new religious resources to enrich their capacities. Others focused on gained knowledge of social structures affecting sustainable living. Over the twelve years I have taught and learned through this class, I too had to grow, adapt, and change my pedagogies, texts, and field-based exercises. I came to view the course as a living system, and that only strengthened my determination to join my students in sustainable hope and action. As one student in my 2005 class expressed it, "I now believe that our actions across the globe interconnect and can greatly affect life, for the better or for the worse."

Stepping into the Fray: Students and Teachers

Graduate-student teaching colleagues and I chose a collaborative teaching style for this course. Initially, our undergraduates struggled to believe that we truly wanted their direct help in shaping components of the course. A senior in the 2008 class, during our third session, responded in an exasperated tone to my suggestion that the class revise our first assignment. "You *really* want our opinion? Well, I mean, I've just never been in a class like this; you're taking student input so seriously." Bewilderment became resistance as students struggled with an outdoor assignment to observe a 12-inch-by-12-inch space and then write about it without using traditional labels and categories. How to talk about "grass" or "insects" without using those words? Challenged to describe what they saw, touched, smelled, and felt using words driven by the phenomena instead of existent ways of knowing, they felt frustrated. What was the "right" answer?

I felt on edge too as I hoped to foster not only alternate epistemologies but also new styles of agency in all of us. As we upended "business as usual" through observation and reflective and analytic writing, we realized how trapped our learning can become. As the semester wore on, however, we grew more comfortable testing the limits of our perceptions and assumptions. Woods walks triggered discussions about what counted as "alive." Closer attention to a deteriorating urban forest drew comparative thinking about the collapse of the surrounding neighborhood. How did causes of pollution interrelate to gentrification? Our default categories and frameworks softened and expanded, enriching our styles of inquiry. As thinking and doing turned out to be multileveled, we kept redefining sustainability, knowledge, and responsibility.

Over the process of the course, we watched pieces of our assumptions break off and reattach to new perspectives amid a growing awareness of our incompetencies. By *incompetency* I mean the recognition that we could not fully analyze or define certain dynamics and relationships. We needed more time to understand the habits of birds while breeding, migrating, and surviving. Specific politics of place now required economic history as well as socio-cultural understanding. More comfortable with the clumsiness of certain models of analysis and action, we learned to wait with the questions that were too difficult to "work through" or find answers for. We recognized more clearly the effects of our discipline-based training and personal stories. Some students found the work in the forest too sentimental, too vulnerable. Others grew up in rural settings, and patterns in urban development took longer for them to grasp. What initially felt like ineptitude became flexibility of minds, bodies, and hearts. This holistic and communal style of inquiry kept us honest, or as Donna Harraway recently said, "staying with the trouble" (Harraway 2011).

Learning as Living Systems

As our corporate confidence strengthened, students realized they *could* teach themselves, and I realized I could trust my teaching instincts. For them, "grass" became "stalks of thin filament reaching." A biochemistry major's site elicited this description of sound: "the absolute lightest softest, nearly non-existent pitter pitter pitter pitter . . . WeeeEEEEEE hummm WeeeEEEEE HUmmmm they go around the discs." New naming and revised assumptions curved our learning and teaching toward adventures we had never imagined. That imagination gave us space to tend to the worlds of bugs, snakes, changeable weather, and necessarily purified water. Focused attention in the moment kept us teetering at the edge of anxiety and delight. Clearly not in charge, awareness also invited us to rest in the here and now as it was. By year three, I asked students with more outdoor experience to take on quiet leadership roles, which helped the whole group navigate anxieties and adventure. As we hiked, for instance, these quiet leaders called regular "water checks," encouraging everyone to drink. They explained how to negotiate a steep trail. We became a learning, living system.

If a drying creek bed invited a "teaching moment," I accepted the chance, asking the class to stop for an eight-minute standing meditation beside it. I used a rising ridge to teach map reading and very simple compass work. We took initiative, grounded in our mutual trust as we moved into new territories together. Especially on our two-night, two-and-a-half day campouts, cold and wet, hungry and adjusting, we grew quieter, slowed down, and increased interior space to notice details. Students recorded these shifts in their portfolio entries.

But camping took a lot of organization, time, and experience. I learned to bring along extra clothes and several camp stoves. When I waffled about going on trips, past students pushed back. The intensity of focus and community, they said, could not be matched by day hikes. So, scaling back from two two-night campouts to one for two nights and a second for one night, I told the incoming class I had to have more help. They invested, organizing gear for everyone and buying and packing the food with less direction from me and my co-teachers. I kept the hikes, but made them closer to home. Whether hiking or camping, I canceled class to honor the time these activities took. For the days we did not have class, our blackboard site listed links where students could find online videos about Atlanta or relevant websites, including the Appalachian Trail Conservancy and the Chattooga Conservancy.

Hiking and camping taught practices of pausing. Students learned to breathe, to wait "in-between" information and questions.[2] Emails from graduated students testify to their continued use of these lessons. Whether in personal decisions or job-related activities, these graduates transform the pressures of such present-moment demands into a short opportunity to settle in their bodies and breathe. Using rational and intuitive skills based on this grounding, they respond without judging themselves or others as they assess next steps. One urban, African American woman who took the class in 2000, for example, learned that semester to make peace with insects, a phobia learned from the aunt who raised her and had coped with insect infiltration in her absent-landlord apartment. But since our class, she has continued to go to a natural setting for what she calls "reconnecting and focusing." Here, she explained, she can pause to think, to listen. One is never sure, as a teacher, what the students are really learning. Will any of this matter for their lives? I have learned not to underestimate the small breakthroughs, for they breed deeper maturation in liberal learning than we often imagine, maturation for life-long study and action.

So, whether through full-scale camping trips, day hikes, or campus walks, students examined the economic, ecosystem, and equity issues of sustainability through community and self. They grew to understand and analyze structural dimensions of racism and poverty as well as to recognize the capacities of human-driven labels to override and/or distort our relations with natural systems. These insights transformed their views and actions. The changes ranged from realizations that sorority and fraternity letters labeled forms of power to recognitions of our campus struggle to completely compost our waste. I did not raise these issues. They arose by the students' integrative work, which broke down their defensive postures, and became levers for changing how they lived. Each year in our last class, we did Joanna Macy's exercise, "Truth Mandala" (Macy 1998, 100–105). Following her design, we sat in a circle with four symbols in the center representing signal experiences of anger, fear, need, and grief. The circle itself represented hope. One by one, upon their own initiative, students shared images and stories reflecting their worries for the planet, for their siblings and parents. They shared struggles with failure and, especially for seniors, fears about the future. Our living community had evolved to the point of naming natural points of collapse, and together finding hope or resilience. The revelations drew caring support, not platitudes. Tears were shed across gender and age.

How We Know Alters What We Do

Cultivating a community that explicitly linked cognitive participation in the classroom to our ordinary lives and other living systems, we challenged more than our epistemologies, assumptions, and interpretations (Zajonc 2006, 1745; Zajonc 2003, 57). Learning about urban development by reading and testing theories locally, we not only enriched our perspectives, but also strengthened analyses for action. Integrating our own narratives and sensory knowledge helped us compare and consider our lives' sustainability with the lives of others in Atlanta's poorer neighborhoods. Linking these place-based approaches with contemplative pedagogies prepared us for critical thinking to link embodied epistemological change to ethical response.[3]

As transformative pedagogies predict, closer attention to information, whatever the form, breeds confrontation with past habits and ideas. For ethical consciousness to mature, it requires and acquires a sense of civic responsibility (Harkavy 2006). One student wrestled with a class reading in her portfolio entry, quoting Parker Palmer: "every epistemology becomes an ethic" (cited in Zajonc 2006, 1744). Her reflection went on: "After our day-long hike in North Georgia, I'm developing a tactile source of knowing beyond my usual approach, human self-absorption. How easily, I get lost inside my own mind, blind to other pathways for understanding—and more important, the consequences." Students described how changes in their ways of knowing began from closer attention to our interdependence with all living things but grew into questions about moral assumptions. One student described her moral assumptions sourced by changes in her spirituality: "I learned more about being "spiritual" in a "non-spiritual" way . . . attending to the living environments . . . our moral obligation to take care . . . I changed." Another commented that "as I paid more attention, I realized the intricate webs of so many levels of life from fallen leaves, to animals' tracks, to the air growing cooler and warmer from patches of light and shade." In his final essay, this same senior wrote, "Now having this knowledge, there is no reason to remain ignorant or not to take action against the environmental and social injustices of my time, no matter where I experience them."

Writing and Resilience

Experientially driven learning transferred and deepened as students wrote portfolio entries about their epistemological shifts, ethical reformulations, and active engagements. The energy required to make these changes flowed from the resilient hope they discovered through our class. Studying their portfolios over eleven years has revealed that resilience and hope. I created the portfolio framework with six optional formats from which students could choose how best to explore their learning and questions: descriptive, analytic, comparative, integrative, reflective, and creative entries. Required to write at least four entries every two weeks, including a reading summary of an assigned text, students revisited their earlier entries to clarify, confound, or continue. Graduate teaching associates and I commented on their entries and invited them to expand further on certain topics or initiate a new direction or critique. Students' final "Presenting Portfolio" consisted of eight entries, which tracked the broad trajectories of their learning and doing over the semester. In addition, they wrote a four-page final reflective essay.

Graduated students view the writing and creative practices of the portfolio as critical steps in life-learning. One athlete described the linkages he found:

What I learned from our class and the portfolio writing has changed my attitudes when I'm running in a track meet. . . . Writing like nature can be very unpredictable. If I had it my way in a meet, it would be always be in the low sixties with no humidity or wind. . . . However, nature does not ask me what I would like every time I step up to the starting line. Nor does reflective writing, if I let go.

The portfolio format gave students a space of their own to explore suffering, resilience, and life as they had not understood it before. A senior described this crucible as "having a 'place' to connect with Atlanta and the lives of other people who have never seen our classroom." Another senior woman wrote: "Through reflection and writing, I realized that if it were not for the group effort, I know I would not have pushed myself. . . . I wanted to be part of this team we had created . . . fully immersed . . . in what everyone was doing. I return to that awareness regularly now." Writing further nourished the confidence we had gained through doing. But below both, I wondered, what fostered the "oomph," the resilience that had kept us going in this class and would keep us going in the future. What were the mechanisms of resilience?

Talking with a colleague from the Environmental Studies Department, I learned about the multifaceted dynamic that feeds thriving living systems, ones that are sustainable. Our class ecosystem had moved through cycles of resource accumulation, stability, collapse, reconstruction, and innovation. Each time we made it through that cycle, never direct or simple, we were tapping into resilience, that multifaceted resource of and for adaptive change.[4] By year six or seven, I explicitly described resilience and the cycling life systems through which it moves and acted. I hoped to quicken our capacities to recognize it and leverage its energy and hope for deeper learning and living. Resilience nourished and reinforced our hope and confidence in the future.

Asking community-related environmental activists to join us in class or on hikes became another opportunity to hear actual practitioners talk about the power of resilience in their lives and work. I continue to think about improving our grasp of this crucial concept. A graduating history major found his own links—from study, to practice, to future life—through resilience. Reflecting on a reading about Arbor Day in the United States, he wrote:

Our reading on the history of Arbor Day stayed with me while watching trees in my campus "place." . . . The invisible force returns and realization sets in. The dominant does not dominate. . . . The force whirls up and combines everything into one. The shy ones, the rusty specks, the webs, the veins, everything. Everything. Even I am part of this force. . . . I am this space and have life.

Transformation

In the fifth year I taught the class, I found a rocky outcropping half a mile from our campsite. It was autumn and a light but steady breeze cooled the rock and anything on it. Would *half* of the nineteen students tolerate sitting through the sequenced meditation exercise by Thich Nhat Hanh that I planned to use (Hanh 2008)? Anxious not to push them, I opened my eyes every minute or three. Were they squirming, lying down, preoccupied with a patch of moss? Very few were not focused—even after twenty minutes. We kept going until thirty minutes passed. In year seven, I arrived in our classroom to discover a video already set up at and primed to play. A subset of students had rallied overnight through email around a clip that they thought well displayed the key points in the day's readings. The first few times this happened, I took it as critique. *I* should have identified a relevant video or assigned them the task. I got over that. By year eight, I rested in the living system of each class, as we explored our territories with and without maps, in and through changing roles, and with and without provisions.

Lingering a bit longer at a stream does not worry me so much now. I am attuned to student hunger for intense engagement and thereby find my own. We need to stay here. If the meditation practice that began class drew us deeper than I expected, I learned to sustain the silence or perhaps add another component to the meditation. When discussions of readings got contentious because people had strong viewpoints, we analyzed and critiqued those beliefs and assumptions without judging or labeling. Although I consistently use a sequenced approach to learning and design assignments moving from understanding to comprehension, then to analysis, critique, and synthesis, I agreed with Lee Shulman: such steps rarely follow a clean learning-taxonomy sequence (Shulman 2002). We woke up and took initiative. We tapped into resilience. We transformed.

Acknowledgments

I would like to thank Leslie Munoz, Leah Abrams, and Caroline Bass who have helped analyze the portfolios written by students in my classes.

Notes

1. *The Miracle of Mindfulness*; *When the Trees Say Nothing: Writings on Nature by Thomas Merton*; and *The Jatakas: Birth Stories of the Bodhisattva* are three examples of texts we used.

2. A phrase foundational to Luce Irigaray's stance in her book, *Between East and West*.

3. In his article "Spirituality in Higher Education: Overcoming the Divide," Arthur Zajonc articulates Platonic epistemological differentiations between rational, deductive thought and perceptive judgment which comes to know through direct engagement with or experience of truth. He goes on to describe a similar differentiation in Buddhist epistemology. The helix of learning drawn from both approaches produces thick knowing capable, even expectant, of ethical reflection and action for the good. Ethical response is an expected outcome of contemplative pedagogies. For more on critical place-based pedagogies see Gruenewald's "Best of Both Worlds: A Critical Pedagogy of Place" (2003).

4. This cycling model of ecosystem thriving is developed in the excellent book, *Panarchy*, by Lance Gunderson and C. S. Holling (2001).

References

Gruenewald, David A. 2003. The Best of Both Worlds: A Critical Pedagogy of Place. *Educational Researcher* 32 (4):3–12.

Gunderson, Lance, and C. S. Holling. 2001. *Panarchy: Understanding Transformations in Human and Natural Systems*. Washington, DC: Island Press.

Hanh, Thich Nhat. 2008. *Breathe! You Are Alive: Sutra on the Full Awareness of Breathing*. Berkeley, CA: Parallax Press.

Harkavy, Ira. 2006. The Role of Universities in Advancing Citizenship and Social Justice in the 21st Century. *Education, Citizenship and Social Justice* 1 (1): 5–37.

Harraway, Donna. 2011. Religion and Animals panel discussion. American Academy of Religion Annual Meeting, November 25.

Kolb, David. 1984. *Experiential Learning: Experience as the Source of Learning and Development*. Englewood Cliffs, NJ: Prentice-Hall.

Macy, Joanna. 1998. *Coming Back to Life: Practices to Reconnect Our Lives, Our World*. Gabriola Island, British Columbia: New Society Publishers.

Mezirow, Jack. 1991. *Transformative Dimensions of Adult Learning*. San Francisco: Jossey-Bass.

Mezirow, Jack. 2010. Sustaining Life: Contemplative Pedagogies in a Religion and Ecology Course. In *Meditation and the Classroom: Contemplative Pedagogy for Religious Studies*, ed. Fran Grace and Judith Simmer-Brown, 148–155. New York: SUNY Press.

Patterson, Barbara. 2005. Practicing Reconciliation in the Classroom. In *Roads to Reconciliation: Approaches to Conflict*, ed. Amy Benson Brown and Karen Poremski, 211–230. Armonk, NY: M.E. Sharpe, Inc.

Patterson, Barbara. 2010. Sustaining Life: Contemplative Pedagogies in a Religion and Ecology Course. In *Meditation and the Classroom*, ed. Fran Grace and Judith Simmer-Brown, 148–155. New York: SUNY Press.

Shulman, Lee S. 2002. Making a Difference: A Table of Learning. *Change* 34 (6):36–44.

Zajonc, Arthur. 2003. Spirituality in Higher Education: Overcoming the Divide. *Liberal Education* 89 (1):50–58.

Zajonc, Arthur. 2006. Love and Knowledge: Recovering the Heart of Learning through Contemplation. *Teachers College Record* 108 (9):1742–1759.

24

Awakening to the Hero's Journey in Teaching and Learning

Christopher Uhl and Greg Lankenau

The Pennsylvania State University is the land grant school for the commonwealth of Pennsylvania. PSU's main campus has an enrollment of 45,000 students and is situated in a fertile limestone valley, surrounded by forest-covered sandstone ridges. The campus, covering almost 300 acres, is located in State College, a town of about 60,000 people.

The year was 1982. I (Chris Uhl) had just accepted a faculty position at Pennsylvania State University (often called Penn State, or PSU) in the Biology Department.[1] Shortly after arriving on campus, I was informed by my chair that I would be teaching Environmental Science (BiSci 3 for short). The course had an enrollment of 400 and was expressly targeted to non-science majors.

I had never taught a college course, much less attempted to *profess* to 400 students, packed into an auditorium, filled to the balcony. In my trepidation, I assumed that I had no choice but to adopt the pedagogies I had been subjected to during my own years of schooling. Yes, I would lecture to my students, aspiring to play the role of the "sage on the stage," filling their empty heads with facts and figures, with a few anecdotes tossed in.

Reading the evaluations at the end of my first year of teaching, I learned to my surprise that more than a handful of my students did not like my course very much. They thought it was a waste of their time and characterized me using words like *arrogant, distant, boring, depressing,* and worse. Ouch! Though I was dismayed to receive these kinds of evaluations, the voice of my ego—"these kids are lucky to have me"—was grander than my capacity to learn from my students' critique. And besides, I reasoned, my primary job as a biology professor was to conduct research; this teaching gig was just a side act. Indeed, in those early years, every chance I got, I went off to the Amazon Basin to figure out ways to help tropical forests grow on lands badly degraded by careless land-use practices.

In sum, my posture as a fledgling college teacher conveyed that my views, my questions, and my assessments were all that mattered. Ironically, my judgments of my students—that they were disinterested, lazy, ignorant, self-absorbed—was an apt characterization of myself. I was the one who was disinterested, lazy, ignorant, and self-absorbed, particularly when it came to truly *seeing* my students.

It is only now, decades later, that I am able to grasp the ways in which this seeing of the other is essential for effective teaching. Real teaching is a relational act. This understanding is situated in the very word education—the root *educe* meaning "to draw out" (not "to fill up empty heads"). Specifically, it means to draw out the innate curiosity, the subsurface yearnings, the burning questions, the capacities for reflection, feeling, caring, and intuitive knowing that lie within each of us, teacher and student alike.

A Fundamentalist

As a beginning teacher of Environmental Science it never occurred to me to ask such foundational questions as: What is the "environment?" Where did it come from? What is "science?" Who says? What does it mean to teach? What is worth teaching? What is worth learning? How does genuine learning occur? These questions never arose because I, like many people in academia, had been successfully conditioned to believe that there was only one way to teach, one way to learn, and that "environmental science" was whatever the textbook writers said it was. Yes, I was a fundamentalist.

So it was that with an environmental science text in hand, I proceeded to "cover the material." There was certainly no dearth of "material" to cover, especially when it came to environmental threats. Everywhere I looked, I saw (or read reports of) wounds—forest clear cuts, acid rain, ozone thinning, polluted rivers, toxins in our food, horrendous waste, wars on all continents—a world seemingly hurling toward its own demise.

All of this woundedness began to get me down; I became sad, angry, and indignant. Indeed, back then, a good class for me was one where I delivered a rant about the latest environmental calamity. I say "good" class because my venting enabled me to experience some measure of personal catharsis. But the larger truth, now self-evident, is that by dumping my angst onto my students, I was acting in an insensitive, self-absorbed way.

Can you imagine being me—Dr. Death—year after year tracking the deterioration in the earth's vital signs? Or perhaps worse, can you imagine being a young person, filled with your own angst, and having to sit in a room with 400 of your contemporaries, receiving information about how the planet is in decline and that there is probably nothing you can do about it?

My Awakening

This phase of my teaching ended when I realized, to my horror, that rather than promoting an ethic of respect and caring for the earth, my negativity was, more likely, engendering a dislike for the environment within my students. One epiphany occurred when I encountered the statement "we teach who we are" in Parker Palmer's seminal book, *The Courage to Teach*. Could that be true? I thought about my most outstanding teachers and realized that, to a person, what they modeled for me (more than the particulars of their prescribed subject matter) was a *way of being* in the world. When it came to their subject, and life more generally, they were curious, reflective, enthusiastic, authentic, vulnerable, compassionate, and more. And what about me? If we teach who we are, as Palmer posited, could it be that I was teaching a way of living imbued with suppressed anger that surfaced as sadness and despair?

A second awakening occurred on the last day of class at the end of my sixth year of teaching BiSci. From my perspective it had been a good year. I had incorporated some new material into the course, and I was becoming more comfortable responding to student questions during class. So, there I stood in a self-congratulatory stance as my students sat with their heads bowed, laboring over their final exam. As the hour wound down, students began to come up, one by one, to hand me their test sheets. I was feeling light-hearted and ready to wish them well and to thank them for taking my course. My students, on the other hand, appeared sullen and downtrodden. Only a handful even made eye contact with me, and, yet, only minutes earlier, I had convinced myself that I was at the peak of my game.

A few days later, still feeling forlorn, I strapped on my backpack and headed to the mountains for a week-long walkabout. The simple act of ambling in Penn's Woods reminded me of the wonder, kinship, and full-bodied delight that I had experienced on sojourns in the wilds, years earlier. It was on this woodland retreat that I realized that I had been teaching BiSci upside down; I was asking my students to care about something—the earth—with which most had little contact, little connection, and to which almost none felt relationship. Like almost everyone else in the United States, my students were indoor people, domesticated, out of touch with rock and soil, free-running water, unfiltered sunlight, gusts of wind, woodlands, and wild animals. How absurd of me, then, to expect them to care about an earth with which they had almost no relationship!

I further realized that by grounding BiSci in the ethos of fear and guilt, I was engendering hopelessness, revulsion, and numbness in my students. What would happen if I were to center my pedagogy on awe, delight, compassion, wonder, and possibility? What if my intention was to help my students fall in love with the earth, to draw back in awe in the presence of a rainstorm? To fall down on their knees, opening their senses, in response to a hilltop oak?

Inviting Students on a Journey

I returned from my walkabout energized and anxious to re-imagine what might be possible in BiSci. Questions bubbled out of me: Did I really need to use a standard environmental science textbook? And, if I found the current texts arid and lifeless, what was keeping me from creating something new? What if I got rid of exams? And how about if I moved away from the safety of the podium, from time to time, and ambled around the room? Too, what would happen if I opened the curtains in the auditorium to let sunlight in? What if I built the course around questions students were harboring? How would it be if I created time for students to explore their feelings, ideas, and experiences during class? And what if I recast my role, not as information broker, but as midwife: one who draws forth understanding from within my students, rather than depositing information into their heads? With all these ruminations, I was, in effect, asking: What's possible here? These deliberations led me to imagine my course not so much as a subject to be taught as a journey to be taken.

A Course Journal

It occurred to me, then, that if my intention was to invite students on a journey, it would be helpful for them to have a journal to record their story. That first year my enthusiasm for journaling, combined with my growing disillusionment with testing, prompted me to announce that I would give no tests in BiSci (yes, there was applause). Instead, I explained, their grade would be determined by the caliber of their journal reflections. To this end, I required that students reflect on each class meeting and on all course readings. So it was that on the last day of class that year, my TA and I collected 400 student journals. This was about 300 pounds of journals, roughly 40,000 total journal pages. The two of us had four days to access these journals. Think of it as reading and offering commentary on seven journal pages a minute for twelve hours a day over a four-day period. Think of it as impossible. Many students received "A"s that semester. It was a fiasco but also a triumph, because I was no longer held hostage to limiting beliefs. In truth, I was ebullient. I had not found a solution, but I had given myself permission to imagine something different. And how fascinating to be finally reading what students were writing about their lives, their discoveries, their long-suppressed feelings. Said one former BiSci student, "I think what helped me the most was the journals. . . . You go home and you think, you have to sit there and think about everything you've learned and put things together and how it relates to your life."

Students Leading Each Other on a Journey
Anxious to initiate still more experiments, I announced on the last day of class at the end of the fall semester, that I was looking to recruit student volunteers to serve as teaching assistants when BiSci was offered again the following fall. Much to my delight, a cadre of volunteers actually did step forward, but then panic struck. Had I once again let my enthusiasm and desperation for change cloud my judgment? After all, these were undergraduates! How could they act as legitimate teaching assistants? Wasn't this status reserved for graduate students? But my fear dissipated as I listened to these TA candidates describe how they had encountered something real in BiSci for the first time since coming to college. Some even spoke about how they were on a journey—their own journey—and they were not done! Moreover, to a person, they wanted to bring something of the awakening they had experienced in BiSci to their peers. Said one TA: "I wasn't ready to stop learning. I wasn't ready to stop my journey yet. . . . This is the best experience I've had in college, I want to stay with this. I feel like BiSci is an underground way of life and I want to bring it to the light and show people, and be like, look at this, this is great. You could do so much, and you have no idea. You have no idea how big you are."

It was January, and I had a semester to prepare these nascent TAs to teach, single-handedly, two weekly break-out sections (with twelve students each) in the fall. Because Palmer's "we teach who we are" dictum had been formative for me, I decided to use it as the centerpiece for the TA course.

We met for four hours on Monday evenings for fifteen weeks. Each night we shared a meal together and then devoted ourselves to experiential learning activities aimed at cultivating relationship with self, the human other, and our planet. By virtue of this simple format, we created a community of care and mutual trust as well as a set of "lab" exercises that TAs would bring to their students in the fall. The labs were designed to allow the TAs to share with their peers experiential approaches to such things as accessing body intelligence, relating to trees, exploring the power of questions, calculating an ecological footprint, practicing the art of truth-speaking, discovering the benefits of slowing down, and creating an ecological meal. By the time the fall semester arrived, the TAs were ready to rock. What they lacked in expertise they more than made up for in enthusiasm and commitment.

Looking back, I realize that each of the fifteen in that first cohort of TAs was, in their own way, embarking on a Hero's Journey, as Joseph Campbell would call it. In the classic formulation, the hero leaves home and endures hardship, ultimately dying to his/her former self (i.e., breaking from his small or false self) before he or she is able to bring home a soulful gift that serves the common good. In doing so, the hero comes to understand him/herself as a part of a much larger whole.

These days, when I begin working with a new cohort of TAs each spring semester, I invite them to see their work as part of a larger quest for self-knowing, and challenge them to seriously question all that has limited them—for example, who they think they are, their so-called certainties, the beliefs that have heretofore limited their understanding of reality. And I warn them that in this process of questioning, they may experience confusion and anguish, as well as the seemingly paradoxical freedom that results when we, as humans, open ourselves to suffering, surrender, and vulnerability. Said one former TA, "BiSci allowed me to see things I didn't want to see, to address things in my life, and also in our society, that I really didn't want to address. I think by becoming involved in BiSci, I realized I could address those issues and face them." This really is a modern-day hero's journey.

The First Day of Class

I often begin my environmental science (BiSci) class by asking my students to look at me and tell me what they see. They observe that I am a male (an assumption, actually), partly bald (apparently true), dressed in a sport coat and tie (true), and so forth. Next, I ask if they have formed any opinions or stories based on their observations. They oblige, often characterizing me as a formal, conservative, eccentric, old professor. This is their story.

Satisfied, I ask them to close their eyes for a moment. Then, I remove my tie and replace my sport coat with a black leather jacket, while wrapping a red bandana around my head. Their eyes back open, I ask them to share their observations and associated opinions and stories. Suddenly, in light of my new garb, I am seen as a laid back, aging hippie professor who probably smokes weed and owns a motorcycle.

I press on, asking students to consider how their different stories, growing from their two sets of observations, might lead them to feel and to act with regard to this course that they just now enrolled in. Some students admit that seeing me in the hippie garb led them to feel anxious and this, in turn, might prompt them to drop the course. Meanwhile, other students concede that the hippie outfit created intrigue and left them feeling excited and committed to stick with the class. As one BiSci TA-in-training wrote: "[Dr. Uhl] was really crazy on the first day, you know what I mean? And I was like, well, if this is the tone . . . I'm going to love every second of this class. Because it's so edgy and different, and exciting. So I immediately thought, 'Yes!'"

My intent in offering this skit is to illustrate how my students' observations of my dress quickly morphed into stories about me; and, then, how their stories affected how they felt and, ultimately, how they might act. Understanding this sequence, Observation → Story → Feeling → Action, offers a window into how each of us, often unwittingly, creates stories, moment by moment, in an attempt to make sense of the world. The problem is that these hastily fabricated stories circumscribe our lives. They keep us safe, but this can be tantamount to keeping us small, caged, asleep. So it is that on the first day of class I lay the pedagogic groundwork for BiSci, knowing that I will return again and again to this four-step sequence (Observation → Story → Feeling → Action) as I challenge students to bring awareness to any and all of the stories and beliefs that are too small—too limiting—for the gift that is their precious life.

The Content of BiSci

A while back, a colleague asked me about my teaching approach in the course. Rather than attempting to offer a sophisticated answer, it occurred to me that the most important thing I do is to simply give my students permission to do cool stuff with the potential to transform their relationships with themselves, with the human other, and with the earth. This simple act of granting permission provides a space for students to awaken to life, challenge their limiting beliefs, and explore what is personally and deeply meaningful to them. Here are three examples: [2]

100 Questions: Geniuses—from Plato and Socrates to Leonardo da Vinci—have known that the cultivation of a questioning mind leads to self-knowledge and wisdom. I share this insight with students by asking them to make a list of 100 personal questions, things about themselves that they would like to understand. Their handwritten list can include any kind of question as long as it is something they deem significant: anything from "How can I save money?" or "How can I have more fun?" to "What is the meaning and purpose of my existence?" I instruct them to create their entire list of 100 questions in one sitting, writing quickly, without worrying about spelling or grammar.

When asked, "Why 100 questions?" I explain that the first twenty or so will be off the top of your head; in the next twenty, themes often begin to emerge; and in the later part of this exercise you are likely to discover unexpected and perhaps profoundly important personal questions (Gelb 2002).

Part of the richness of this exercise comes afterward as students study their questions, noting themes and paying special attention to questions that seem to bubble up from some deep place. As students review their questions I ask them to consider such things as the feelings they experienced as they were doing this exercise, the patterns or unifying themes they see in their questions, the things (perhaps unexpected) that their questions reveal about them, the questions that hold the most energy for them, and the steps they could take to begin to answer some of their more intriguing questions. A TA recorded this journal entry: "I think that the course is helping me to develop my relationship with myself. . . . Along with the questions, that whole writing 100 questions thing for the first field study, I complained about that to my friends so much, but then when I sat down and actually did it, I was shocked at how much came out."

A Class on Insects

I start my class on insects (the most species-diverse life form on the earth) by asking students the first words that spring to mind when they hear the word, "insect." Students shout them out: *gross, annoying, creepy, itchy, frightening.* Hearing such reactions, I suggest that this is a case where the things that we fear may have important things to teach us. In this vein, the Dalai Lama, when asked what he thought was the most important thing to teach our children, responded, "Teach them to love the insects!" Taking this spiritual leader seriously, I suggest that loving an insect could begin with an invitation to be in relationship with one.

I then invite the fifteen TAs down to the front of the room and give each one a Madagascar hissing cockroach to hold. Adults of this species are about two inches long with a lustrous deep-brown carapace. While holding one of these beautiful creatures in my hand, I tell students about their fascinating biology. My intent is to prompt students to question common stories about cockroaches being dirty, dangerous, or disgusting. Next, the TAs introduce students to the delicate beings that they are holding. At first there is chaos in the room, but gradually class members summon the courage to transcend the strictures of their stories by holding a cockroach in their hands. This act of extending one's hand to an insect, which for many is the ultimate "other," represents a giant step away from fear and toward relationship. In the words of one student,

The cockroaches especially [changed my point of view]. It was so interesting when [Dr. Uhl] said it's not actually the cockroach that scares you, it's your perception of the cockroach. Because he brought them in, and we looked at them, and there was obviously nothing to be scared of. And so you looked at them, and you knew, okay, they're not going to hurt you, but there was this intense fear. It makes you more aware of your perception of things in the world, and how they might be disabling you. . . . The journey was definitely about discovering yourself, but at the same time, it was about the world around you, too.

Walking on Water

When it comes to giving students permission, the biggest challenge I give my students is to "walk on water," the final assignment of the semester. The assignment, inspired by Derrick Jensen 2004, asks students to "commit a miracle"—to do the impossible! I introduce it by positing that what we are unwilling to experience limits our lives. For example, if we are afraid of failing, we close off possibilities for learning and growth; if we are afraid to make ourselves vulnerable, we live without intimacy. Each fear that we give in to diminishes the potential fullness of our lives.

As a means of getting started, students complete the following open-ended sentences:

-If only I had the guts, I would_____
-If I didn't care about how people might judge me, I would_____
-If I weren't worried about my future, I would_____

Their responses to these questions point toward how they might walk on water. In the process of choosing what to do, it is common for some to detect a little voice inside that says, "No, not that, I absolutely could not do that!" When this happens, I suggest that this little voice is actually revealing what it would truly mean for them to walk on water.

On the last day of class, students gather in circles with their TAs to tell their walking on water stories. Imagine the scene: Rachel begins by saying that prior to this project she has never told her mom and dad that she loved them, nor had her parents ever spoken these words to her. Rachel's walking on water plan was to speak "I love you" to her parents during a weekend visit. She described how she fretted and agonized during their first meal together on Friday night, the words, "I love you," trapped in her throat. On Saturday, she waited for the right moment; it never came. Then, suddenly, it was Sunday afternoon and her mother and father were getting into their car to drive home. It was then that Rachel finally did what she had deemed impossible to do. She declared, "I love you," first to her mother and then to her father. Hearing her words, Rachel's parents embraced their precious daughter.

After Rachel, others step forward with their stories: Sarah tells how she had been led to despise Arabs after her Israeli cousin was killed in the Middle East, but now she has done the impossible: she has befriended an Arab student. Josh, who was freaked out by the sight of blood, walked on water by volunteering to donate blood. Sam summoned the courage to tell his parents—both doctors—that he was not going to follow in their footsteps but instead pursue his own passion, theater.

Walking on water, doing the impossible, shows students that they do indeed have the capacity to respond to the call for heroism.

Wrap Up

My own journey since 1982 has been a process of asking questions about what it means to teach, what it means to learn, and what is worth teaching. The journey is ongoing.

I now know more clearly than ever that my mission in BiSci is to ground my teaching in the healing of the fractured relationships we have with ourselves, each other, and the earth that is our larger body. This involves coming to realize that it is *not* the earth that belongs to us, but *we* who belong to the earth. As Richard Nelson (1991, 249) puts it: "There is nothing of me that is not earth, no split instant of separateness, no particle that disunites me from the surroundings. I am no less than earth itself. The rivers run through my veins, the winds blow in and out with my breath, the soil makes my flesh, the sun's heat smolders inside me. . . . The life of earth is my own life. My eyes are earth gazing at itself." I tell students that being able to say, "I am earth," and to realize the deep truth in this statement necessarily expands and deepens their identity, their consciousness. As all of us—student and teacher alike—begin to step into this new consciousness, the work to create a sustainable world will no longer feel like a chore. Why? Because we will see the earth not as object, not even as *other*, but as the beloved—our beloved—and that will make all the difference!

I should be clear: I am not suggesting that a college class with 400 students and a cadre of undergraduate TAs can singlehandedly create self-actualized, ecologically conscious adults. It cannot. What it can and does do, I believe, is validate for many young people that there really is more—much more—to life than our culture has led us to believe. It can help them activate aspects of their humanity that have become atrophied—such as their capacity to express curiosity, creativity, innocence, lightness, awe, and compassion. It can encourage them to consider that often things are not as they at first seem, and, in so doing, challenge them to question the so-called certainties—the untested stories—that have governed their lives. It can invite them to cultivate the habit of truth-speaking—only speaking what is authentic, genuine and free of hubris. It can affirm that each of them has a gift to give the world, and that their gift is to be found where their deep joy in living meets their felt pain for the world's suffering. It can coax them to slow down—if only a little—and explore what it is like to be a genuine human *being* rather than a mindless human *doing*. In all these ways BiSci can awaken an appetite in young people for growing into full and resplendent human beings who feel a kinship with other beings and the earth. As one student noted,

[BiSci is] about waking up to things that are dictating your life that you don't even know. And it's about finding all the wonderful things that lie within you, even though you might not think they exist. And it's about finding this connection, you know, that word relationship.' It's about finding this wonderful, rich, fulfilling relationship with, first of all, with yourself, then with other people, then with the world as a whole, and finding this level, this capacity of compassion and care and selflessness that exists in everyone.

. . . And that is a heroic journey worth taking.[3]

Notes

1. The "I" in this story refers to Christopher Uhl. Interview quotations from former students and teaching assistants are provided by Greg Lankenau, who studied BiSci 3 as part of his dissertation research at Penn State.

2. See: www.chrisuhl.net and http://www.personal.psu.edu/cfu1/index.shtml for more examples of field studies, descriptions of the weekly experiential learning labs led by student guides, and details on the use of role play, ritual, and body awareness work in the course.

3. During the first half of my career, I divided my time between research and teaching. Like other professors I thought of research as scholarship, whereas teaching was simply telling students what I believed to be true. Given this formulation, it took me a long time to realize that teaching and scholarship need not be mutually exclusive. Indeed, BiSci—a seemingly ho-hum general education course at Penn State—has turned out to be the primary source of my scholarly endeavors over the last decade. For example, my dismay with cookie-cutter environmental science texts was the catalyst for writing *Developing Ecological Consciousness: The End of Separation* (Uhl 2013). In a similar vein, the lessons learned in introducing ten generations of BiSci TAs to the craft of teaching prompted me to write (in collaboration with my colleague Dana L. Stuchul) *Teaching as if Life Matters: The Promise of a New Education Culture* (Uhl and Stuchul 2011).

References

Gelb, Michael. J. 2002. *Discover Your Genius*. New York: Harper Collins.

Jensen, Derrick. 2004. *Walking on Water: Reading and Writing and Revolution*. White River Junction, VT: Chelsea Green.

Nelson, Richard. 1991. *The Island Within*. New York: Vintage.

Uhl, Christopher. 2013. *Developing Ecological Consciousness: The End of Separation*. Lanham, MD: Rowman and Littlefield Publishers.

Uhl, Christopher, and Dana L. Stuchul. 2011. *Teaching as if Life Matters: The Promise of a New Education Culture*. Baltimore, MD: Johns Hopkins University Press.

About the Contributors

Wendy B. Anderson is a professor of biology at Drury University in Springfield, Missouri. She earned a BS and MS from Baylor University and a PhD from Vanderbilt University, with emphases in plant, community, and ecosystem ecology. When she is not studying the ecology of the San Juan Islands of Washington with students, she leads Drury's sustainability initiatives as director for both the Environmental Programs and Campus Sustainability.

Peggy F. Barlett is Goodrich C. White Professor of Anthropology at Emory University and faculty liaison to the Office of Sustainability Initiatives. She has co-led the Piedmont Project for sustainability across the curriculum for ten years. She received a BA from Grinnell College and a PhD in anthropology from Columbia University.

David Barnhill is the director of Environmental Studies and a professor of English at the University of Wisconsin Oshkosh. His publications include *At Home on the Earth* and *Deep Ecology and World Religions* as well as a two-volume translation of the Japanese poet Bashô. His courses include American nature writing, Japanese nature writing, and bioregionalism. He received his BA in political science and his PhD in religious studies, both from Stanford University.

Sherry Booth is a senior lecturer in English at Santa Clara University whose teaching, research, and publications focus on ecofeminist theory and sustainability education. She directs undergraduate research projects in sustainability through the Environmental Studies Department and serves on the University Sustainability Council. She received her BA from Virginia Polytechnic Institute and State University, and her PhD in English from Texas Christian University.

John Callewaert   is the Integrated Assessment Program Director for the Graham Environmental Sustainability Institute at the University of Michigan. The Integrated Assessment Program includes several large-scale interdisciplinary initiatives covering topics such as climate adaptation in Great Lakes cities, sustainable redevelopment in Detroit, campus sustainability, livable communities through sustainable transportation, and water and global health.

Geoffrey W. Chase   received a BA in English from Ohio Wesleyan University and a PhD in English from the University of Wisconsin–Madison and has been the dean of undergraduate studies at San Diego State University since 2002. He was also a founding board member of the Association for the Advancement of Sustainability in Higher Education (AASHE) and served as chair of that board from 2008–2011.

Clayton J. Clark II   is an associate professor in the Department of Civil and Environmental Engineering at the Florida Agricultural and Mechanical University–Florida State University (FAMU–FSU) College of Engineering. His research specialties are hazardous remediation and sustainability. He is editor of three books and author of over twenty publications. His bachelor's degree is in chemical engineering from FAMU; his master's and PhD degrees in environmental engineering are from the University of Florida.

John Cusick   coordinates the Environmental Studies program and advises the Ecology Club, a chapter of the Ecological Society of America's Strategies for Ecology Education, Development, and Sustainability (SEED) program at University of Hawai'i Manoa (UHM). He received a PhD in geography from UHM and a BA in geography, Latin American studies, and Spanish from California State University, Chico.

Kate Davies   is a core faculty member in the Center for Creative Change at Antioch University Seattle and teaches courses on sustainability, reflective practice, and social change. She has a doctorate in biochemistry from Oxford University, a master's degree in cultural anthropology and social change from the California Institute for Integral Studies, and her undergraduate degree from Sheffield University was in biochemistry.

LaRae Donnellan   is a professor and Public Relations Sequence Coordinator in the School of Journalism & Graphic Communication, as well as an adviser to the FAMU Green Coalition. Her research interests include the climate crisis, social media, and white privilege, and her public relations experience includes working with agricultural scientists. She received her doctorate from Rensselaer Polytechnic Institute in communication and rhetoric and did her undergraduate work in journalism at the University of Minnesota.

Marie Eaton returned to the faculty at Fairhaven College of Interdisciplinary Studies at Western Washington University after twelve years as dean to teach in areas of creativity, human development, and sustainable food pathways. She has a doctorate in special education and curriculum design from the University of Washington and a BA in English literature from Pomona College.

James W. Feldman is an associate professor of environmental studies and history at the University of Wisconsin Oshkosh. He received his BA from Amherst College and his PhD in history from the University of Wisconsin. His publications include *A Storied Wilderness: Rewilding the Apostle Islands*. He is currently writing a book on the history and sustainability of radioactive waste disposal in the United States.

Margo Flood was the Chief Sustainability Official, a President's Advisory Council member, and executive director of the Environmental Leadership Center at Warren Wilson College until 2011. Prior to 2000, her career as an experiential educator culminated as managing director of North Carolina Outward Bound School. She has a BA and graduate work in English from the University of Florida.

Michael Gillespie returned to Washington after years of teaching philosophy in the University of Nebraska Omaha's Department of Philosophy and Religion. His teaching concerns include the humanities and interdisciplinary efforts. He recently retired again, this time from the University of Washington Bothell's program in Interdisciplinary Arts and Sciences. His undergraduate work at Whitman College and his MA and PhD from Southern Illinois University were all in philosophy.

Richard D. Schulterbrandt Gragg III is associate professor of environmental science and policy in the School of the Environment at Florida Agricultural and Mechanical University and chair of FAMU's Environment and Sustainability Council. His research interests include environmental justice, environmental health disparities, environmental policy, and sustainability. He did his undergraduate work at Binghamton University in biochemistry and his doctoral work in pharmaceutical science at FAMU.

Leslie Gray   directs the Environmental Studies Institute and is an associate professor in the Department of Environmental Studies and Sciences at Santa Clara University. Her research focuses on environmental change and food security issues in Sub-Saharan Africa and food justice in California.

Angela C. Halfacre   is a professor of political science and sustainability science at Furman University. She is the founding director of Furman's David E. Shi Center for Sustainability established in 2008. She received a BA in political science from Furman University and a PhD in political science from University of Florida. Before coming to Furman, Halfacre spent ten years at the College of Charleston as a political science professor and Department of Environmental Studies graduate program director. Her teaching and research focuses on understanding the perceptions, policies, and practices that characterize local and regional "conservation culture."

Karen Harding   taught chemistry and environmental science at Pierce College for thirty-three years. Since retiring, she has been managing a project that supports Pierce College faculty as they integrate service learning into their courses. She has an MS in environmental chemistry from the University of Michigan.

Krista Hiser   is an associate professor of English and teaches eco-composition in developmental and college-level writing courses. With an MA in English composition from San Francisco State, she recently completed a PhD in educational administration at the University of Hawai'i at Manoa, focusing on student perspectives on sustainability in the academic curriculum.

Andrew J. Horning   serves as deputy director of the Graham Environmental Sustainability Institute at the University of Michigan, where he conceptualizes and develops new initiatives that advance sustainability efforts throughout the university. His research and teaching interests include sustainability leadership development and the role institutional structures play in promoting or impeding sustainable behavior.

Viniece Jennings   is a doctoral candidate at Florida Agricultural and Mechanical University who researches the role of urban tree cover as a human health indicator. Along with her service in numerous campus initiatives, she is a senior fellow with the Environmental Leadership Program and alumnus of the Youth Encounter to Sustainability program. Her undergraduate work was in environmental science from Delaware State University.

Lindsey Cromwell Kalkbrenner is the director of Santa Clara University's Office of Sustainability. She was hired as SCU's first sustainability coordinator in 2006. She has a master's in business administration and is also a master composter.

Greg Lankenau is an assistant professor of interdisciplinary environmental studies at Florida Gulf Coast University; he received the doctorate in geography and women's studies from the Pennsylvania State University, an MS in systems science from Portland State University, and a BS in computer science and mathematics from Colorado State University.

Katherine Lund was an Integrated Assessment Specialist for the Graham Environmental Sustainability Institute at the University of Michigan from 2009 to 2012. In this role, she helped coordinate sustainability projects and their faculty-led research teams. She also worked to engage stakeholder groups and decision makers into project planning and product development. She is currently working on coastal management projects on the East Coast.

Jean MacGregor is a senior scholar at the Washington Center for Undergraduate Education at The Evergreen State College. She also teaches in the Masters of Environmental Studies Program. After twenty years of leadership work on behalf of curricular learning communities, she created the Curriculum for the Bioregion initiative in 2004. Her undergraduate and graduate work was at the University of Michigan School of Natural Resources in Wildlife and Fisheries and Resource Planning and Conservation.

Grant A. Mack earned a political science and history degree from San Diego State University and currently serves as an adviser to Robert B. Weisenmiller, chair of the California Energy Commission. Before that position, Mack worked at the California Center for Sustainable Energy as the Policy and Regulatory Research Analyst intern and before that was the 2011–2012 Associated Students president at San Diego State University.

Ryan Mitchell is the Environmental Health and Safety Coordinator at Florida Agricultural and Mechanical University. He serves on the board of directors of Sustainable Tallahassee and the Tallahassee Area Association of Environmental Professionals. Mitchell is also CEO of ISIS Energy Trinidad Ltd, a foreign-based sustainable energy solutions consultancy firm. His undergraduate work at Florida A&M University was in environmental science, and he holds several certifications in environmental health and safety.

Julie Newman   received her doctorate in natural resources and environmental studies at the University of New Hampshire and a BS in natural resource policy and management from the University of Michigan. She is the founding director of the Yale University Office of Sustainability and holds a lecturer appointment with the Yale School of Forestry and Environmental Studies. In 2004 Julie co-founded the Northeast Campus Sustainability Consortium to advance education and action for sustainable development on university campuses in the Northeast and maritime region.

Sharon Daloz Parks   holds an MA and a ThD, and is a senior fellow at the Whidbey Institute at Chinook. She teaches at Seattle University, and formerly served in faculty and senior research positions at Harvard University in the schools of Divinity, Business, and Government. She teaches in the areas of human and faith development, leadership, and ethics.

Bobbi Patterson   is a professor of pedagogy and founder of Emory's experiential learning program who uses integrative approaches that challenge students' personal and culturally framed assumptions. Currently emphasizing place-based and contemplative pedagogies, she has developed learning exercises and formats which highlight linkages among history, ecosystems, and community for analytic insight, ethical decision making, and action. She received her AB from Smith College in Religious Studies, her MDiv from Harvard Divinity School, and her PhD from Emory University, Institute of Liberal Arts.

Charles L. Redman   has been chair of anthropology, director of the center for environmental studies, and most recently the founding director of Arizona State University's School of Sustainability since joining ASU in 1983. His interests include rapidly urbanizing regions, sustainable landscapes, urban ecology, and sustainability education. Redman received his BA in physical sciences from Harvard University and PhD in anthropology from the University of Chicago.

Donald Scavia   is the Graham Family Professor and Director of the Graham Environmental Sustainability Institute at the University of Michigan, as well as Special Counsel for Sustainability to the U-M president. He is also a professor of natural resources and of civil and environmental engineering. He has published over 100 peer reviewed articles, co-edited two books, and led dozens of scientific assessments and program development plans.

Amy Shachter   is associate provost for Research and Faculty Affairs at Santa Clara University where she is also associate professor of chemistry. She has been involved with campus sustainability efforts for twenty years. Shachter currently administers the SCU Sustainability Research Initiative and serves on the Campus Sustainability Council.

Mike Shriberg   is the education director for the Graham Environmental Sustainability Institute and a lecturer in the Program in the Environment at the University of Michigan. Serving as the North American editor for the *International Journal of Sustainability in Higher Education*, his expertise is in organizational change and sustainability leadership.

Julie Snow   is an associate professor in the Department of Geography, Geology, and the Environment at Slippery Rock University in Pennsylvania. She received a doctoral degree in chemical oceanography from the University of Rhode Island, and her undergraduate degree was also in chemistry, from Wittenberg University. Her previous research on air quality in western Pennsylvania led to her strong interest in energy conservation and sustainability.

Beverly Daniel Tatum   is president of Spelman College. A clinical psychologist and author, her books include *Can We Talk About Race? And Other Conversations in an Era of School Resegregation* (2007) and *Why Are All the Black Kids Sitting Together in the Cafeteria? And Other Conversations About Race* (1997). She earned her BA in psychology from Wesleyan University and her MA and PhD in clinical psychology from the University of Michigan.

Mitchell Thomashow   is the director of the Presidential Fellows Program at Second Nature, working with college and university presidents on sustainability initiatives, climate action planning, and effective change management. He is the author of *The Nine Elements of a Sustainable Campus* as well as *Bringing the Biosphere Home* and *Ecological Identity*. Thomashow, the former president of Unity College and former chair of Environmental Studies at Antioch University New England, received his BA from NYU in Urban Problems and doctorate from University of Massachusetts Amherst in Future Studies.

William Throop   has been provost at Green Mountain College since 2002. After earning a PhD in philosophy from Brown University, specializing in philosophy of science and epistemology, he published extensively in the field of environmental philosophy. He currently serves as chair of the board of directors of AASHE.

Christopher Uhl   is a professor of biology at Pennsylvania State University. He earned a BA in Asian Studies from the University of Michigan and a PhD in Plant Ecology from Michigan State. In the 1970s and 1980s he conducted ecological research in Amazonia; his research efforts shifted to campus sustainability during the 1990s. These days his primary focus is on teaching and writing.

William Van Lopik   is a faculty member at the College of Menominee Nation and currently chair of the Social Science Department. He teaches courses in sustainable development and geography. He received a BA in Sociology from Calvin College and has advanced degrees in Geography, Human Resource Leadership, and Resource Development from, respectively, Western Michigan, Azusa Pacific University, and Michigan State.

E. Christian Wells   is founding director of the Office of Sustainability, deputy director of the Patel School of Global Sustainability, and associate professor of anthropology at the University of South Florida. Trained as an environmental archaeologist, he received his BA from Oberlin College and his MA and PhD in anthropology from Arizona State University.

David Whiteman   is a faculty member in the Department of Political Science, where he teaches green politics and political communication. He is also affiliated with the Environment and Sustainability Program and the Film Studies Program. Whiteman's primary research interest is the role of documentary film in contemporary green activism.

Jim Zaffiro   is a professor of political science and coordinator of the Office of Global Sustainability Education at Central College, Pella, Iowa. He received a BA from Marquette University in political science and a PhD in Political Science–African Studies from the University of Wisconsin-Madison. He teaches undergraduate courses in global sustainability and US environmental history and policy and manages Central College's organic garden.

Index

Urban and Industrial Environments

Series editor: Robert Gottlieb, Henry R. Luce Professor of Urban and Environmental Policy, Occidental College

Eran Ben-Joseph, *The Code of the City: Standards and the Hidden Language of Place Making*

Nancy J. Myers and Carolyn Raffensperger, eds., *Precautionary Tools for Reshaping Environmental Policy*

Kelly Sims Gallagher, *China Shifts Gears: Automakers, Oil, Pollution, and Development*

Kerry H. Whiteside, *Precautionary Politics: Principle and Practice in Confronting Environmental Risk*

Ronald Sandler and Phaedra C. Pezzullo, eds., *Environmental Justice and Environmentalism: The Social Justice Challenge to the Environmental Movement*

Julie Sze, *Noxious New York: The Racial Politics of Urban Health and Environmental Justice*

Robert D. Bullard, ed., *Growing Smarter: Achieving Livable Communities, Environmental Justice, and Regional Equity*

Ann Rappaport and Sarah Hammond Creighton, *Degrees That Matter: Climate Change and the University*

Michael Egan, *Barry Commoner and the Science of Survival: The Remaking of American Environmentalism*

David J. Hess, *Alternative Pathways in Science and Industry: Activism, Innovation, and the Environment in an Era of Globalization*

Peter F. Cannavò, *The Working Landscape: Founding, Preservation, and the Politics of Place*

Paul Stanton Kibel, ed., *Rivertown: Rethinking Urban Rivers*

Kevin P. Gallagher and Lyuba Zarsky, *The Enclave Economy: Foreign Investment and Sustainable Development in Mexico's Silicon Valley*

David N. Pellow, *Resisting Global Toxics: Transnational Movements for Environmental Justice*

Robert Gottlieb, *Reinventing Los Angeles: Nature and Community in the Global City*

David V. Carruthers, ed., *Environmental Justice in Latin America: Problems, Promise, and Practice*

Tom Angotti, *New York for Sale: Community Planning Confronts Global Real Estate*

Paloma Pavel, ed., *Breakthrough Communities: Sustainability and Justice in the Next American Metropolis*

Anastasia Loukaitou-Sideris and Renia Ehrenfeucht, *Sidewalks: Conflict and Negotiation over Public Space*

David J. Hess, *Localist Movements in a Global Economy: Sustainability, Justice, and Urban Development in the United States*

Julian Agyeman and Yelena Ogneva-Himmelberger, eds., *Environmental Justice and Sustainability in the Former Soviet Union*

Jason Corburn, *Toward the Healthy City: People, Places, and the Politics of Urban Planning*

JoAnn Carmin and Julian Agyeman, eds., *Environmental Inequalities Beyond Borders: Local Perspectives on Global Injustices*

Louise Mozingo, *Pastoral Capitalism: A History of Suburban Corporate Landscapes*

Gwen Ottinger and Benjamin Cohen, eds., *Technoscience and Environmental Justice: Expert Cultures in a Grassroots Movement*

Samantha MacBride, *Recycling Reconsidered: The Present Failure and Future Promise of Environmental Action in the United States*

Andrew Karvonen, *Politics of Urban Runoff: Nature, Technology, and the Sustainable City*

Daniel Schneider, *Hybrid Nature: Sewage Treatment and the Contradictions of the Industrial Ecosystem*

Catherine Tumber, *Small, Gritty, and Green: The Promise of America's Smaller Industrial Cities in a Low-Carbon World*

Sam Bass Warner and Andrew H. Whittemore, *American Urban Form: A Representative History*

John Pucher and Ralph Buehler, eds., *City Cycling*

Stephanie Foote and Elizabeth Mazzolini, eds., *Histories of the Dustheap: Waste, Material Cultures, Social Justice*

David J. Hess, *Good Green Jobs in a Global Economy: Making and Keeping New Industries in the United States*

Joseph F. C. DiMento and Clifford Ellis, *Changing Lanes: Visions and Histories of Urban Freeways*

Joanna Robinson, *Contested Water: The Struggle Against Water Privatization in the United States and Canada*

William B. Meyer, *The Environmental Advantages of Cities: Countering Commonsense Antiurbanism*

Rebecca L. Henn and Andrew J. Hoffman, eds., *Constructing Green: The Social Structures of Sustainability*

Peggy F. Barlett and Geoffrey W. Chase, eds., *Sustainability in Higher Education: Stories and Strategies for Transformation*